Formula 1 Fanatic

Formula 1 Fanatic

Koen Vergeer

Translated from the Dutch by David Colmer

BLOOMSBURY

First published in The Netherlands as
De formule 1-fanaat in 1999 by Uitgeverij Atlas

First published in Great Britain 2003

Bloomsbury Publishing Plc, 38 Soho Square, London W1D 3HB

A CIP catalogue record for this book
is available from the British Library

ISBN 0 7475 6214 8

10 9 8 7 6 5 4 3 2 1

Typeset by Hewer Text Ltd, Edinburgh
Printed in Great Britain by Clays Limited, St Ives plc

Contents

As much as you can try to give those people, somehow it is nothing compared to what they live in their own mind, in their dreams . . .

Ayrton Senna

F1 has to be the ultimate or else why should it be called Formula One?

Jacques Villeneuve

Demo

It's come back at last. Packed trains crawl towards Zandvoort. Every fifteen minutes a crowd pours out on to the platform, the small old-fashioned train station is bursting at the seams. I wonder what Bernie Ecclestone will make of it all.

It's summertime, but today it's more than that. Flags flutter over the colourful procession: Ferrari, Ferrari, Villeneuve, Adeus Ayrton.

Of course, some of the passengers are on their way to the beach, but they're easy to pick – with big bags filled with towels and food, they're kitted out for sand and sun. Today most people look different, they're not going to the sea, instead they turn right, heading for the circuit. It's a strange, indeterminate crowd. The people in it aren't shoppers or a pop-festival audience; they're not soccer, skating or tennis fans. There's nothing identifiable about them at all, they're an almost repulsively perfect cross-section of the population: respectable families – mum, dad, two teenagers bounding ahead – cuddling couples, giggling coltish girls, serious-looking boys, churchgoers, shopkeepers, civil servants, bumpkins with ice chests and wives in tow; there's young and old, and very young – parents struggling with whining four-year-olds, wet two-year-olds, buggies and dummies. More important is the elated festive atmosphere, the excited voices – something's about to happen.

And still the waves flutter in the wind: Ferrari, Ferrari, Villeneuve

. . . But a closer look shows that the majority are red, white and blue, with the same simple rhyme: Jos the Boss.

Silently, I stroll along with the rest. Crossing jam-packed car parks, joining one of the long queues for a ticket, waiting to have it checked at the gate, eyeing the total fans, the ones who have got out their most beautiful gear, the outfits that most express their commitment, their involvement. They'll be hot today.

And as always when passing through a gate with a crowd, I wonder why. What has brought me here? I don't even like cars! But you don't need to, we're on our way to something that's in a completely different category.

It's 4 August 1996 and today the sixth Marlboro Masters of Formula Three will be held here at Zandvoort. The Masters is one of the most important Formula Three races of the year. The up-and-coming stars of the various national Formula Three competitions will all be competing against each other here today. Traditionally the winner has an excellent chance of breaking through to motorsport's top category, Formula One. David Coulthard once won the Masters; so did Norberto Fontana, Pedro Lamy and the Dutchman Jos Verstappen.

Jos. Jos the Boss. In 1993, the year he became German Formula Three champion, Jos Verstappen won the Masters. Like a rocket, he shot through to Formula One. He was an immediate sensation with Benetton, a leading team. Jos was quick, he scored points, podium places. OK, he made mistakes as well and, after Benetton, he had to make do with more modest teams, Simtek and now Arrows, but even with this inferior equipment, he has shown time after time that he's a born racer. Jos has what it takes, the whole world knows that by now, and today he's come home to Zandvoort.

That's what's drawn such an enormous crowd. Eighty-five thousand people. They haven't come because the sun's shining or because it's free. They're not here to see the Ferrari-Porsche Challenge or the Citroën Saxo Cup, not even the Masters. Sure, a

Formula Three race is interesting and nice enough, the competition is ruthless and those guys really do give their all to get ahead, even running each other off the track when they need to, but still . . . It won't be until after the Masters, that's when it's going to happen: Jos Verstappen will give a demonstration in his Arrows FA 17. For the first time in years, a Formula One racing car will tear through the dunes. Eighty-five thousand people are here for just one car, a Formula One racing car. With Jos at the wheel.

Once they've had their tickets checked, the crowd pours into the narrow path that leads to the circuit. A lot of them dawdle by the race simulator, the pit-stop game, the Formula One show tent or the beer tent. Nowadays visiting a race is supposed to be a full day trip with lots of attractions. I might be a purist, but it seems like nonsense to me. There's only one attraction: the circuit, the cars, the speed.

Still, even I can't turn a blind eye to the merchandising. Model cars, T-shirts, caps, sweaters, scarves, flags . . . fetishes are part of the game. Some people stock up without a second thought. Others know what they're looking for and expand their collections carefully. Fathers buy gifts for their children. And suddenly I spot the loner. A boy of about fifteen, staring silently, pondering with an almost religious intensity whether or not this is the right moment to buy Ayrton Senna's FW 17 Number 2. Fifty guilders. Half his budget. He walks away, looks at stalls further along, but I know he'll come back later. Apart from the prices, not much has changed in the last twenty years.

I buy a Damon Hill T-shirt.

Then I want to get to the circuit. Past the promo-girls, past the chip stalls, into a subway, at the other end the dunes start . . .

But when I emerge from the short tunnel, there are even more grinning girls handing out freebies. I don't want another *Penthouse* or Marlboro sticker, I want to see the dunes, feel the wind, the sea. But somehow they're not there. It's full, cramped, and only now do I realise that the old circuit is long gone. Sometime in the late eighties the circuit was shortened, from more than four kilometres to two and a half. No more Scheivlak or Panorama corner, no Tunnel Oost. The old track had to make way for a recreation park. The place where Roger Williamson once went up in flames is now the site of a holiday home with all mod cons: cable TV, bathtub, fireplace . . .

Holland has never had a real culture of motor racing or, more specifically, Formula One. Too small, is the favoured explanation. Nonsense, look at Belgium with its fabulous racing history. Too sober, too prudish, too careful – they sound more plausible to me.

All the same, Holland was right there in 1950 when the first Formula One world championship was held. A few enthusiasts came out of the woodwork and built a circuit on the war debris in the dunes. The winner of the first Dutch Grand Prix was Louis Rosier in a Talbot.

Two years later there were even two Dutch drivers: Dries van der Lof and Jan Flinterman. Flinterman finished ninth in a Maserati, seven laps behind the winner, Alberto Ascari.

Ten years later Ben Pon tried his hand at Formula One at Zandvoort. He flew off the track after just a few laps. Carel Godin de Beaufort did better. Between 1958 and 1964 he drove in no less than thirty Grands Prix. He scored four world championship points and cut a dashing figure in the orange Porsche 718 he'd inherited from Stirling Moss. In 1964 Godin de Beaufort died on the Nürburgring during practice for the German Grand Prix.

Seven years passed before another Dutchman appeared in Formula One: Gijs van Lennep, who drove in nine Grands Prix and scored two points. A Dutch Formula One team even saw the light of day when HB Bewaking bought Ensign. But neither Van Lennep nor Roelof Wunderink were able to get their cars moving, and the team ended up sinking in a financial morass.

After that Boy Hayje and Michael Bleekemolen drove a few Grands Prix, but they didn't get anywhere either. It wasn't until the late seventies that a really talented Dutch driver emerged: Jan

Lammers. At just fourteen, little Jan was already demonstrating perfect spins at Rob Slotemaker's skid course. He became European Formula Three champion in 1978, and in 1979 he started in Formula One, with Shadow. Highly promising, but no results. And without any lasting support, Lammers's decline was as fast as his rise: ATS, Ensign, ATS, Theodore, twenty-one starts, eighteen failures to qualify, not a single world championship point. In 1992, he launched a comeback with March, but after just two races the team went bankrupt . . .

Mistrust and disappointment typified Holland's relationship with Formula One. Huub Rothengatter made another attempt. Between 1984 and 1986, he started twenty-seven times but his results were uninspiring. Told you so: Formula One's just not our thing.

The last Grand Prix on the Zandvoort circuit was held in 1985. Winner: Niki Lauda. Afterwards the circuit was just a burden. A source of noise pollution, environmentally unfriendly, economically scarcely viable, a historical and cultural site of . . . Historical and cultural? Come on, don't make us laugh . . .

The fire, inasmuch as it had ever existed, now seemed totally extinguished. But the emergence of Jos Verstappen brought the Formula One virus back with a vengeance. More than that, Jos the Boss set off a true rage: commercial TV station RTL4 began broadcasting the races with the verve they deserved – even the qualifying and the warm-up! Special Formula One magazines shot up like mushrooms, Jos's fan club exploded, Formula One trips were organised, there was an annual speed expo . . . 'You have a potential world champion, why don't you have a Grand Prix?' asked Ken Tyrrell, who had fond memories of Zandvoort.

Yes, why not? Times have changed. A self-respecting prosperous nation *should* host a megalomaniac media spectacle like Formula One. Noise pollution? Listen: the Zandvoort business community can't get enough of it. Environmentally unfriendly? It's all electronic these days, isn't it? Historical and cultural? Exactly! In 1998 Holland had a centenary to celebrate: one hundred years of Dutch motor racing! A century earlier the first racing cars had driven over Dutch soil in the Paris–Amsterdam–Paris road race. Suddenly anything is possible. The politicians have turned around, the circuit regains a whole range of permits and is allowed to expand. The Scheivlak re-emerges from under the sand and a few new corners around the holiday homes restore the circuit to an acceptable length. The antiquated stands and the musty pits are demolished and replaced with an ultramodern set-up. Out of the corner of his eye, Bernie Ecclestone follows developments. No one dares to say it out loud, but by 1999, when the work's finished, Zandvoort will be ready for Formula One.

And the fans, the fans are more than ready. They can't wait. In their thousands they cross the borders every year, headed for Spa, Hockenheim and even further abroad, but Formula One in the dunes . . .

Jos. It's time for Jos. Once the Formula Three is over, I head for the main stand opposite the pits. It's chock-full but right at the top, on a row of paving stones, I find a space. It's actually an incredibly shoddy stand. Stone, grass and sand, the Ancient Greeks used the same ingredients. But there's something comforting about it, something intimate. The sea breeze gently carries the expectant buzz out from under the roof of the stand. This is Zandvoort, I feel a tingling in my innards, something's going to happen. I stretch to see what everyone's looking at.

On the other side of the track, in front of the first pit box, it's crawling with photographers and officials. But between all those people, I can just make out the red and the blue, and the shape of the Arrows. Jos is already behind the wheel. I even catch a glimpse of him tracing circles in the air with his right index finger, signalling that it's time to start the engine. The sound of the engine, a Hart V8, unleashes cheering in the stand. This is what everyone has come for.

And immediately the horde of photographers parts and Jos turns out of the garage. Oh God, the sight of the Arrows flashing down the pit lane almost brings tears to my eyes. Flags wave, hooters sound, people cheer and the car storms out on to the track, full throttle, that's our Jos. Gracefully he steers through the Tarzan Corner, the Gerlach Corner behind the pits, braking for the Hughenholtz – the sound from the stands almost drowning out the engine – then accelerating all the way up the Hunzerug before waving from the crest of the hill and disappearing out of sight.

Opposite the stand an enormous screen shows Jos on the far side of the circuit. That doesn't count. The cheers die down. Breathless, it seems, everyone listens to the sound of the Formula One car in the dunes.

The cheering builds up again the moment Jos comes on to the straight at Bos-uit. The silhouette of the car coming towards us through the silvery seaside haze, against a sandy backdrop, this is as beautiful as Formula One gets . . . But immediately all noise subsides. Jos turns off to the right and drives into the pits. Of course, we'd been warned, it was only a set-up lap to check the car. But we can't wait any longer.

At last, a Formula One car at Zandvoort. The real thing, a genuine racing car. Not a museum piece, not a show model or a hand-me-down from the year before, but a car that races every second week in a world championship Grand Prix, competing with Hill, Schumacher, Villeneuve and Coulthard.

Well, competing . . . everyone knows the score as far as Jos is concerned this year. The Arrows is too slow, it's too unreliable, parts tend to fall off a little too often and the engine's a disaster – rather than being the boss, Jos is usually at a loss. But that's irrelevant now. Today Jos is bringing Formula One to life, he's turning all those TV broadcasts from Monaco, Silverstone and Monza into reality.

Again the Hart V8, and when Jos comes out on to the track for the second time, he means business. You can tell straight away. In the papers, Jos has cautiously announced an attempt at the lap record, set by Jan Lammers in a March CG911 in 1992. That was the last time a Formula One car was seen at Zandvoort. But Lammers's appearance drew nowhere near the crowd or evoked the intense feeling of Jos's appearance today. Nobody believed in it back then, Lammers hadn't had the results or the media attention they generate.

As far as that's concerned, Jos was lucky to start in a top team. In one go, he scored more world championship points than all of his illustrious Dutch predecessors put together. Suddenly everyone in Holland knew who Jos Verstappen was. What's more, he livened up his Benetton year with a number of spectacular crashes, cart-wheeling at Interlagos and engulfed by flame in the pits at Hockenheim. The eyes of the world were upon him.

Jos was a big name in Formula One. And here he comes. At Bos-uit. Gliding over to the outside of the track, not lifting off this time, coming closer, coming closer and racing past at full speed.

Complete euphoria surges through the stand. This is it: the sound of the engine cuts through the ground, it doesn't just reach you through your ears, it comes through your feet, your legs, your knees, your gut. It hurts, but the pain is sweet. It is the joy of Formula One. The sound is the instantaneous, corporeal link to the racing cars. That's why mufflers mean the death of motor racing, that's why it doesn't help to turn the TV up full blast, and that's why CDs with racing noise invariably disappoint: the sound has to go through the ground.

Jos has gone over the Hunzerug again. An attempt on the lap record is not without a certain risk. There's a lot of sand on the track, the asphalt hasn't been worn in. That's why Jos wants to find out how the car handles on the smooth surface first, making sure he's got the right set-up. The last thing he wants is a shunt during a demonstration for his own fans.

In that regard, all the media attention works against him. Every mistake is noted mercilessly. There are plenty of journalists who are keen to label him a bungler. They've forgotten about all the shunts caused by over-keen Laudas, Mansells and even Schumachers. And they forget that Jos, driving with inferior equipment post-Benetton, has to push beyond the limit much more often just to keep in the picture. Or is that the very thing he shouldn't be doing? Have his successes with Benetton made Jos too impatient? According to Jackie Stewart, Jos was thrown into the deep end too soon, he should have ripened more slowly, in something like Formula 3000.

Maybe Stewart's right, but now it's summer, August, and Jos comes tearing down the straight, past the stand, his first fast lap . . . a fraction over Lammers's 52.4. Jos buckles down. He turns in closer to the kerbs, even cutting over them. He's close to losing the rear of the Arrows, slipping . . . Tension builds, he could easily push too hard.

Anxiously, everyone watches Jos on the screen. You can see him working hard, steering, correcting in the Toyota corner and coming through Bos-uit a little wider. Faster than last time, you can feel it. He shoots past in front of us and the clock stops at 52, then corrects down even further to 51.68 as Jos brakes again for the Tarzan. He's done it! No doubt the team, also concerned, has radioed the time through to Jos, who immediately slows down.

But that's just the beginning: the lap record turns out to be the prelude to a fantastic show. In the following laps Jos stops in front of the different stands. People take photos and wave to Jos in his cockpit. The blue-and-red Arrows shines in the sun. Jos revs the engine for a test start, the car pulls wildly left and right, wheels spinning, smoking as he shoots off. Leaving thick black stripes behind him on the asphalt like a signature. The fans go wild: this is Formula One for them alone.

After about ten laps, Jos stops in front of the main stand and gets out. A man with a microphone comes out on to the track. And in the silence after that glorious noise, a brief interview follows. Jos talks about the dangerous, slippery track and his uncertain future: he's negotiating with various teams. 'It's looking good,' he concludes as usual. Finally a bottle of champagne is brought out to celebrate the brand-new lap record and the party is complete.

And suddenly there's something lonely about the way he's standing there with the bottle next to his Arrows. The man and his machine. The cork pops, Jos runs up to the stand and the liquid just reaches the front rows; obediently the fans remain in place behind the fences. When Nigel Mansell won the British Grand Prix in 1992, his fans stormed the track even before the slowing-down lap was over. Mansell was dragged out of his car and hoisted up on to their shoulders like a hero. Bullfighters get carried all the way home or to their hotels, their enraptured admirers sing in the streets until morning.

I've always had my reservations about Jos; his lightning career seemed so unreal. His achievements have often been praised beyond proportion, and too many Dutch journalists, dependent as they are on his successes, have begun flaunting his fame. But today I saw Jos as he really is. His presence, his notorious rattletrap of a car, the lap record on a track which is doomed to disappear in just a few years' time, and that wonderful, no-holds-barred show has touched me and another 85,000 Formula One fans in our hearts. A day like today must have been lying dormant in Jos on the morning of his First Holy Communion, when he heard the go-karts shrieking in his village and went to check them out with his father. Despite all his great races, his podium places and his world-championship points, I still see this as the pinnacle of his racing career: the day he, like a true motor-racing hero, brought Formula One back to Zandvoort, in Holland. Jos the Boss for ever.

PART 1: HEROES

Origin of an Obsession

Ancient history. A race report, found in a primary-school exercise book, grade three: *Vroom ladys and gentle men this is the homemade race. Ickx has the lead then Steward and behind him Oliver. Smash! Bang! Crash! Oliver spins off the track and now Werben is third. Final lap. Wow!!!! Ickx is number 1 Steward 2 Werben 3. We now return you to the studio in Bussum.*

The exercise book is full of stories about machines of all shapes and sizes: hovercraft, robots, bulldozers. They obviously fascinated me – I must have been about eight.

I hadn't yet thought much about immortality, but that was definitely part of it. Machines never die. You can take them apart, you can figure them out, you can repair them. But once assembled they have something extra, a soul. A soul that manifests itself above all in functionality and beauty, but that too was something I had hardly thought about. I was a very ordinary child.

As machines, racing cars too held a certain attraction, albeit slight. They were too remote. You almost never heard anything about them and you saw them even less. But on those rare occasions when news from the world of motor racing did reach me, it was immediately charged with tension, thrills and drama. I remember Jochen Rindt crashing at Monza, 5 September 1970.

During the last qualifying session on that scorching Saturday afternoon, Rindt flew off the track going into the Parabolica. A broken brake shaft, as it turned out later. At over 200 km/h, the Lotus veered left and slammed into the barrier. The car bounced back, spun over the track and ended up in the sand on the inside of the curve. Panic and yellow flags, while the cloud of sand dispersed. Rindt was slumped inside the ravaged car like a lifeless dummy. Blood everywhere. Crying, his friend and manager Bernie Ecclestone carried his helmet back to the pits. In the contest for the world championship, Rindt had built up an enormous lead over Ickx, and ultimately that lead proved sufficient. Rindt became the first posthumous world champion.

I was eight. I probably heard the news on the radio. It was far beyond my comprehension. All I remember is a strange, numbing sense of shock.

Other machines weren't like that. Most other machines were useful, everyday objects. Racing cars were special, they inhabited a world apart, with its own turbulent history, a story of its own. The kind of story I had written in my exercise book.

Where I got it from is a mystery. Grand Prix statistics do not include any races with a comparable result or similar events. But why should they? My eight-year-old self admitted from the start that the race was homemade, in other words, fiction. Thirty years later, I am proud of myself – I had already compacted things, distilling them, going straight to the essence.

The name Jack evidently stood for fast, fearless and smelling of motor oil, because all the leading men in my story are called Jack: Jacky Ickx, Jackie Stewart, Jackie Oliver, Jack Brabham – Werben, my Dutch phonetic adulteration of Brabham's name, suggests an oral source.

I probably knew more about Jacky Ickx, if only how to spell his name correctly. Ickx is the hero of the piece, even if I can't explain why. Given the lack of homegrown talent, it is likely that the young, promising Belgian received disproportionate coverage in the Dutch media. Driving a smaller, Formula Two car on the Nürburgring in 1967, he had shown up virtually the entire Formula

One élite, and less than a year later he won his first Grand Prix. But he had not yet won in the wet at Zandvoort in 1971. Otherwise it would definitely have been raining in my story, and I would have mentioned the make of his car: Ferrari.

Oddly enough my race report does not include a single marque, no Ferraris, no Marches, no Matras or BRMs. Still, the cars are emphatically present in the sound effects: the roaring engine that starts the story and the crash when Oliver writes off his car. I know that for me Ickx only became Ickx when he was sitting in his racing car. Man and machine were one. The further he sank into the cockpit, the closer he came to non-existence and immortality.

I was a very ordinary child. I didn't realise any of this in so many words, but I am convinced that these perceptions fit the way I experienced these things as a child. Why? Because more than anywhere else, it is in car racing that that child has been preserved.

Play

Writing and playing are not so very different. They are both brave attempts to grasp some aspect of reality.

Of course, I too had a collection of toy cars: Matchbox, Corgi and Dinky toys. The usual recipe: fire engine, ambulance, police car, tractor, trucks and a few dragsters, futuristic vehicles with lots of glass and showy engine blocks. Ridiculous little things, but they went like the clappers.

I had one racing car. A dilapidated 1950s Maserati, engine up front, spoked wheels, and the driver in the grimly determined, Nuvolari-like pose you only ever see on old posters. The rest of my fleet was fine, but I didn't like that Maserati.

On holiday in Italy I discovered a brilliant racing car at the weekly market. It was white, without a single logo, just a red dot at the front. More important, however, was the realistic engine block at the rear and, especially, the big aerofoil above it. This was an up-to-date racing car, a real one. I was getting closer.

In reality I was already a few years behind. In 1968 at Spa-Francorchamps, Ferrari and Brabham had been the first to use wings on their cars; the birth of modern, aerodynamic Formula One. Lotus adopted the idea immediately, mounting enormous, adjustable wings above the engine block. But the forces on these large aerofoils were enormous, and after Jochen Rindt crashed with a broken wing at Montjuich in 1969, they were banned. From then on, smaller wings were attached firmly to the rear of the car. How was I to know that?

That same summer Ickx won the Dutch Grand Prix in the wet. Besides Rindt's death, this is my first conscious memory of motor racing. Headlines: 'Ickx: The Rain Master'. I remember the full-page coverage, the blood-curdling duel with Pedro Rodriguez – afterwards the winner called it the most difficult race of his career – and the photos: Ickx taking the lead for the last time, Rodriguez's BRM virtually invisible in the spray.

Rain Master. In summery Italy the description of the race came from an immeasurable, almost divine distance. It never once occurred to me that Zandvoort was closer to home than Italy, that Ickx and Rodriguez were just as real as I was.

The next market day I bought my white, winged racing car. Carefully I carried my treasure home. A thousand lire, I was suddenly broke. At the back of the tent I took it out of the box and weighed it in my hand. The metal was heavy and gratifying, the car sat perfectly in the palm of my hand, scale 1:36.

Immediately the most beautiful races started in my mind. The first signs of voodoo. In the pouring rain Ickx wiped the floor with the competition. Only Rodriguez and Stewart were able to keep up, but ultimately they too were no match for the Ferrari. I turned my car upside-down: Honda F1. I didn't care. I had a racing car, a real one, and from now on, this car belonged to the invincible Ickx.

Television

One minuscule school composition and a holiday souvenir: my obsession was still in a mild, dormant state, a mixture of casual interest and childish fantasy. Ultimately it was television that set it all off. I was eleven years old and reality was beginning to encroach on my life.

On a Sunday evening in the summer of 1973, an episode of *Studio Sport* ended with highlights from the Monaco Grand Prix. A sparkling throng of racing cars wormed their way through a maze of crash barriers, fences, balconies, zebra crossings, road signs, extravagant balustrades and even a tunnel. Familiar and unfamiliar names flashed across the screen: Peterson, Stewart, Fittipaldi, Lauda, Ickx, Regazzoni, Cevert . . . Crammed together, shuddering and juddering, they disappeared around a blind corner.

In 1973 Bernie Ecclestone had founded the Formula One Constructors' Association, and thanks to television rights this pressure group would expand Formula One over more than twenty-five years into the megalomaniac circus it has now become. 1973 was also the last year of the era of Jackie Stewart.

Stewart was without a doubt the best driver of his day, only Rindt was faster, and at the end, maybe Peterson. Stewart was smart, he knew when to go fast and he rarely made mistakes. But he was no robot; he wasn't a calculating driver who shunned danger. His 1968 victory on the Nürburgring is legendary. Driving in the wet, he finished more than four minutes ahead of runner-up Graham Hill. Yet Stewart was no fan of the Ring. In his assessment it was much too dangerous.

> In those seven minutes on the Nürburgring, every racing-car driver experiences more adventure, tension, horror, danger and closeness to his vehicle than any other person in their whole life. There's one spot where you literally take off – and that's while you're going around a corner! You come out of the corner

> airborne! Worst of all is the Karussel. You approach it doing 230 km/h up a steep slope. You can't even see the corner. You don't know where to brake, you've got nothing to go by, you just aim the car at one of the spruce trees on the side of the track, Dan Gurney taught me which one. And then the car falls into that bowl-shaped semicircle, its own impetus drags it around the corner. You can't feel the suspension at all. The car rams the shock-breakers, it rattles and shakes. You can't see a thing because of the shaking, but you mustn't straighten up too soon, because if you do you'll shoot into the undergrowth anyway. Madness. I drive so fast here because I can't wait to get it over and done with.

Stewart was the first to criticise the terrible safety provisions on and around the circuits. His was the voice of experience. After a pile-up in the first corner at Spa-Francorchamps in 1966, he sat trapped in the cockpit of his BRM while it slowly filled with fuel. Graham Hill only succeeded in freeing him after first collecting a screwdriver from a nearby spectators' car park. In the hospital, or the establishment that lay claim to that title, Stewart lay surrounded by cigarette butts and empty beer cans . . . But too many race organisers were members of the old guard, they'd seen Fangio driving in his polo shirt and they brushed aside Stewart's criticism. Wasn't the risk one of the sport's greatest challenges? And who was going to pay for all those safety measures anyway?

'At night,' Dan Gurney once related, 'they come back, the dead. The friends you left behind on the track, you count them, he's dead . . . so is he . . . and Christ, he's already dead as well . . .' Stewart was the most sensible. While driver after driver died, Stewart gave up in late 1973 after three world championships and twenty-seven Grand Prix victories. He didn't start what would have been his hundredth and final race. The day before, his team-mate François Cevert had been killed in a crash. Stewart could say 'that's motor racing' with an inimitably caustic edge to his voice, but the Flying Scot still said goodbye with tears in his eyes.

That same year Stewart's successor appeared on the scene, in Monte Carlo of all places. Niki Lauda had already been fastest during a rainy practice session, and in the race itself he spent a long time in third place, in front of Ickx's Ferrari, until his BRM once again let him down. But among the TV viewers in faraway Italy was Enzo Ferrari, who called his race manager: 'Who was that, in the BRM? Who'd you say? That's right, get him to come to Maranello sometime.'

Of course, I didn't know any of that then, I scarcely remember the course of the race. There is really only one image that has stayed with me: Peterson and Stewart roaring out of the tunnel. In his sleek, gold-and-black, wedge-shaped Lotus with the wing at the very back, Peterson looks faster, but behind him Stewart sits enthroned in that round blue Tyrrell with the self-assurance of a winner. The colours of the TV are too shrill, now and then they blur together. Like flickering demons, the cars tear along the waterfront, over the zebra crossings and the lines and arrows on the road. The ultimate racing cars. Stewart and Peterson tear into new, uncharted realms of my consciousness, where no one will ever overtake them.

In utmost concentration, I watch the images and let the commentary carry me away. The voice of Frans Henrichs chases the drivers along the waterfront, past the swimming pool, Rascasse, the former Gasometer, then back up over start–finish towards Sainte Dévote . . . It's as if he's taking part in the duel himself, influencing it. Sometimes he's a little bit ahead: 'Watch now at Mirabeau. If Peterson leaves any kind of gap at all, Stewart will be in there!' He looks back, where Fittipaldi is coming up, then at the balconies 'you'd have to lay down a couple of months' wages for' or into the pits, where Ickx has retired with a defective rear axle, then back at the track again, where Peterson and Stewart swoop down to Loews, under the flyover, through Portiers and into the tunnel . . .

Henrichs starts talking about Zandvoort. About the circuit, which has regained Fédération Internationale de l'Automobile accreditation, 'so this summer you can go and see them again yourself, 29 July, in the dunes . . .' In that same moment I myself shoot out of a tunnel into light. The television bursts like a cocoon and I am catapulted into the world. You can go there, you can go and see them yourself . . . That glittering world I'm watching on the television – it really exists.

The Crash

So there I was, suddenly surrounded by racing fans with their flags, their racing jackets, their scarves and their T-shirts. Everything had become real. Packed trains, long queues at the ticket office, men peddling official programmes, fish vans and, rising above it all, the roof of the main stand. A voice boomed out of the PA and through the dunes.

My father bought the tickets. While I stood there waiting, three implausible blondes approached me. They were wearing shiny leather boots, hot pants and tight black John Player Special T-shirts. They smiled and one of them pushed a book of matches into my hands. Startled, I slipped it into my pocket.

Once inside, I couldn't believe my eyes. A long row of market stalls proved an inexhaustible treasure-trove. Arrayed on the first stall was really everything there was to do with Ferrari: photos, flags, umbrellas, jerseys, windcheaters, jackets, ties, ashtrays . . . The next one had everything from Tyrrell, then came Lotus, McLaren, Surtees, BRM . . . I grabbed free stickers wherever I could, but also discovered some magnificent toy cars. Brilliant models, racing cars that would soon emerge on the track. It confused me, this giddying realisation that the world of my toys could come so close to the great big world of reality, that they could almost touch . . . My father was calling, we had to go on, otherwise we'd be too late.

A tunnel under the track admitted us to the dune circuit. Sun, the sea breeze and now, all around us, the track. A great event was about to take place.

We found a good spot on top of a dune. My father set his camera up on a tripod. We were just in time for the warm-up, the last practice before the race. During the warm-up, the teams check the final set-up while the drivers wear in their brakes and get the feel of how the cars will respond soon, with full tanks.

Cars drove past on the track, ordinary cars. The last one carrying a fluttering green flag: all clear. The announcer's voice buzzed through the dunes. Just a few more seconds. In the background we heard the building snarl of engines, then suddenly everything was drowned out by an enormous racket – the cars were driving out on to the track.

They're coming. I keep my eyes fixed on the small piece of distant asphalt where the first real Formula One cars I would see in my entire life would soon appear. Here they come, for a moment they disappear into a deeper curve, then they tear past in front of me.

It really is tearing. They go so fast it's impossible to grasp what's happening. I didn't even see who they were, there was only a sense of tearing or, better, of being torn. It hurts and at the same time it's sweet. And the next ones are already on their way. They race past, the shriek goes through the ground, through my bones, through my gut. Peterson! It was Peterson! And there go the Tyrrells – Stewart, Cevert – and then it doesn't stop: BRMs, McLarens, Brabhams and lots and lots and lots of cars I don't even recognise.

It's almost too much to bear. The sound. The speed. I shudder and give myself over to this stream of mad, roaring birds of paradise. They don't stop, they thunder past and return. Peterson again, the Tyrrells, Regazzoni, Fittipaldi, Reutemann . . . From now on there is no turning back. I have been touched. Formula One has found me, and I've found Formula One.

They drive past, lap after lap. But gradually there are less and less of them, gaps open up, it gets quieter. In the end there is just Mike Hailwood driving lonely laps in his Surtees. Then the warm-up is over.

The start of the race was still a long way off. The support programme consisted of a Group Two Touring Car race. But after just two laps I wrote it off as a hopeless muddle. Of course, the cars drove bumper to bumper, nudging and shoving their way around the corners, the competition was merciless – but competition alone was nothing. Formula One was much more than that, I'd seen that at once.

I immersed myself in the programme. A new world had opened up and now it opened wider. I went through the list of entrants, reading names I had never heard before: George Follmer, Ricky von Opel, Roger Williamson, Motor Racing Development Ltd, Brooke Bond Oxo – Rob Walker – Team Surtees, LEC Refrigeration Ltd. It had begun, now I was going to get the hang of it, I was part of it.

Unlike Ickx. To my horror I realised that I hadn't even noticed his absence. My father read it out loud, it was in the newspaper he'd brought with him. Ickx, who had won here two years before, was not racing. Ferrari's results had been so disappointing this year that Enzo Ferrari himself had decided to suspend racing until the new car was ready, maybe in Austria. Ickx, my hero, my idol . . .

In retrospect I was spared his humiliation. The Ferrari 312 B3 really was a soap box and, demotivated as he was, all Ickx was doing was stirring up the Italian hornet's nest; the parting of the ways was imminent.

As ruthless as motor racing itself, I immediately transferred my allegiance to Stewart. In the battle for the world championship, Stewart had a one-point lead over Fittipaldi. But yesterday Fittipaldi had gone off the track at speed, and the resulting ankle injury prevented him from playing any significant role in the Dutch Grand Prix. Lotus was relying on Peterson, who on Saturday had driven the fastest practice lap, his sixth pole position this season.

Again I hear the sound of the engines. Restrained this time, they come past singly or in small groups on their way to the starting grid. Peterson leads the softly growling procession. I see Revson, winner of the British Grand Prix, and bringing up the rear, a pair of magnificent black cars, the Shadows driven by Jackie Oliver and George Follmer.

They're lining up on the far side of the circuit, in front of the main stand, but the grim snarling of the engines is already audible everywhere. Their menacing impatience feeds back over the speakers. Then the flag falls.

At once all the cars scream together, setting off a scream inside me that is just as furious. Everything I know about Formula One, everything I have thought, dreamed and hoped, is contained within this one race. They're coming. Through the dunes. Tearing, tearing up everything. It's almost frightening, this distilled rage, this terrible pack passing over such a narrow stretch of asphalt – there's no knowing the damage they could cause.

Here they come. In the distance they flash over the circuit. Black in front of blue, Peterson in front of Stewart. The next moment they're shooting past, followed by Pace, Cevert and the rest, a tangled mass, a confusion of cars, Hailwood and Fittipaldi dangling along behind.

This is it. This is Formula One. It is the absolute pinnacle of my eleven-year-old existence. I am part of it. And here they come again: Peterson, Stewart, Pace with Cevert at his heels, then a group of white cars, two BRMs and the rest. The field has already spread out a little, it's a pulsing avalanche of noise, of speed, of virtually untameable energy. This is what brought me here.

I sometimes think that those first eight laps of the Dutch Grand Prix were the peak of my existence to date. Never again has my mind been so open, my consciousness so clear and so unbiased, on the edge of knowledge but still free of inhibiting fear. That eleven-year-old with his great expectations of life is, in any case, the reason why I will never again be able to extricate myself from Formula One.

But just as often, I wonder what would have come next if

nothing had happened, if the Dutch Grand Prix had simply been a race like so many others. Where would the euphoria and the excitement have gone? Would my attention have waned under the onslaught of Stewart's and Cevert's somewhat monotonous pursuit of Peterson? Or would the ecstasy have built up ever higher and would I have returned home overflowing with Formula One? I will never know. I brought a dead man home with me instead.

Carried away by an exhilaration that was growing lap by lap, I walked down from the top of the dune to the mesh fence behind the barrier so that I could get an even closer look at the cars. Here they came again: Peterson, Stewart, Cevert, Pace now following at a distance, the white cars, the BRMs and the rest. I felt like I was being drawn through the fence, sucked along behind them, I could almost touch them . . . Peterson, Stewart, Cevert, Pace clearly in difficulty, only just in front of the white cars, Regazzoni and Beltoise's BRMs and suddenly there was a smash.

On the other side of the track, a car was flying through the air – five, maybe six metres above the ground. I had a bird's-eye view of the car, silhouetted against the sky. I was looking straight into the cockpit.

People rushed down the dune, running towards where the car must have landed. In the chaos I was pushed up against the wire. I turned and saw my father above the crowd. Shocked, he was standing next to his camera and pointing into the distance where a thick cloud of black smoke was rising . . .

I can be glad I didn't see the rest. The car, it was Roger Williamson's March 731, landed upside-down on the track a hundred metres further along. It slid another two hundred metres on the roll bar before stopping on the side of the next corner. As it slid, parts and components broke off the car: panels, radiators, wheels, fuel tanks . . . immediately the March burst into flame. Upside-down and trapped in his car, the driver struggled to free himself. David Purley, who had been engaged in an intense battle with Williamson, stopped at once, tore a fire extinguisher out of someone's hands and tried to douse the flames. But the hand extinguisher was much too small and soon empty. Throwing it down on the side of the track, Purley now struggled to right the wreck. In the flames, Williamson screamed. Purley shouted that he would save him. Hellish scenes ensued: a maddened Purley tugging at a rear wheel sticking up out of the sea of flames, gesturing furiously at the track marshals, none of whom was wearing fireproof clothing, desperately trying to flag down the drivers who were racing past. No one stopped.

The marshals warned Purley to get a grip on himself. Some of them assumed that Purley had been the driver of the burning car. The fire brigade crawled up. Once the flames were extinguished and the wreck could finally be turned over, Williamson's charred, lifeless body sat slumped in the cockpit.

Everyone where we were standing was overcome by horror and uncertainty. The enormous column of smoke and the flames visible above the treetops were clearly ominous. The sudden, cold thud against the barrier had shocked us all, no one knew what to say. I didn't even know who it had been. The silhouette kept flashing through my mind, but I couldn't place it. I don't know what made me think so, maybe a vague recollection of my homemade race – 'Smash! Bang! Crash!' – whatever the reason, I was convinced that it had been Jackie Oliver. I checked off the passing cars and saw that Oliver was no longer among them.

For days I was certain that Oliver had been killed in the crash, until later I happened to see a photo of the wreck and read that it had actually been Williamson. Oliver had dropped out in the second lap, after skidding off the track on the Hunzerug.

The race continued. But now there was nothing to it. Peterson had built up an enormous lead. According to the experts, he had taken advantage of the situation. Whereas Stewart had held off near the site of the accident, Peterson had kept going mercilessly. The sun had disappeared, an unpleasant breeze blew up, and all I felt in my bones was that terrible crash into the barrier.

Towards the end of the race, the lead became less convincing. Stewart was visibly catching up. There was a fresh moment of excitement, but finally Peterson gave in. Stewart passed him easily and two laps later Peterson retired with engine failure. Stewart won, but so what? The euphoria had gone up in flames.

Without a word my father telescoped the legs of his tripod, he'd already packed away the camera. Now that the engines were quiet, we became aware of the oppressive silence around us. Without speaking, the dismal crowd filed over the narrow path and through the subway. Behind the wire fence the bushes looked white and grey. Somewhere on that circuit a drama had taken place. In the pocket of my coat I felt the book of matches. The announcer told us that Stewart's victory had taken him to the top of the all-time ratings with a total of twenty-six Grand Prix victories, one more than Jim Clark. He added that, with his sixth place, local boy Gijs van Lennep had won his first Formula One world-championship point.

When we arrived home, one of the kids from up the street stopped us. 'Another one kicked the bucket, didn't he?' He saw our astonished faces. That's right, he'd seen it all on telly: dead as a doornail. We went inside. We'd actually known it all along. This too was Formula One.

Borne by the Seasons

The sound of the March smashing into the barrier echoed through my mind for a long time. For weeks, maybe even months, I felt numbed, anaesthetised by that cold, dull blow, the thought of denting metal and the car disappearing out of sight.

I've never seen any of the television images, even though the disaster happened in front of the cameras and was broadcast live into millions of homes. The sport was under attack. Right-minded people everywhere called for the abolition of Formula One, of motor racing in general. The controversy passed me by unnoticed. I wanted to cry, but didn't dare. Because what did I know about Roger Williamson? I didn't know him at all. What's more, they knew what they were doing, didn't they? It was part of it. I was too young to realise that I was grieving for something very different. I bought a racing car and held it up against the light, studied its outline and ran my fingers over its flanks, the wheels, the ripples of the radiators, the fuel tanks . . .

My fleet of racing cars expanded rapidly. The pride of my collection was the Ferrari 312 B2, the car Jacky Ickx had driven at Zandvoort in 1971. Now I actually owned it, even the number was right. When Corgi brought out a series of cars from 1973, I was beside myself with joy.

In the attic at home I drew my own advertising signs and built models of the circuits. I organised races, world-championship

Grands Prix. They were fantastic seasons: full of drama, knife-edge duels, rain, tactical struggles, massive pile-ups, restarts and chases. I sat in the middle, moved the cars and provided the commentary. Tireless, I listed the field: Ickx, Stewart, Cevert, Fittipaldi . . . Gradually I became aware of my calling: motor-racing commentator. An omnipresent voice, merging with the race he described, or rather sang, thus determining both the course and the result. The most terrible accidents turned out well, and Ickx gloried as the new world champion.

Collecting

And everything began anew: 1973 was over and suddenly it was a completely new season. Brand-new cars rolled out of the pits and on to the track with new numbers, new colours and new names.

1974. A lot had changed. Stewart had given up racing and Cevert had died at Watkins Glen; Tyrrell was starting from scratch with Scheckter and Depailler. Fittipaldi had turned his back on Lotus, Peterson was joined by Ickx. Fittipaldi had joined McLaren, which simultaneously scored a major sponsor with Marlboro. At Shadow, Revson became team-mates with Formula Two champion Jarier; courtesy of Oliver and Follmer. Hill started with Lola. Ferrari poached both Lauda and Regazzoni from BRM. BRM was left destitute with Beltoise and no sponsors. Merzario opted for ISO-Marlboro, March came up with Stuck and Brambilla. Hunt remained loyal to Hesketh, Reutemann to Brabham, Pace to Surtees.

There were new cars, too: the Ferrari 312 B3 had been totally overhauled and looked like a sharp, eager winner. Tyrrell presented the 007, a delicate car, nothing like its squat predecessors. The Shadow DN3 was nowhere near as beautiful as the DN1, and you could tell at a glance that the Lotus 76 would be a flop. McLaren still believed in the old M23.

I saw a calendar and was initiated into the names of the circuits and their trusted place in the year: Interlagos and Kyalama in early spring; Monaco in May; Zandvoort in June; Brands Hatch alternating uncomplainingly with Silverstone in the summer; then the Nürburgring, August; Zeltweg and Monza, September; and in autumn, Watkins Glen, the title decided. In 1974, Lotus and McLaren were clear favourites, and maybe Ferrari . . .

It was overwhelming to discover all this, feeling all those names underneath my fingers again like the pieces of a puzzle. But not just any puzzle, you could put this one together in a slightly different configuration and it would still fit perfectly. Solving the puzzle seemed to make the tragedy of Zandvoort disappear, but at the same time, I knew that there was no better way of preserving it. For the first time I felt the security, the hidden comfort of Formula One. The sport was so much bigger, it had a wealth of history, traditions, fixed customs. Formula One came from somewhere, it swept you up and carried you through time, it divided time. Not just the past, but also the present, because there were always new races, over and over, as tokens of time's comforting progression, the return of the seasons.

At the start of March, for example, there was the traditional Race of Champions. I saw the highlights on TV. The race, at Brands Hatch, did not count for the world championship, but in pouring rain Ickx and Lauda fought a classic duel. A struggle for prestige. With the new Ferrari, Lauda was on his way to the top, whereas Lotus had already peaked – Ickx too, actually. But on the hilly, twisting circuit, with its potentially fatal embankments and trees and with spectators almost standing on the track, the rain master gave his all one last time to defeat his ungrateful former employer.

Constantly, the combatants swapped places, red and black phantoms, chasing each other, floating through veils of rain, will-o'-the-wisps in the spray on Clearways, Druids, Portobello Straight, sometimes pursuing, then alongside each other again. Towards the end of the race Lauda seemed to have a firm grip on the lead. But Ickx pressed him, corner after corner: Bottom Bend, South Bank, Dingle Dell. Lauda didn't give an inch. But on the washboard of Pilgrim's Drop, Ickx simply planted his Lotus next to the Ferrari. Braking, drifting through Hawthorn Bend, with visibility practically zero, Lauda backed off and Ickx was past. It was his last Formula One victory.

Caught up again by the television pictures, I started collecting everything I could find about Formula One. I wanted to hold it all in my hands, everything, all the pieces of that big puzzle. Stickers, posters, cartoons, calendars, pictures, photos from TV guides, sensation mags, newspaper clippings – no matter how obscure, I wanted it all.

The crux of my collection became the series of postcards of the teams and drivers from the period 1970–1973. Magnificent cards with a photo of the car on the left between black-and-white checked stripes and an oval portrait of the driver on the right between branches of laurel. Holy cards.

I fastidiously pasted them into ring binders and noted the vital information alongside. Tyrrell 006/2: tyres, Goodyear; fuel, Elf; sparkplugs, Champion; shock absorbers, Koni. I also noted the drivers' achievements. My cherished dead were commemorated with an extra line, written in beautiful, curly capitals. Solemnly I noted that François Cevert and Peter Revson were unforgettable. I seemed to realise intuitively that sorrow – sorrow? Did I know the guys? – the unutterable sorrow they left behind needed to be embellished, decorated and celebrated. Only then could it be contained.

My avid collecting was a form of mourning. I mourned those dead heroes. But at the same time I tried to ward off death. Formula One was such a beautiful, grand and entrancing spectacle. I knew that death was inextricably tied up with it all, but I still couldn't come to terms with it just by collecting, by embellishing.

And then, at last, I discovered the books, the annuals that brought it all together. Suddenly you had a whole season, a whole year in your hands. Race reports, statistics, maps, starting positions, technical details, photos . . .

The *Grand Prix* series by Ulrich Schwab in particular won me over. From 1968 on he described all the world-championship races in clear unpretentious prose. All the heroes from that hazy pre-history came to life: Ickx, Rindt, Hill, Oliver, Brabham . . . I read, to my surprise, that in 1970 another racer had already died in flames at Zandvoort, Piers Courage, driving in the team of some guy called Frank Williams.

The most recent volumes consisted of magnificent, intimate race reports. If it happened to be raining in Canada, then it was raining in the story as well, and they re-emerged out of the mist and the veils of rain, that row of names: Stewart, Ickx, Peterson, Revson, Fittipaldi, Amon, Hulme, Reutemann . . . in a whisper I counted them off.

My heart went wild one afternoon when I opened the volume for 1973. Cautiously I leafed through the season I'd barged into so abruptly. 1973 too had once begun full of optimism and speculation about new cars and combinations. I saw all those magnificent vehicles before me, arrayed calmly in the pits: the Tyrrell 006, the Lotus 72 D and the Shadow DN1. I saw Peterson and Stewart racing through Monte Carlo, Ickx in his ramshackle Ferrari and the pile-up at Silverstone, an error by Jody Scheckter that wrote off eight cars. I saw the start at Zandvoort and the rest . . . For the first time I saw the March landing on the asphalt, sliding, breaking, tearing and showing the first signs of fire . . . I was shocked but no longer turned my head. I studied the photos calmly and respectfully, they were now part of a series of inescapable events, of a whole season full of hope, tension, uproar and magnificent cars.

Schwab's books finally gave my obsession a direction, a direction I had sought from the very beginning – a way to become one with Formula One, to give voice to this ecstasy, and finally to preserve that voice, in other words: writing.

Writing

I began writing my own race reports. At first it went no further than adapting newspaper articles. Often these were the briefest of summaries, without a trace of enthusiasm and chock-full of mistakes as well. Fortunately, more and more races were being broadcast on television.

On the Wednesday before the Grand Prix, I started with a preview, tracing and discussing the circuit, and sometimes considering the background situation in the country, such as when the race was being held in South Africa. I commemorated the dead and introduced new cars. After presenting an overview of the statistics from previous years, I would compile a list of favourites. Juggling names, reading tea leaves, holding forth on the history, and doing it all with the authority of an insider. Pure delight.

When Formula One came to Holland, I naturally went to Zandvoort. Alone. Thirteen or fourteen. I didn't share my obsession with anyone. I only went to the practice sessions – that was enough to see the cars, hear them and feel them. The Grand Prix itself was too expensive. I preferred spending my money on model cars, photos, brochures and stickers.

On Sundays I sat in front of the TV with pen and paper ready. Television gave you an overview, you saw all the incidents and accidents – no misunderstandings possible – and it was much easier to note the positions. At a glance I could easily identify a sequence of ten, maybe fifteen cars, and in a flash I'd jot down the whole litany on my scraps of paper. That string of names – that was what it was all about.

I wrote Schwab-like reports: glowing, naïve, close-up. I was there, following motor racing at firsthand, on top of it all and in the middle of the action. It was a wonderful sensation to start one of those big folders: turning the first flimsy pages, knowing it would be bulging by the end of the year. And once filled, they slotted into an impressive series. They were bibles. These books gave me tremendous strength. They incorporated me into an ongoing history, giving me a real role within it. Borne by the seasons, I felt invulnerable. I even included the crashes.

And there were quite a few crashes. In late 1974 during the United States Grand Prix, the young driver Helmuth Koinigg shot off the track. His Surtees slid under a barrier and Koinigg was beheaded.

The following year, during the controversial road race on Montjuich in Barcelona, Rolf Stommelen's rear wing broke off. Just like Rindt's Lotus six years earlier, Stommelen's Embassy-Hill was immediately airborne. The car bounced over the track, scraped over the barrier, burst through the fences and mowed down dozens of people. Five spectators died. Stommelen survived.

Later that year, during the rainy warm-up for the Austrian Grand Prix, Mark Donohue ran into a barrier at 240 km/h. When fellow drivers lifted him up out of the wreck, he mumbled: 'I don't know what happened. Whack, suddenly I was off the track. It went like lightning.' A day later Donohue died in hospital: head injuries. Shaken, I recorded the tragedies, swaddling fate in summaries and career overviews, pacifying it.

With all these accidents, the calls for more safety in Formula One became increasingly strident. Niki Lauda in particular was concerned about the large numbers of, in his view, unnecessary accidents. 'It is stupid to practise a modern sport under Stone Age conditions. Just one more catastrophic crash, because we drivers have not recognised the risks in time, and we can forget all about Formula One,' pronounced Lauda in early 1976.

After Jackie Stewart, Lauda more than anyone else determined the face of Formula One. Stewart himself called Lauda 'the most intelligent driver in Formula One'. That had been apparent from Lauda's first tests with March in 1972. While team-mate Peterson deployed all his magic to force faster times out of the car, Lauda declared the vehicle undrivable. The team brushed aside his criticism: 'Once you have Ronnie's experience, you'll be able to handle her too.' Unfortunately the course of the season proved Lauda right: 'There are no bad cars, just as there are no good ones. A good car doesn't come out of nowhere, you have to make it. Some of my colleagues forget that. "I'm really good," they say, "but the car is useless." Come on now. If they took the trouble to make the car better, success would follow automatically.'

Lauda brought this attitude to Ferrari in 1974 at exactly the right moment. With Lauda, Ferrari went through a true renaissance. Although technical failings kept the title out of his reach in his first season, he reigned supreme in 1975 and brought the championship back to Maranello for the first time in eleven years.

But the new, clever champion was not loved everywhere. He was no virtuoso, reckless racing hero like Clark or Rindt had been. Lauda did his sums, second or third counted for the championship as well. He was soon nicknamed the Computer, later, even the Rat. Too much brain, too little emotion. Lauda's blunt opinions did the rest, like after Williamson's crash at Zandvoort in 1973. When a journalist kept on badgering him, Lauda snapped, 'I'm paid to race, not to rescue.' It took him years to live it down, but Lauda's image left him cold: 'I never give it a second thought. I'm not a romantic and I'm happy.'

Like Stewart, Lauda's criticisms concentrated on the poor safety arrangements at the Nürburgring. But unlike Stewart, whose picturesque descriptions of the Ring were always tinged with adoration for the danger, Lauda's rejection of the Ring was unambiguous, analytical and virulent. The Nürburgring was too long. A modern circuit was about five kilometres, the Ring was twenty-three. Safety could not possibly be optimised along that kind of length: some sections were inaccessible, rapid assistance was out of the question. Furthermore, the climatic conditions were often different on different sections of the track: with start-finish dry, the back of the circuit could be wet and extremely slippery. And then there were the trees, the waiting ravines, the rocks, the earth banks. The cars bounced around at 260 km/h – 'Only God can help you,' according to Lauda.

The sponsors were with Lauda: they thought they weren't getting enough exposure for their money. Twenty-three kilometres meant just fourteen laps, their expensive brand names were only appearing fourteen times.

But the spectators didn't seem to mind. Each year the Ring drew some 300,000 fans. Ken Tyrrell knew why: 'Campsites, beer, a big barbecue, what more could you ask for on the first Sunday of August?' For a modest fee, people were even allowed to take their own cars out on to the track to imitate their heroes between events. Fifty-seven people had already died doing just that. Add that to seventy-seven dead drivers, and Lauda's rejection of the Ring made good sense.

And yet . . . in 1975 Lauda was the first and only driver to break the magical barrier of seven minutes for a lap of the Ring.

In 1976, when Lauda is world champion and holds even more authority, he forces the issue. Lauda calls the Nürburgring a false myth, no longer in keeping with today's Formula One. 'The Nürburgring is dangerous,' he explains in an interview. 'If I come off the track on a modern circuit, my chances of surviving are 7 to 3, but if something goes wrong with the car on the Ring, the chance of dying is 100 per cent.'

Organisers and journalists call Lauda a coward who's only in it for the money. Even the public get involved in the debate, unfurling banners with slogans like 'The Ring forever, Lauda never!'.

The day before the race, Lauda takes a few journalists for a ride around the circuit. Just as they are about to leave, a fan begs a signature. In return he slips Lauda a photograph . . . of Jochen Rindt's grave.

Out on the circuit, one of the journalists has a tape running. Lauda pans every section of the track, all those infamous, photogenic spots where the cars take off. Between Ex-Mühle and Bergwerk, he says: 'Here you come down in fourth, full throttle, about 240, 250, I think. Look, it's like this . . . If you get a blowout here . . . You either crash into that, or go down there, or hit that.

You're a goner. Look around: there's rocks, trees, and nothing! You'd plunge straight down . . . Do you know how far down that is?'

1 August 1976 is a day with that typically deceptive Eifel weather: occasional showers, light, here and there. It's just after two o'clock and most drivers avoid the risk and start the German Grand Prix on wet-weather tyres. Lauda messes up his start. At the end of the first lap he's tenth and has discovered, like most drivers, that the track is drier than expected. He pulls into the pits for a tyre change. At the rear of the field now, he storms back on to the track. Determined to make up lost ground, Lauda flies through Hatzenbach, past Flugplatz, Schwedenkreuz, through Aremberg and Adenauer Forst, green hell, trees, rocks, embankments . . .

Just past Ex-Mühle, on his way to Bergwerk, Lauda's left wheels hit the kerbs on a fast left-hander and suddenly the Ferrari deviates from its line, swerves to the right, spins and runs backwards into an embankment. It mows down twenty fence posts and is catapulted back on to the track in flames. Guy Edwards tears past within inches, but Brett Lunger has nowhere to go, brakes and slams into the Ferrari. Harald Ertl tries to slip through on the right but there's no room and he hits the spinning wreck, which collides with Lunger's Surtees a second time.

Lauda is slumped forward in the cockpit, helmet gone, the Ferrari ablaze: polyester, rubber, magnesium, fuel – temperatures must be between eight and nine hundred degrees Celsius.

Edwards, Lunger and Ertl sprint up to the sea of flame, Arturo Merzario is there as well. 'Lauda screamed,' relates Merzario later, 'he screamed terribly.' Ertl looks around for a marshal with a fire extinguisher. No one in sight. Then a man emerges from the woods with an extinguisher. But the fire is everywhere. Merzario dives into the flames and manages to unbuckle Lauda's safety harness. Together the drivers succeed in dragging Lauda out of the cockpit, Lunger up to his ankles in a burning mass of plastic – his shoes are charred.

Lauda lies in the grass, his face and hands badly burnt, blood everywhere. John Watson cradles Lauda's head. Lauda is conscious and asks what he looks like.

'Not too bad,' lies Watson.

'Face?'

'It's perfectly OK, Niki . . .'

Five minutes later an ambulance arrives with a stretcher and emergency dressings. Hans-Joachim Stuck has to show the driver the shortest route to the hospital . . .

The entire field, backed up at the level of Ex-Mühle, returns to the grid. The organisers announce that Lauda is fine: 'He's already flirting with the nurses.' The race is resumed and won by James Hunt.

For days Lauda balances on the edge of death. Cheekbone broken, jaw broken, face burnt, but worst of all, damaged lungs. He receives the last rites: 'I'm going to die,' thinks Lauda, and a doctor whispers to his parents that they shouldn't count on him making it.

The world waits. Every day there are press releases. Helicopters circle above the hospital and photographers try to bribe the staff for a photo. The overwhelming pile of mail includes a toy car: 'Because your Ferrari is broken, you can have mine . . .'

And Lauda makes it. Don't fall asleep, he tells himself, don't slide away into that comforting black hole. He wants to come back, as soon as possible, he still hasn't lost the championship. And Lauda comes back. Marked by the fire – his scalp still raw, no hair, his right eye half closed and his right ear reduced to a stump of flesh – Lauda reports in to Ferrari: 'No one, not even Enzo, knew what to do with me. Because what kind of a Lauda was I now? Scared? Foolhardy? Mad? Unpredictable and full of complexes? And how were people supposed to look me in the face?'

Six weeks after the crash, determined, with his head wrapped in gauze, and tortured by the pain from the vibrations, bumps and sweat inside his helmet, Lauda steers his Ferrari into fourth place at Monza. Weeping, his mechanics climb on to the car. The greatest comeback since Lazarus, according to the headlines.

But Lauda is haunted by fear and Hunt keeps getting closer. Before Germany, Lauda had a lead of thirty-five points, by the eve of the last race, in Japan, it has been whittled back to three.

In Japan the rain is terrible. In places the water is ten centimetres deep. Most of the drivers don't want to start, but the organisers insist. After three laps in the rain and the mist, Lauda drives into the pits and gives up: 'The rain has totally destroyed me. We were drifting across the track at 150 an hour. Sitting there panic-stricken, rain lashing down, seeing nothing, just hunched down in the cockpit, shoulders tense, waiting for someone to run into you. Everybody is skating and spinning; it is crazy.'

Hunt comes third and takes the title with a one-point lead, but the whole world praises Lauda's wisdom. 'The courage to be scared,' is the headline of one Italian newspaper. Only Ferrari disagrees. They question his courage first, then his sanity. If only he'd stayed in hospital, then at least they would have lost in style.

Lauda decides that he has overstayed his welcome, but is smart enough to realise that only Ferrari offers him a real chance at the title in 1977. He stays and wins it with ease. With two races left to go, he has already secured the world championship and leaves Ferrari.

Enzo had seen what was coming and made Lauda an offer that was financially far beyond anything he had ever offered to anyone. Lauda refused. Furious, Ferrari roared that his 'dearest son' was 'worse than Judas' and 'selling himself to the opposition for thirty salamis'. Quite a few ex-Ferrari drivers grinned with perverse delight. Because there were only actually two ways to leave Ferrari: feet first or bum's rush. Lauda was the first to beat *Il Commendatore* at his own game.

⋆ ⋆ ⋆

The year that Lauda grabbed his second title saw one of the most gruesome accidents in Formula One history. Doing more than 300 km/h down the straight at Kyalami, Tom Pryce hit a marshal who was trying to cross the track to put out a harmless fire in the car of Pryce's team-mate Renzo Zorzi. The Shadow completely shredded the fireman, whose body spun through the air and splattered the tarmac. His fire extinguisher, however, hit Pryce full in the face. Literally beheaded, Pryce drove on at full speed towards Crowthorne Corner. Slowly he deviated from his line, mowing down the signs giving the distance to the corner and finally crashing into an unsuspecting Jacques Lafitte. The cars spun into the fences. An angry Lafitte jumped out of his Ligier and stormed over to call Pryce to task – then looked into the cockpit of the Shadow.

Again that strange, unreal sorrow needed to be described, tempered with sentences, flourishes and statistics. Just two years earlier Pryce had taken my breath away at Zandvoort, behind the wheel of the most beautiful Formula One car ever, the Shadow DN5.

It became increasingly difficult. These extremes were something I couldn't explain to anyone, not even to myself. And I noticed that I was starting to hide my obsession. I didn't let anyone else read my annuals, they were mine alone, just like all of Formula One was something I was better off keeping to myself. And yet my love for the sport was neither an escape nor some kind of autism. My school grades were normal. I had friends, too, even girlfriends. I just kept the best I had to offer in reserve, for Formula One.

I was seeing the first signs of shame. I was ashamed to admit giving myself over with so much passion to something that was, in essence, totally pointless – it wasn't even art. I felt a change coming. Just *one* more of these catastrophic crashes and I could forget all about Formula One. These were the last skirmishes of my childhood.

Monza, 10 September 1978

As usual I started the 1978 Italian Grand Prix with a preview. It would be a race like so many others this season. The Lotus 79 was unbeatable and at Monza Andretti could already seize his first world championship. The only theoretical threat came from his team-mate Peterson. Theoretical, because Peterson's contract decreed that Peterson was the number-two driver. Up till now Peterson had scrupulously obeyed this stipulation, they had already crossed the line a few times in tandem: Andretti in front of Peterson. They'd done it just a fortnight ago at Zandvoort. But Monza was different. The high speeds and the challenging corners suited Peterson down to the ground. He had already won here three times before and Andretti's title was virtually secured. Would Peterson be able to resist the temptation at Monza?

On Sunday morning during the warm-up, Peterson's brakes fail. The 79 shoots off the track at high speed. Miraculously, Peterson escapes unharmed – the car is written off. A few hours later, with very sore legs, Peterson drives to the grid in an old Lotus 78.

This is the first of a series of fatal events.

At the end of the warm-up lap, the extended field heads for the starting positions. Andretti, on pole, has already stopped under the red light, but the last cars are still speeding out of the Parabolica. This is lost on the celebrity guest starter, Gianni Restelli, who only has eyes for Gilles Villeneuve's Ferrari. The moment it takes up position next to Andretti, the jittery Signor Restelli presses the green button.

Much too soon. The front cars are taken by surprise and the drivers at the back get a flying start. The field concertinas. Twenty-six Formula One cars storm full throttle down the straight that leads to the first chicane. Unfortunately the straight at Monza splits into two halfway down: the track to the old speedbowl curves off to the right; to the left, or rather straight ahead, the drivers follow the modern circuit. The result is a narrowing of the track, a narrowing that only now becomes apparent. Riccardo Patrese sees the bottleneck looming in front of him. He's done well from Restelli's fumbling and moved quickly up the field on the inside right. Already doing more than 200 km/h, Patrese now tries to merge left. There's no room. Hunt is forced to swing aside to avoid a crash and touches Peterson's Lotus in the process. The Lotus shoots to the right, smashes head-on into the barrier, bounces back and is immediately transformed into a fireball. Drivers try to dodge it left and right, cars spin over the track and into the barriers, fire and smoke everywhere. Regazzoni, Lunger, Depailler and Brambilla have no choice but to go straight through the flames. No one can say who hits who. Daly and Reutemann just miss Hunt's McLaren. Stuck gets hit in the head by a wheel, and Pironi rolls away from the scene of the disaster in a completely devastated Tyrrell.

I sit frozen in front of the television with my scraps of paper on my lap. The scenes that follow, shot from a helicopter, are etched image by image in my memory. In the middle of the wreckage, the burning Lotus with Peterson sitting motionless behind the wheel. Two firemen try, but fail, to douse the flames. Clouds of smoke curl up past the camera. I feel soot and grit in my eyes. Suddenly Hunt clambers up on to the burning car and, helped by Merzario and Regazzoni, succeeds in pulling Peterson out of the wreck. In panic, they drag him a few metres over the asphalt in his bright yellow overalls and suddenly four, maybe five people are standing around him. I see Peterson move his right arm, lift his head . . .

It is still chaos. Over on the right they discover Brambilla, comatose in his Surtees. By now the Lotus is completely gutted. Drivers wander aimlessly between the wrecks. Peterson is carried off on a stretcher. Stunned, he looks down at his hands and at his legs, broken in numerous places.

Hours later they start again. The race has been shortened due to imminent nightfall. Andretti wins, ahead of Villeneuve, but, because of a false start, both are given a one-minute penalty, making Lauda the official winner. Andretti has secured the world championship, but the Lotus team is more concerned about their protest against the one-minute penalty and then, suddenly, Peterson.

Because initially Peterson's condition had not seemed critical. Professor Sid Watkins, engaged at Bernie Ecclestone's request in an investigation into Grand Prix safety, relates that Peterson had discussed his injuries calmly and clearly with the doctors at the Monza medical centre. In hospital, however, a late-night decision was made that an operation was needed to save his right leg from amputation. X-rays revealed twenty-seven fractures. Overnight his condition worsened, and early in the morning, Peterson died from emboli in his lungs, brain and kidneys.

Once again motor racing became the subject of heated discussion. Calls for a ban went up on all sides. Monza had to go. The drivers themselves pleaded for professional starters. Some of them, led by Hunt, pointed an accusing finger at Patrese. Niki Lauda was furious about the course of events in the hospital: they should never have been allowed to operate; they should have stabilised the driver's condition first; the doctors had failed; Peterson's death had been unnecessary. Bernie Ecclestone asked Prof. Watkins to form a professional medical team for each Grand Prix.

Far from all commotion, in my ring binder, I mourned the loss of my hero. I realised that Peterson had been there from the very beginning – all the others had died, fallen far behind, or stopped racing.

I started my report as solemnly as I could: 'Super-Swede is dead.' But while I wrote these words and followed them with an overview of Peterson's career – 'The master drifter who literally melted his car through the bends', 'faster than Stewart, than Fittipaldi', 'the king of the pole, but never world champion, he always bet on the wrong horse' – while I wrote all this, I knew that it was over. That I wouldn't go on writing. My naïve, childish bent for Formula One was gone, it had died with Peterson.

Finally I stuck in a photo. A photo of the dead driver, laid out with a slender candle burning beside his unblemished face. It had been insane foolishness, an introvert dream world, fiction. Death was real, it wasn't something to casually note in your scrapbook. I didn't turn against motor racing, there was nothing wrong with motor racing itself. I didn't plead for the abolition of Formula One, I didn't rant about twenty-six irresponsible idiots racing full tilt into a much too narrow corner. I simply lost faith in my own approach. I clicked my pen shut and put my folder and all my other Formula One gear away, far away. It was time for life to come up with some real ecstasy for once.

The Turbo Era

'It's a total waste of energy and a source of pollution, isn't it? Just think of all those tyres and all that petrol . . .' With a triumphant grin, Christa leant back against the tall windows of the canteen. She watched me struggling to find the right words. I mumbled something about the car industry, about tests and safety, but I knew I'd lost.

Yesterday in the schoolyard, Dick had come up to me as well. Dick, the laid-back counterculture guru from the form above mine. He looked at the Texaco-Marlboro team badges on my coat, the badges I'd got as a birthday present just the week before. 'Do you realise,' he said, tapping the badges, 'that they're very dubious multinationals?'

As if that wasn't bad enough, Walter had taken to following me around. 'Do *you* think Patrese will get a new contract with Ferrari?' Walter was always shouting, he wore a signet ring and a leather jacket with a fur collar, and his friends never talked about anything except mopeds. Hotted-up Kreidlers and Zündapps that did sixty coming down the big bridge – with bored-out cylinders, carburettors and disc brakes. I kept him at a distance by playing the expert. In a calm voice I analysed the Patrese problem, summed up the various options and rounded off with a touch of motor-racing philosophy. Preferably I avoided Walter altogether. It mystified him anyway.

It mystified everyone. I was a Yes fan too, wasn't I? Music in search of a higher consciousness. I wrote poems in secret and I was interested in Buddhism, what was I doing in that world of machos, money and fire-spitting engines? That world of crass commercialism and women as sex objects?

'And all those accidents . . .' Christa didn't feel the slightest inhibition. 'What's so great about seeing one of those blokes burn to death in his car?'

Christa could drop dead as far as I was concerned, except that she was Marian's best friend. Marian would never ask all those questions, not like that anyway. Marian loved me. Even if she wasn't *in love*, no, she'd told me that just the other day, she wasn't in love.

'It's a disease. An addiction. It's not the kind of thing you can explain. Once you get into it, you never shake it again.'

Christa laughed scornfully. But I knew that I had given the only correct answer, even if I myself found it less and less convincing.

Schisms

Of course, it was my fault that Formula One and I grew apart in the early eighties. But Formula One was to blame as well.

The sport was in crisis. Turmoil and disunity were rife. Politics. Formula One was changing, but for the time being those changes produced nothing but a variety of obscure schisms that robbed the sport of its appeal. It was no wonder I almost lost sight of Formula One.

In retrospect the changes are understandable. After all, what had Formula One been until the late seventies? A group of fanatics, who had more or less agreed to meet and race each other on a fortnightly basis. The transport and media facilities were virtually prehistoric, as were the safety arrangements for mechanics and even spectators. Change was long overdue.

It was the spirit of the times. There was money to be made in Formula One. Big money. The growth of the mass media, particularly television, meant exposure for sponsors, and that meant money, big money that Formula One wanted to pocket for itself.

Formula One sponsorship went back to 1968 when brilliant Lotus owner Colin Chapman made a deal with the Gold Leaf tobacco company. His team was rechristened Gold Leaf-Team Lotus, name and logo appeared on the cars, the sponsor's money accelerated and improved development, and the victories began. In no time, sponsorship took off. Five years later, Marlboro chose Formula One as its chief shop-window, under the pretext that adventure still existed. And the advertising paid off. After investigating the effects of advertising through motor racing in the late seventies, cheese manufacturer Parmalat swapped its personal contract with Lauda – good for some 75,000 dollars – for a long-term contract with Lauda's boss Ecclestone to the tune of almost 2 million dollars annually.

Ecclestone. He was the first to really catch on. Long, long ago, Ecclestone himself had tried to qualify for the Monaco Grand Prix. And failed. Afterwards he dedicated himself to things financial. But racing had a hold on him. In 1970 he managed Jochen Rindt. A year later he bought Brabham's entire team. As a team owner he soon saw Formula One's enormous financial potential, but also the appalling amateurism blocking this development.

He responded by founding FOCA in 1973. The Formula One Constructors' Association began representing the interests of those who actually made Formula One, the teams. The organisation started by streamlining various aspects, particularly those regarding safety and the media. It also became involved in the contracts with circuit owners and sharing out the prize money. FOCA's influence grew.

This expansion did not, however, proceed without growing pains. The emergence of FOCA was resisted by FISA, the sporting arm of the FIA, the Fédération Internationale d'Automobile, the leading body in the world of the motor car. The late 1970s saw a major clash. The stakes were power and money, but the struggle was fought out on the circuit in a technological and regulatory sparring match that seriously damaged the sport's image.

The conflict concentrated on two technical innovations, both of which appeared on the circuits in 1977.

In 1977 Renault introduced the turbo engine. For years a passage about turbo engines had lain dormant in the FIA regulations, but no one had ever dared take advantage of it. Now that Renault had introduced theirs, pitying smiles were the response. Turbos were much more powerful, it was true, but they were also more expensive, less robust, unpredictable – in short, doomed to failure. An extra problem was the so-called turbo lag. The engine did not deliver its extra power until the turbo pressure was high enough – the powerful boost came a second or so after the depression of the accelerator. In situations that revolved around tenths of seconds, this made things complicated and risky.

The Renault turbo made its debut in England and promptly broke down. Told you so! But through the following season, the monster remained whole more and more often and regularly showed its muscle. And in 1979 it won its first Grand Prix, at home in France.

Gradually it became clear: the turbo was the future. For teams that built their own engines, like Ferrari and Alfa Romeo, it wasn't such a problem – they were already carrying out secret tests – but for the rest it was a disaster.

For years most Formula One teams had put their faith in the Ford Cosworth engine. And rightly so. With 155 Grand Prix victories and twelve world championships, it was the most successful engine in history. But the turbo was putting an end to its hegemony, and as Ford itself originally had no turbo plans, the Ford teams were all forced to go in search of a new engine partner. BMW, Porsche, Honda – they were all keen, but developing a turbo was extremely costly and very time-consuming.

For the mean time, the Ford users had to rely on that other innovation of 1977, the wing car.

The wing car was yet another of Colin Chapman's ideas. By shaping the bottom of the car like an upside-down aircraft wing, the air passing under the car sucked it tight to the surface of the track. This 'ground effect' was magnified even further if the openings between the car and the asphalt were closed off on the sides by durable PVC strips or 'skirts'.

Hugging the track, the wing cars were able to corner at higher speeds and were an immediate success. In 1977 Andretti won five races. The following year Lotus obliterated allcomers. By 1979 everyone was experimenting with wing cars.

FISA considered ground effect too dangerous and attempted to ban the wing cars. *Attempted*, because the majority of the constructors, united in FOCA, resisted. Suddenly FISA and FOCA were adversaries; suddenly there were FISA teams and FOCA teams. The FOCA teams – the Ford users, led by Ecclestone – saw FISA's measures as an attempt to promote the advance of the turbos. This was not entirely fanciful: the president of FISA (and of the FIA), the rather dictatorial Jean-Marie Balestre, was also chairman of the French motor sports association and Renault was a French state enterprise . . .

FOCA's angry response was to circumvent the rules. To reduce ground effect, FISA ordained a minimum ride height in 1981. The FOCA cars satisfied this requirement perfectly during pit inspections, but once out on the track the teams were able to lower the cars to optimise ground effect. A blatant con trick.

In 1982 the FOCA teams began manipulating their weight. The cars were simply built fifty kilos lighter and fitted with a water tank that was only filled for inspections. The water, they claimed, was for cooling the brake discs. Lies.

FISA intervened, banning the tanks and disqualifying numbers one and two of the Brazilian Grand Prix: Nelson Piquet and Keke Rosberg. Stupid. Twenty-two cars had driven with water tanks, twenty-two drivers should have been disqualified. Now it was abundantly clear that one driver in particular had gained from

FISA's intervention: the original number three, Alain Prost in – you guessed it – a Renault.

The outraged FOCA teams decided to boycott the San Marino Grand Prix. The schism was a fact. Only fourteen cars started at Imola. This wasn't helping anyone, Ecclestone and Balestre both understood that, and they publicly settled their differences. But the cheating went on. As long as there was no restraint on the turbos increasing their output, the FOCA teams were equally unrestrained about fiddling their weight. Some used extra-heavy wings for the inspections, others had weighted-down bonnets, lead was slipped in under seats, and water tanks were still being used. It was a disorganised mess. On his way to an inspection, a mechanic stumbled and kilograms of lead clattered over the pit lane.

Jackie Stewart shook his head. 'The greatest show on earth is busy self-destructing. Formula One no longer has any public, financial or political image, it's all been ruined. There's no longer any question of communication or co-operation. They're constantly at each other's throats.'

Safety?

There was one area where FOCA and FISA agreed: safety on and around the circuits. Drivers like Stewart and Lauda had called for improved safety provisions years before, but the improvements generally came too late.

Ecclestone realised that Formula One would only really become attractive to sponsors when bloodbaths, burning wrecks and other catastrophes could be avoided. After Peterson's accident, Ecclestone had given Professor Sid Watkins the job of establishing a medical team to formulate and watch over the primary safety requirements for Formula One races.

It was a big job. When, after a labyrinthine search, Watkins walked in to inspect the Brands Hatch medical centre, the on-duty ambulance-men had just opened up some beers and couldn't find the spanner that turned on the oxygen supply. In Sweden the medical centre was in a caravan; at Hockenheim it was a bus. And after a bad crash in America, Jacky Ickx had to lend the ambulance crew a few dollars to buy gas to get to the hospital.

Gradually, however, permanent, well-equipped, accessible medical centres were established. Doctors with appropriate skills were employed – in other words, anaesthetists and neurologists, rather than gastroenterologists who happened to like car racing. Everyone attended courses on extricating injured drivers from their cars, and medical staff were given permission to drive their fast emergency vehicles on the track. If organisers put up any unforeseen resistance, Ecclestone took up position at the end of the pit lane and no one drove anywhere until Watkins had had his way.

The safety precautions were a bitter necessity. The turbos became more powerful every year. Whereas the first Renaults had generated only 700 horsepower, by 1986 the thousand was passed easily, during training BMW even reached 1,300 horsepower. As early as 1982, Grand Prix chronicler Heinz Prüller wrote: 'Turbo cars no longer obey the laws of racing cars, but rather the laws of ballistics.' At Zeltweg that year, Patrick Tambay approached the magical limit of 350 km/h. 'A terrific, horrifying, sensational adventure. All you feel is the incredible power. You feel like you're sitting on a bomb and the chassis is being pulled along behind.' The drivers *were* sitting on a bomb. While testing at Hockenheim in August 1980, Patrick Depailler came off the track in the lightning-fast Ost Kurve. The collision was enormous. Depailler was dead and the car was so twisted that it was impossible to ever determine the cause of the accident.

And the drivers weren't just sitting on a bomb, they were sitting on the *front* of a bomb. Engine, turbo and cooling took up so much room that the drivers were strapped in at the very front of their car, their feet protruding beyond the front axle. 'Our feet are the bumper,' complained Lauda. It was not uncommon for a career to end with crushed feet and ankles: Jabouille, Surer, Pironi . . .

But even more worrying were the wing cars. Their cornering speed went beyond terrifying. The cars gripped the asphalt so tightly that they could no longer actually be steered, they had to be *thrown* into the corners, hoping that the driver had aimed well. It was even too much for Gilles Villeneuve, a champion at rough and tumble:

> I used to enjoy every corner, often fifteen times a lap, now it's maybe once in the fifteen laps. No one outside of Formula One can imagine how lousy these cars are to drive. There are moments, for instance, when you bounce over a bump while steering into a curve, everything goes black. You see everything in a haze. The centrifugal force is unbearable, you're pulled off to the side, the steering wheel is as heavy as a big truck's. You keep on bashing your back, your legs and your head against the side, after a while you're hurting all over . . .

But the biggest danger of the wing cars was the loss of ground effect through damaged skirts. The car became instantly uncontrollable, it could even become airborne, with all the consequences that brought with it. Niki Lauda: 'Before it was never a problem to scrape over the kerbs, nowadays it can be the *coup de grâce*: the skirts break, the aerodynamics is gone and you take off . . .' One of the worst flights was René Arnoux's at Zandvoort in 1982: when he braked for the Tarzan corner his Renault went off the track and became airborne. Arnoux was lucky: the car landed on top of a tyre barrier. Hours later, the spectators in the stand behind the tyres were still green around the gills.

In late 1982 wing cars were banned. To the relief of all Formula One drivers. Jackie Stewart: 'At last the car is not "the master of going faster", it's possible to win races with talent again. The flat bottom returns feeling and control to the driver. What's more: those who make mistakes will no longer be punished by a serious accident, they'll just get overtaken.'

The reason for the ban was probably much more banal: by 1983 most of the FOCA teams already had turbo engines at their disposal. And much sadder: the ban came too late.

A sport dominated by conflict and deceit, cars as uncontrollable, murderous rockets that required stuntmen rather than drivers, it was no wonder that the heroes Formula One produced in those years were so unappealing.

Of course, Lauda's heritage needed to be dealt with first. In 1979 Lauda abruptly turned his back on Formula One. After wheedling a contract worth millions out of Brabham boss Bernie Ecclestone, Lauda realised after the first test drives that it was all over: 'Racing cars had nothing to offer me any more. No love, no emotion, it was all gone. I was fed up with driving around in stupid circles.'

Ecclestone thought it a sensible decision. But he too must have asked himself: who's left for heaven's sake? Lauda was the last of the post-Stewart generation. Peterson was dead, Hunt had stopped racing, so had Andretti, and Fittipaldi – who had been bringing up the rear with his own team for years – suddenly stopped in 1980 as well: 'I looked around me on the grid and asked myself: who's left of those who did battle with me in 1970?' That same year Depailler died and Regazzoni crippled himself. Suddenly Formula One had an obvious lack of top drivers, there were no real stars.

The problem with the heirs-apparent was that they were either too nice, too charming and too lazy, or else they were too rough, too wild and too impatient.

The first category definitely included Jacques Laffite and John Watson. Jackie Stewart considered Watson 'much too nice a guy to win'. Watson himself: 'I just happen to be an old-fashioned driver. I race for my own pleasure, not for the money, and I hate the politics.' But his sponsor lamented: 'John has no charisma, we can't sell him.'

The same applied to Laffite, who saw his team, Ligier, as his family, and life as one big holiday 'with car racing, golf, fishing and skiing'. But fisherman Laffite failed to keep Ligier on the ball in 1979 and the title went to Jody Scheckter and Ferrari. Scheckter was no longer the daredevil who'd made his debut in the early seventies. He scraped his points together and partly owed his title to Villeneuve's bad luck and loyalty. The following year the reigning champion failed to impress. Scheckter scored just two world-championship points, and when he couldn't even qualify in Canada, he too gave up.

In 1980 the title was for Alan Jones, the rashest of all, who pushed his Williams wing car around the circuit at phenomenal speeds. Frank Williams loved his Aussie die-hard, but in late 1981 Jones suddenly gave up as well. He had had enough of 'strife-torn Formula One politics' and didn't want to let himself 'be destroyed by the wing cars and their hard suspension'. Lauda's judgement was merciless: Jones was 'fat, fast and drab'.

Perhaps Jones was most disappointed by the fact that he was shown up by Carlos Reutemann in 1981. By that time Reutemann was one of the old guard. 'He looks like an Indian and he's completely insane,' grumbled Rindt in 1970 after Reutemann had forced him off the track. The Indian had a difficult character for Formula One: gruff and mistrustful, but also easily upset. Reutemann kept his mouth shut and drove. But ever since his glory days with Brabham, he'd always fallen just short: with Ferrari, with Lotus and finally with Williams. Even though Reutemann had a good chance at the title in 1981 (partly because he ignored team orders in favour of Jones), the Williams team consistently gave Jones the best equipment. Unappreciated, bitter and plagued by obscure problems, Reutemann just missed out on scoring in the last race of 1981 and was passed at the last moment by Nelson Piquet, who took the title.

Piquet was Reutemann's opposite, a real Mr Nice-guy. When Piquet had to drive out on to the track in 1978 for his debut with Brabham, he squeaked that he didn't even know the circuit. 'Out of the pits, turn left, the rest will come to you,' snapped Ecclestone.

Seemingly carefree, Piquet went on to amass three world-championship titles. Racing was fun, but it wasn't everything. Piquet was just as keen on aeroplanes, yachts and women. He liked to play the glamour boy, he was full of mischief, jokes, ridiculous answers, gossip and rumours. Star status left him cold. People claimed that he didn't take things seriously. 'But why should he?' answered a friend. 'Everyone loves him.' Jackie Stewart: 'Formula One can only afford one Nelson Piquet, no more.' His layabout image. But meanwhile Piquet drove thousands of test kilometres, often in secret, and he knew exactly how to attract and hold major sponsors and concerns.

Of course Piquet was an excellent driver, but it's undeniable that he profited in each of his championship years from the failings of others. In 1981 it was Reutemann, in 1983 Prost and in 1987 Nigel Mansell.

In 1983 Piquet was the first turbo champion. Again the decision came in the last race. And while Prost dropped out with turbo failure, Piquet's third place was enough to give him the title.

Renault hit the roof. In 1981 Prost had been seven points short, in 1982 ten points, and now it was just two. And that despite having enjoyed a fourteen-point lead three races earlier. The advertising space that Renault's PR department had bought up all over the world in anticipation was taken over by an obliging, cheerful BMW.

Renault blamed Prost. He couldn't stand the pressure. It was true. But it was also true that the pressure had been phenomenal. In France questions had been raised as to why a state company should be spending so many millions on one man. In response Prost was elevated to the status of national symbol and the whole country was pasted with gigantic posters: '*Allez* Alain!' Prost was also tormented by personal problems. Rumour had it that Prost was even more crazy about women than Piquet was. In retrospect it's difficult to say whether that influenced his 1983 racing results, but when asked about future lives and reincarnation, Prost replied that he would like to come back as 'a eunuch'.

Insiders blamed Renault. Faced with real competition in 1983, they should have thoroughly tested the engine, and that was when it failed. Renault had made history with its turbo adventure, but the company had gone unrewarded: it had failed. Prost was fired.

Looking back, it was the best thing that could have happened to him because in 1984 Prost joined McLaren-Porsche as Niki Lauda's team-mate: the start of a new era in Formula One.

That's right, Lauda. In 1982 McLaren had lured him back to Formula One. Finally the circus had a superstar again. At a big price, because Lauda knew exactly what he was worth. When the sponsor wondered whether he would be fast enough, Lauda answered: 'Fine, just pay me one dollar for my driving, the rest is for my PR value.'

There was no turbo available for Lauda in 1982, Porsche wasn't ready until midway through the 1983 season, and the year after that Lauda promptly won the championship. 1982 was the last year that the title went to a wing car, the Williams with Keke Rosberg at the wheel. Rosberg, according to Lauda, 'the biggest maniac in Formula One', grabbed the title with just one Grand Prix victory, and that was his first ever. But Rosberg only became champion after the Ferrari team had literally and figuratively driven itself to its own destruction. 1982 was a disastrous year for Formula One.

The Last Romantic Racing Hero

At the start of 1982, Gilles Villeneuve had become especially angry about the cheating and conniving in Formula One: 'What needs to be changed in the regulations? Everything! Formulate positive, straightforward rules and then enforce them tightly. Don't write any of these damn rules that everyone can manipulate, where there's always some way around it and room for constant deception. Probably one of us will have to die first, before these idiotic rules are changed.'

Only in retrospect – through and after his death – did Villeneuve become the hero, more than the hero even, of the turbo era. Villeneuve had many admirers before then as well, but it was the very way he blossomed just when Formula One was turning its back on romanticism and mythology – and showing its face as a ruthless business – that made the legend take off in Formula One's collective memory, racing ever faster, becoming ever more spectacular, ever more moving. Villeneuve was the last romantic racing hero.

Villeneuve made his début in a McLaren in the 1977 British Grand Prix, the race in which Renault first rolled out its turbo. Villeneuve ended eighth. In Italy, Enzo Ferrari had once again sat down in front of his television at just the right moment. By the last races of that same year, Villeneuve was already driving as Lauda's replacement.

Villeneuve was a man after Ferrari's heart. The small French-Canadian reminded him of Nuvolari, a Ferrari legend from the very beginning. *Il Commendatore* didn't mind Villeneuve regularly writing off his cars: 'He continually brought us face to face with our limitations, with the most extreme tests for our cars that our engineers had ever encountered. Transmissions, gearboxes, drive shafts, everything was subjected to the utmost punishment. He was a high priest of destruction, but his way of driving showed us how much we had to improve those parts.'

His mechanics affectionately called him 'The Aviator'. But sometimes Villeneuve took the nickname a little too literally. In Japan, during his second race for Ferrari, Villeneuve hit Peterson. Villeneuve braked too late or not at all, his Ferrari flew into Peterson's Tyrrell, launched through the air, landed upright on its nose, then did a few somersaults, ending up on the other side of the barrier, where the wreck mowed down nine people who had slipped under the fences. Two of them did not survive the accident.

Two races later the two naturals crashed again, it could no longer be seen as a coincidence, and Peterson was understandably furious about the reckless newcomer: 'The man is a public menace!'

But Villeneueve also lived up to his nickname with fabulous, pure motor racing. In 1979 he beat that other cowboy, René Arnoux, after a breathtaking duel on the circuit of Dijon. In the battle for second place behind Jabouille, they tore around the long sweeping curves side by side for the last three laps. Drifting, sliding, sometimes even off the track, Arnoux and Villeneuve were locked in a life-and-death struggle. With smoking tyres and shuddering, almost uncontrollable cars, they matched each other's every manoeuvre. It was a duel beyond all limits. 'My greatest *souvenir* of racing,' Arnoux said later. 'You can only race like that, you know, with someone you trust completely, and you don't meet many people like that. He beat me, yes, and in France, but it didn't worry me – I knew that I had been beaten by the best driver in the world.'

Even tough guy Alan Jones felt sorry for Gilles after Jones's victory in Canada in 1979. In the much quicker Williams, he was still unable to shake off Villeneuve: 'As soon as I backed off a fraction, there was that bloody red shitbox in my mirrors again – he never gave up. He just drove the wheels off the thing.'

Villeneuve pushed his car to the limits and preferably beyond. Trying to make up lost ground at Zandvoort in 1979 he ended up beside the track in the Tarzan corner. Undaunted, he threw the Ferrari into reverse and roared back on to the track with a damaged left rear wheel. The spinning shreds of rubber smashed the suspension, the rear of the car slumped, lifting the right front at least ten centimetres off the ground. Sparks and flames shot out behind the Ferrari but Villeneuve raced to the pits, almost a full lap. Enzo Ferrari was proved right, because Nuvolari had done just the same half a century before, also at Zandvoort. In the pits a dumbfounded Villeneuve resigned, he really was convinced he only had a flat tyre.

Two years later on the same circuit, team boss Forghieri admonished Villeneuve to take it easy at the start to save his tyres: 'You're on the fifth row. If you overtake three before the first corner that's more than enough.' But Villeneuve wanted to get past everyone and immediately flew off the track. 'Sorry,' he defended himself against Forghieri's rage, 'forgot.'

Leafing through an overview of 1981, he nodded in agreement: 'A lot of crash photos of me, but that's what it was like.'

And soon after, at Zolder 1982, Lauda watched Villeneuve shoot off the track on the first corner of the first lap of practice. 'How do you manage it . . .' stammered Lauda afterwards. And Villeneuve: 'Niki, it's the only way I know.'

Of course, Villeneuve never became world champion. He wanted to win races. If you just did that enough, the world championship would naturally follow. Backing off to score points . . . ridiculous. Later the story went that Villeneuve didn't want to win races, just laps, and later not even laps, just time. When Villeneuve met Professor Watkins he said: 'I hope I will never need you.'

The same Professor Watkins once accepted a lift from Villeneuve in Brazil. The astonished neurosurgeon watched Madame Villeneuve cowering on the floor in the back of the car. A little later he knew why. Villeneuve drove through the streets of São Paulo as if he were on a circuit: foot flat to the floor, ignoring red lights, and simply bouncing off cars that got in his way. At the same time, as Watkins tells it, he never stopped talking. Villeneuve explained that he had a theory, on the track, but off it as well. That theory told him to do everything at top speed, because everywhere and anytime there would be a gap somewhere, a place to get through, a space to move into, a hole, an escape. The professor politely declined the ride back.

Only his children dared to sit next to Villeneuve on the front seat, cheering him on: 'Faster, faster!' Gilles had done just the same with his own father.

But sometimes, as one of his biographers related, 'Gilles relaxed the pace of his speech. Whenever he talked about his feelings for racing, it was with quiet and reflective emotion, almost as if speaking of the love of his life. Probably, he was.'

Besides racing, his family meant the world to Villeneuve. When he came to Europe, he shipped over a large motor home so that the family could travel from circuit to circuit. 'We don't like hotels,' declared Joann Villeneuve, 'I'd rather eat my own cooking and Jacques is happy as long as he gets a steak. Sure, we live like Gypsies. But we like it and I don't think we'll change.' In his contract with Ferrari Villeneuve requested a special item covering travelling expenses for his family. He didn't see racing as a profession, it was his life. 'Motor racing was a romantic thing for him,' smiled team-mate Jody Scheckter. The myth was growing, only one thing was missing.

1982 was going to be Villeneuve's year. After two years of struggling with ground effect, Ferrari, which already had a turbo engine at its disposal, finally put a winner out on the track. Villeneuve and his buddy Pironi were a super-fast duo. The championship beckoned.

Villeneuve's fame had grown and the world of glamour had gradually taken hold of 'the hick from Berthierville'. The family had settled on Monaco as permanent home, and, away from the track, Villeneuve developed a taste for ever-faster toys: cars, helicopters, speedboats. 'Everything in Gilles's life moved at 300 km/h, whether it was driving, playing Monopoly, flying helicopters or spending,' laughed Patrick Tambay. Finally his marriage began to suffer from Villeneuve's superstar status. In Italy Villeneuve liked to go out on the town with Pironi. Things became really problematic when Villeneuve fell in love with another Canadian, who was regularly sneaked into Grands Prix or flown to hotels. The Gypsy romance was drawing to a close.

Prost won the first two races of the season and Lauda triumphed in the labyrinth of Long Beach, but then it was Ferrari's turn. During the FOCA-boycotted San Marino Grand Prix at Imola, the 126 C2 showed its true character for the first time. Villeneuve and Pironi dominated all weekend. The competition was trounced and Villeneuve went into the last lap in the lead. But Pironi was behind him. Two Formula One aces. Nothing had been agreed, there was no clear hierarchy within the team. But Villeneuve didn't feel an inkling of danger; he had turned the race to his hand and he'd been loyal to Ferrari for so long . . . But Pironi was faster and unable to resist temptation. He surprised Villeneuve in one of the last corners and won the race. Villeneuve felt betrayed by Pironi and, even worse, by Ferrari.

Witnesses tell that he was gloomy, bitter and angry in the fortnight leading up to the next race: the Belgian Grand Prix at Zolder. The problems at home had grown: Joann wanted a divorce, she hadn't accompanied him to Belgium.

During practice Ferrari immediately confirmed its supremacy. Pironi clocked up a pole time that no one else could equal, unless perhaps Villeneuve. A little before two, at the end of the last qualifying session, Villeneuve left the pits, determined to show who was really the fastest.

They were typical Villeneuve laps; the driver in a constant battle with his car. Endlessly correcting, slipping, bouncing dangerously over the kerbs, throwing up clouds of sand, fidgeting through the gears and, wherever possible, full throttle.

After a few laps, it was clear that Pironi's lap time would stand. The team realised it as well and called Villeneuve back in, but Villeneuve ignored the signal and never came back.

On the far side of the circuit, between the trees, he pushed his Ferrari through the chicane into a left-hander that led straight into a downhill right-hander. Villeneuve must have seen Mass in front of him, but lifting off . . . nonsense. Slowly driving back to the pits in his March, Jochen Mass saw Villeneuve at the very last moment and quickly cut off to the right to leave the best line open for the speeding Ferrari. But in that same moment, Villeneuve had already decided to pass him on the right. His theory that at top speed he would always find a gap to slot into had failed him.

Professor Sid Watkins was one of the first on the scene. Villeneuve had been thrown out of his car and lay, still strapped to his seat, near the catch fencing. He'd stopped breathing, his eyes were wide open. 'I hope I never need you.' He was put on a respirator, but the professor already knew that Villeneuve had a fatal fracture of the neck.

Pironi arrived in his Ferrari, but was sent away by a still-shaking Mass. With Villeneuve's helmet in his lap, Pironi returned to the Ferrari garage. In Italy the newspapers would write about fratricide.

It was a typical racing accident. Villeneuve gambled on the wrong side and hit Mass's right rear wheel at full speed. The Ferrari, sucked down tight on to the asphalt a fraction of a second earlier, now catapulted metres high into the air, cartwheeled dozens of times, shucked off wings, wheels and driver, and finally slid back on to the track an empty carcass, a destroyed monster.

A frightened silence descended over Zolder. It took a long time before anything happened. At Ferrari they had already closed the shutters.

Policemen and marshals held up blankets to hide the sight from inquisitive eyes, and 'The Aviator' was transferred to the waiting ambulance. Later he was rushed to Louvain by helicopter. At twelve minutes past nine he died in the presence of Joann, who had rushed to his bedside.

More than anything else it is his death that has turned Villeneuve into a legend. Looking back, the myth of Ferrari's Number 27 adds colour to a messy, bloody and scarcely glorious era in Formula One history. The crash at Zolder was a turning point. The romanticism of racing died with Villeneuve. And that's the very thing that keeps his memory alive.

It was only natural that he should die in a car from the team that even today still cherishes the last smouldering ember of racing romanticism: Ferrari. Ferrari and Villeneuve were made for each other. Ferrari was his delight, but it was also his lot. The judgement of John Watson, who went on to win the race in Belgium, was scathing:

> Perhaps Ferrari were the worst team for Gilles Villeneuve. The gift and talent he had as a racing driver were misused at Ferrari because they, as a team, loved the caricature of the racing driver that Gilles was. Had he been signed up by McLaren or Williams, Brabham or Ligier, those were the teams that had really begun to capitalise on the ground effects at that time, and had Gilles gone there he would have learned things that he was totally ignorant of. Gilles's potential was exploited as the result of the adulation and mythology that grew up around him (. . .) It was a waste of a driver, a waste of a life, and a waste of a charismatic man and a family man as well. If he had been in Ligier or Brabham, they would have taught him about being a Grand Prix driver, rather than just getting in and driving it to death, and he would have won more Grands Prix, he would have been world champion and he would probably be living today.

There was more to come for Formula One that year. Two races later Riccardo Paletti was killed in a crash on the starting grid of the Canadian Grand Prix. It was Paletti's first race. In previous races he had tried but failed to qualify. Now he had done it. His mother had flown over from Italy just to be there. Pironi was on pole, but stalled at the start. The immediate result was enormous chaos, but everyone succeeded in dodging the Ferrari – except Paletti. As inexperienced as he was, he ploughed into the stationary Ferrari at more than 180 km/h. Paletti's Osella burst into flame, but the fire was immediately extinguished by the marshals, together with Pironi – who had quickly leapt out of his car. It was too late to help Paletti: the steering wheel and column had crushed his chest. Worst of all, according to Watkins, was Paletti's mother, who ran out on to the track in tears and stood by while her son's dead body was lifted out of the car.

Soon fate caught up with Pironi as well. In pouring rain at Hockenheim, Pironi crashed at top speed into Alain Prost's car, which was invisible in the mist and the spray thrown up by Derek

Daly's Williams. The Ferrari took off, flew over Prost and crashed down on to the asphalt. 'I only remember the treetops,' Pironi said later. It took a good twenty minutes to free him from the wreck. He had multiple fractures in both legs and his right foot was crushed. Pironi's Formula One career was over. He had a tremendous lead in the battle for the world championship, but three races before the end of the season Rosberg passed him. After twenty-four operations, Pironi spent years working hard on a Formula One comeback. Crying from the pain, he got behind the wheel of a Ferrari again in 1984. It was beyond him. Two years later, with AGS and Ligier, it was still beyond him. In 1987 Pironi died in a speedboat race off the Isle of Wight.

Intermezzo: Racing

Sometime in the early seventies a French furniture-maker, holidaying on the Mediterranean, takes his fifteen-year-old son to a funfair next to the motorway linking Cannes and Monaco. It's one of those sweltering August days. The asphalt trembles. Cars race by the whole damn afternoon.

The fair is still asleep when they swing into the car park. A cluster of white buildings between palm trees and cacti. 'Disco! Dancing!' is the empty promise above the closed doors. Only the casino is open, but nobody wants to test their luck at this time of day. The bored croupiers and bouncers are gathered around an undersized fan.

A shabby place, but you have to do something with a kid this age. Not yet old enough for girls, but already eager, hungry for the world.

There's a go-kart track behind the white buildings, that's what they've come for. For a moment father and son pause at the edge of the asphalt. It's their Rubicon, but how were they to know that?

Then they cross it and crunch over the gravel to the operator's wooden booth. The karts are next to the whitewashed booth, parked neatly in angled spaces.

The operator is there, he's listening to a transistor radio. Dad does the talking, pays, and the taciturn kart operator comes out from behind his counter. While he walks over to the karts, the boy looks at the photos mounted behind the counter: Jack Brabham, Jochen

Rindt, Jackie Stewart. He doesn't recognise them, he wants to be a footballer.

But going for a ride on one of these karts looks like fun, too. Curious, he sits down on the sputtering kart. He feels the vibrations of the engine against his back. The operator, still holding the steering wheel with one hand, points with the other: '*Gaz! Freins!*' Then he steps away from the track, nods to the boy's father and climbs back in behind his counter.

Slowly the boy drives off, without waiting, moving intuitively, searching out the responses of the machine he now has control of. Calmly he takes the first corner, feeling the grip of the small tyres. On the second corner he checks the strength of the brakes, then he puts his foot down. All the way.

Twenty-five years later this boy will have become one of the most successful Formula One drivers of all time: 199 Grand Prix starts, 51 victories, 106 podiums, 798.5 world-championship points, 4 world titles, 41 fastest lap times. His name: Alain Prost.

I was fifteen, on a family holiday in Italy, when my father took me to *Italia in Miniatura*, a theme park dedicated to scale models of Italian tourist attractions. In the weeks before, we had visited quite a few duomos, monuments, tombs and colosseums together, and now suddenly we had them all in one place. It gave you a sense of power, of godlike superiority, and our voices echoed cheerfully off the plastic Alps and Apennines.

'Look, Dante's grave.' My father pointed out a tiny house next to a bloated red basilica and lowered his voice solemnly: 'Abandon all hope, ye who enter here . . .' As if *I* knew who Dante was. It reminded me of Dr Who's TARDIS and I calculated that there would be room inside for just a single Matchbox toy.

It was probably because of the heat, but we were the only visitors there that afternoon. The restaurant was shut. We were walking around it when my father stopped and pointed: 'Look, Monza . . .'

Off to one side, away from the other models, was a kart track.

And even though my father couldn't tell one circuit from the other, it was in fact laid out like Monza, albeit without chicanes. At the level of start-finish there was a wooden booth, a fat stomach and two legs protruding.

'Come on.' My father strode over to the track. I saw what was going to happen here in a flash. I didn't want to, but I had no choice. With my overblown interest in racing, I had brought this confrontation down on myself.

Mumbling that we had interrupted his afternoon nap, the kart operator fished an orange crash helmet up out of a box in the waiting room. He showed me the chinstrap and gestured that I should do it up nice and tight. Three karts were parked against an iron rail. Shaking his head, the operator pulled one out into the middle of the track. I looked around and saw that the rail enclosed the entire circuit. The operator looked at me impatiently. I quickly pulled the helmet on to my head and immediately a suffocating warmth descended over me, along with the murmur of the voices of thousands – no, millions – of other racers; I was suddenly on another planet.

Fidgeting with the chinstrap, I walked over to the waiting kart. For the briefest moment I imagined myself in a picture of Michel Vaillant, my favourite cartoon hero. It was from the album called *Fate*. Michel is on his way to his car to start in the French Grand Prix, the race which, after an endless series of mishaps, will finally, finally . . . I jump out of my skin when the engine starts up. This is no comic book, it's not France, it's Italy. It's Monza, it's hell.

With lead in my shoes I settle into the plastic bucket seat. In his autobiography Nigel Mansell explains what a revelation the karts were to him: 'To a child, the karts looked like real racing machines. The noise and the smell made a heady cocktail and when you pushed down the accelerator, the vibrations of the engine through the plastic seat made your back tingle and your teeth chatter. It was magical. It became my world.'

Not mine.

All I felt was a machine that was capable of pushing me all the way to my death. I didn't understand a word the kart operator said as he bent over me, mumbling and pointing at the pedals at my feet. Did I say pedals? They were actually two bent bars, just waiting for a chance to slip out from under the soles of my shoes . . .

The kart operator walked off without a second glance. My father gestured, 'Go on, drive!' I didn't even know which bar was the accelerator. No one ever told me anything! I looked ahead, there was the Curva Grande, the corner where the entire Formula One field fanned out so beautifully – abandon all hope, ye who enter here. I pressed down on the right-hand bar. Immediately I was thumped in the back, I shot forward, the kart got away from me. In a reflex I stamped on the brake and stopped instantly. After just one and a half metres, my racing career was already over.

But the engine was still running. Carefully I touched the right-hand bar again: another shock – in me, in the machine, as if a spasm had passed through both of us. I let go, but the kart was still rolling, rolling forwards. Again I pressed down a half centimetre on the accelerator, and again. Mistrustfully, I looked down at my distant feet, forgot to steer and drove into the outside rail of the Curva Grande. Bump. Startled, I pushed the accelerator down by accident, tore across the Roggia, took the first Lesmo in a panic, clipped the rail in the second, and more or less managed to stop in the Serraglio. I took the Ascari smoothly, if crawling. But in the Parabolica I rammed the rail again. The kart flew through the air, three wheels off the ground, and landed crossways in the middle of that famous corner. I'd had enough, this wasn't what I'd wanted at all, I wasn't made for this, this wasn't what I loved.

But giving up wasn't an option. Cautiously tapping the hysterical metal bar, I turned the machine around for the straight; you can reach 300 an hour down there.

Where did *she* suddenly come from? During my third lap – hardly scraping the rail at all – I saw a girl talking to the kart operator. Black curls, animated gestures. She must have heard the noise. Grinning, she grabbed a silver helmet from the wooden shelter. I went by on the straight while the kart operator pushed a second kart out from the rail. My orange helmet felt even more claustrophobic, the strap stuck wet to my chin.

Even before the first Lesmo, she'd whizzed past. I watched her go, saw how fast she was and how tightly she moved the kart through the corners. And after the Parabolica, she really put her foot down.

Where could I go? The track suddenly seemed ten times as narrow, she was coming up again. I heard her engine shriek, drowning out my pathetic puttering. In the Ascari she cut through on the inside. I watched her kart bouncing, sliding, almost turning sideways, pulling straight, squealing tyres. Recklessly, she swung into the Parabolica, shooting round it laughing. I saw that my father too only had eyes for her. That was how you were supposed to do it: she had her kart dancing around the bends, doing exactly what she wanted it to and loving it, and she in turn allowed herself to be dragged along by the machine.

While I juddered out of the Ascari, she tore over start-finish. For a moment we looked at each other. She grinned, happy, with mischievous sparkling eyes: 'Come on, play with me . . .' But I couldn't – no, I was too scared. I didn't dare surrender to the speed of a machine, no matter how much I myself was generating it.

Beyond her, I saw my father waving furiously. Faster! Easy for him to say. He wasn't sitting in this thing, he wasn't feeling those treacherous vibrations in his back, those stupid metal bars under his feet, his legs vulnerable between all kinds of tubes and bars. He didn't feel the forces at work on the whole vehicle, the vicious little tyres, the grip of the asphalt. He didn't need to think about guard rails, somersaults, grazes and cuts, crushed ankles, multiple leg fractures, brain damage and fire . . .

After nine laps, the operator gestured that my time was up. Relieved I immediately steered the kart over to the side. No slowing-down lap necessary. I got out, took off my helmet. Never again, I was sure of that.

Vacantly I watched the girl with the black curls do a few more laps. Of course, she came here every day, she knew the operator, the track, the karts.

'I wanted to know everything about the machines, how they worked and more important how to make them go faster. I wanted to test their limits, to see how far I could push them through a corner before they would slide. I wanted to find new techniques for balancing the brakes and the throttle to gain more speed into corners. I wanted to drive every day, to take on other children in their machines and fight past them. I wanted to win.' Yes . . . Mansell.

I turned away. Behind the plastic mountains, our bus was waiting.

PART 2: SUPERSTARS

Nigel Mansell: The Lion

Monaco 1984. The forty-second Grand Prix in the principality's streets turns into a water ballet – surfing with a thousand horse-power. And the turbos didn't like Monaco to start with. Because of the turbo lag, the surge of power can come at the most inconvenient moments, and that on a circuit where the leeway is measured in millimetres.

There's not much to see of the start. At the front of the grid Prost and Mansell throw up so much spray that the rest of the field disappears in mist. Immediately, at Sainte Dévote, the two Renaults, cut off by Arnoux, collide and write each other off. Prost laughs up his sleeve and takes the lead.

Behind him the destruction grows. De Cesaris gets hit and drops out. Fabi aquaplanes into the barriers. The same thing happens to Hesnault and reigning champion Piquet, who loathes Monaco anyway. Everywhere visibility is terrible: barriers and signs loom up out of the mist like ghostly forms. At the swimming pool, driving fast is gambling against the odds: a car could be turned sideways anywhere on the track, taillights disappear into the void around the corner – hallucinatory.

Most drivers are cautious, looking twice before turning into Mirabeau, crawling around Rascasse – slipping half a metre here could be fatal. Most drivers . . . but not Nigel Mansell.

Mansell – the fanatic, the daredevil – in second place behind

Prost, his gold-and-black Lotus is continually weaving back and forth. Prost isn't worried, he knows that no one can overtake in the wet in Monaco. Mansell disagrees and, in the eleventh lap, he sees his chance. Coming out of Portiers, Prost sees the marshals pushing Fabi's Brabham over to the side of the track and hesitates. Mansell doesn't think twice and shoots into the tunnel in the lead.

The drudge, the man who had the longest row to hoe – he can't believe his luck. For the first time in his career, Mansell has taken the lead in a Grand Prix. And not just any Grand Prix – it's Monaco! He shoots ahead, immediately building up his lead over Prost, who doesn't even try to keep up. Prost knows how treacherous the wet can be. For three laps all goes well, four laps, then Mansell pushes too hard on the climb to Beau Rivage.

Jackie Stewart's first lesson: 'Avoid the white lines when it rains in Monaco!' The stripes, the zebra crossings, the direction arrows and the speed limit indications all get extremely slippery.

In his enthusiasm Mansell goes too fast, his car starts to slide and ends up with one of the rear wheels on a white road marking. Out of control, the Lotus smashes into the barriers – left then right. The back of the car is wrecked, the wing is dangling alongside the chassis and the rear wheels are pointing in different directions. End of story. Whether Mansell agrees or not. Stubbornly he drives, swerves and slides on. Prost passes, then Lauda, Arnoux, Senna . . . Mansell parks his unsteerable car on the pavement.

In the pits Lotus team manager Peter Warr is furious. Even before the start of the season, he'd wanted to swap Mansell for Ayrton Senna, but his sponsor, John Player, had resisted: Mansell had market value in Britain. And now Mansell has given away a Grand Prix he'd already won. And not just any Grand Prix – he's given away Monaco!

Slipped on a road marking. Sponsor satisfied? English fans satisfied? 'Mansell will never win a Grand Prix,' fulminated Warr, 'as long as there is a hole in my arse.'

There is no further information as to Warr's anatomical peculiarities, but a year later Mansell did win his first Grand Prix, and from there he went on to win thirty more *and* the world championship, but not with Lotus.

Because at the end of 1984, Warr had his way: Senna replaced Mansell. And this time Warr was right: Senna was a born winner, unlike Mansell. But John Player had done their sums correctly as well, because the British fans weren't bothered by this at all. On the contrary, most fans, and not just in Britain, enjoyed Mansell's fumbling and plodding, his setbacks, his pigheadedness and his perseverance. 'Against all odds' became his battle cry.

Mansell had sold his house to race in Formula Three, he'd worked as a window-cleaner on the side – freezing his hands and doing his back in – he'd sent hundreds of begging letters to potential sponsors and been turned down every time, and he'd ended up in hospital maybe even more often, after yet another terrible crash. Mansell was the working man's champion. Win or lose, it didn't matter.

His unbridled dedication, his reckless street-fighting style, that was what mattered. Often, after a race in which Mansell really had given his all, he needed to be lifted out of his cockpit. Even if Jackie Stewart saw this as a weakness rather than a strength: 'As far as I'm concerned Mansell won't be a truly great driver until he's able to walk away from his car after a race without immediately collapsing or stumbling over everything in his path. Look at Prost and Senna: compared to you they're puny little runts – but they have more stamina. Cool it, Nigel.' Fat chance! Unforgettable images from Dallas 1984, when Mansell ran out of fuel and tried to score one last world-championship point by ignoring the subtropical temperatures and pushing his car over the line. It was too much: Mansell succumbed and ended up unconscious on the asphalt.

Theatrics, was Gerhard Berger's ice-cold judgement. Berger had been Mansell's team-mate for a year at Ferrari. Long enough to see right through him. Behind Mansell's appealing, crowd-pleasing behaviour, Berger discovered an extremely mistrustful loner. But, he added: 'Mansell already had people like Piquet after him, he was a wounded elephant.'

'People like Piquet' added even more lustre to Mansell's heroism. Because his whole life long, Mansell had to do battle with smooth, sharp, sly champions like Piquet, Prost and Senna. He beat them often enough on the track, but off it, in the world of contacts and contracts, they ran rings around him. No less than three times, Mansell stood by helplessly while a car in which he was convinced he could have become world champion was whisked out from under his nose. And nothing less than the championship would do, he'd set himself that goal in the very beginning. Again, this blind commitment was what made him the people's champion.

For thirteen years he fought and suffered for the title. Sometimes he came close, very close, but the championship always proved one notch too high. Jackie Stewart knew why:

> Mansell's problem is that he still thinks he has to prove how good he is. If he weren't so desperate to prove himself, he'd be a better driver.
>
> His head is down there between his feet instead of up on his shoulders. He gets too agitated and does things he later regrets. It's a matter of self-control and discipline. But Mansell still isn't capable of leaving emotions out of it – that's wrong: your head has to rule your heart, you can't let your heart be the boss.

Wise words and Stewart was no doubt right, but it was those very emotions – including all those failings, blunders and theatrics – that made the Lion so real and so appealing, so much less distant than all those other champions with their innate superiority.

Mansell became my hero as well. By finally winning races, he drew me back into Formula One. I too gradually discovered that adult life was more drudgery than rapture, but when a drudge won, it was fun to be there alongside him. Of course, he sometimes got carried away with his role as clown, outcast and loser, but for a long time he also generated Formula One's most beautiful, enjoyable and moving stories. Mansell was the voice of dissent in Bernie Ecclestone's increasingly commercialised, streamlined, result-obsessed circus.

And Mansell became world champion. At last. In 1992. 'When it was actually too late,' according to Berger. And Berger was right. The true Mansell fan had experienced his finest hour six years before, during that unforgettable race in Adelaide.

The Duffer and Sunday's Child

In 1980 Mansell made his début with Lotus. The tone was set right away: Mansell drove forty whole laps with pain searing his back; there'd been a spillage during refuelling. Afterwards he could barely walk and the next day saw him in hospital having the blisters lanced. But Colin Chapman saw something in the self-made man. When Mansell qualified as third in Monaco in 1981 and still looked gloomy at the dinner table, Chapman asked him what was wrong. Their money was almost all gone and Mansell's wife Rosanne wouldn't be able to travel to the remaining Grands Prix. Whereupon Chapman tapped his glass and announced that he was immediately doubling Mansell's salary, because Rosanne belonged there with the rest of them. The good old days.

But after Chapman's death in 1982, Mansell's position at Lotus suddenly became insecure. Heroism and blisters left Peter Warr cold, he wanted to bring home the occasional winner as well.

At the end of 1984 Mansell departs for Williams. Williams think they've snapped up an outstanding number two, but suddenly Mansell turns out to be a winner. In front of a home audience at Brands Hatch, he wins his first Grand Prix. And in 1985 and 1986 Mansell keeps on winning. Much to the annoyance of his new team-mate, Nelson Piquet. Piquet, spoilt by years as Brabham's unchallenged number one, discovers that Williams play by different rules. 'Don't run each other off the track,' is the only order Frank Williams gives to his drivers.

Thus begins a two-year battle for supremacy. A classic duel between the duffer and Sunday's child. The differences are clear: Williams pay Piquet 3.3 million dollars a year and 10,000 dollars for every point he scores. Mansell gets 800,000 and no bonus at all. It's the working-class hero versus the multi-millionaire, the family man versus the playboy with the yacht and the private plane. The double world champion has to pull out all the stops to keep in front of Mansell. That's why he regularly provides Mansell with disinformation, keeps new material under wraps, monitors Mansell's radio and tries to wind Mansell up every chance he gets: 'Mansell is just a dressed-up racing dummy, he realises that his car can go faster than his brain and that's what makes him so unbearable.'

Still, in direct confrontation Mansell is generally quicker, more aggressive and more persistent, like at Brands Hatch 1986.

The race begins with a pile-up: Jacques Lafitte breaking his legs and pelvis – the end of his career. Mansell is lucky. His Williams gave up the ghost just after the start. Now, for the restart, he's able to change over to the spare car. Since the spare car is Piquet's privilege, Mansell has to drive with his rival's set-up. What's more, there's no drinking bottle on board and the straps are much too tight. Against all odds. It becomes a blistering wheel-to-wheel battle between the two team-mates. Mansell is second for a long time, then he gets used to the car and exploits a minimal error from Piquet to take the lead. After the pit stops Mansell, on cold tyres, blocks Piquet any way he can for a whole lap. Piquet is furious, but Mansell wins: drained, dehydrated and five kilos lighter. Mansell mania sweeps England.

In Italy Enzo Ferrari has seen the race on television. Like Lauda and Villeneuve before him, Mansell is summoned to Maranello for an audience. Flattered and overwhelmed, Mansell signs various documents, only to realise on his way home that a contract with Ferrari will bury his title aspirations with Williams. Mansell phones Ferrari to cancel. He insists that he had only signed a declaration of intent, but Ferrari later admits to demanding a significant pay-off.

Whatever the truth of the matter, by the end of the season it seems money well spent. With a lead of six points over Prost and seven over Piquet, Mansell arrives in Adelaide for the decisive last race.

Finally a race to get me up in the middle of the night again. Mansell mania has reached me too. Especially now that the duffer is about to become world champion, I wouldn't miss it for anything.

Adelaide is on the Grand Prix calendar for the second time. A street circuit. Piquet hates street races, Mansell adores them, even if he's never won one.

It turns into the race of the tyres. In Mexico Berger has just won his first Grand Prix by surprising everyone and driving on without a pit stop, but no one is convinced that the same trick is possible in Australia. Mexico had also been Mansell's first chance to secure the title, but he hadn't even been able to drive, laid low as he was by Montezuma's revenge. 'To make it even worse,' Piquet later confessed, 'I stole all the toilet paper from the Williams pit.'

In Adelaide Mansell has everything under control. Things can hardly go wrong again: both Prost and Piquet need to win, and even then Mansell only needs to come in third.

Frank Williams is a guest in the BBC television studio. A terrible car crash at the start of the year has left Williams almost totally paralysed – the long trip to Australia is beyond him. The presenter runs through a few questions with him in preparation: there's one list for if Mansell becomes world champion, another one in case it's Piquet; they don't consider any other result possible.

On the other side of the globe, Piquet takes the lead after the start. But he's using too much fuel and is forced to lower turbo pressure. Rosberg, driving his last Grand Prix, takes over. Mansell is third, fourth, comfortable, nothing to worry about. He feels even more comfortable when Prost gets a flat tyre after a shunt with Berger. A pit stop puts the Frenchman way back; his hopes seem gone.

The experts from tyre supplier Goodyear inspect Prost's tyres and find few signs of wear. The teams are informed that they can drive on without pit stops. Williams had intended on stopping, but now there's a change of plan, partly on Piquet's advice: 'Slight vibration, but I'm not coming in.' Mansell too drives on.

The television is turned down low, everyone else is asleep. I'm the only one watching, the only one in the whole world, that's what it feels like.

The sixty-third lap, nineteen to go, and Rosberg gets a flat front tyre. But the veteran driver thinks it's engine failure and parks his car on the side of the track. Suddenly the television viewer knows more than the drivers: the tyres won't last the whole race after all. The most terrible, the most dramatic ninety seconds of the season begin . . . Piquet has taken over the lead from Rosberg, and Prost, going fast with new tyres, passes Mansell at the same moment. But third place is still enough. Mansell is more than a full minute ahead of number four, Stefan Johansson. 'Change!' I scream, whispering desperately to myself when Mansell appears on the screen, 'Change!' A minute ahead of Johannson. A wheel change will secure third place and give Mansell the title! But Mansell drives on. Why doesn't he pit? Williams says: we were ready for him. Mansell: the team kept me out there.

What follows is Nigel Mansell's ultimate moment. At more than 300 km/h on the Jack Brabham Straight, Mansell's left rear tyre explodes. Sparks, madly spinning rubber. The car swings to the side, jolts and touches the wall, again and again. Mansell wrestles with the wheel like a man possessed, struggling to follow the line of the wall. It's terrifying. I can't scream, can't stamp my feet, can't pound the chairs, everyone's asleep. The car slides straight ahead, but it's lost its momentum. Finally, doing 40 at the most, it hits the wall at the end of the escape road and stops.

My hands over my mouth, trembling knees, pounding heart. For seconds Mansell stays sitting in the car. Goodbye, title.

Of course, he's got off lightly. What if the car had got away from him? If it had started spinning or rolling, and that at 300 km/h? Mansell has just given a demonstration of superior car control. But what does he care about that?

Slowly, completely disillusioned, he climbs out, forcing himself to wave to the crowd. The helmet comes off, marshals approach cautiously and lead the broken, exhausted hero to safety. This is typical Nigel Mansell. He's just short of considering quitting right then and there, that comes later.

On the track a panicky Piquet rushes into the pits for new tyres and Prost seizes the title. The British TV studio is given over to a distraught silence.

A year later Mansell is close again. He wins six Grands Prix to three apiece for Prost and Piquet. Again, there are scenes of euphoria in England: in a fantastic chase at Silverstone, Mansell comes up from being twenty-eight seconds behind Piquet, then outsmarts him on Hangar Straight with two fabulous dummies.

In 1987 Mansell is definitely the quickest, but once again he misses out on the title. Partly because Piquet plays his usual games – keeping a new suspension system secret, for example – and partly because of a few absolute blunders of his own creation. Like at Spa, where he tries to overtake Senna in the first lap in a place where Senna thinks overtaking is impossible. Senna analyses:

> Mansell launches an all-out attack, I don't do a thing. It's pointless, no one can overtake there. People often try – but they always drop back at the last moment. I thought Mansell would do the same thing. I never thought he'd take such a risk. We both hit the brakes, changing down, six – five – four. Suddenly I realise: he's really going to do it. I'm in the middle of the track and already into the corner. Damn it, I think, we've had it. It's as if we're pouring into a funnel, I hope we'll slide apart some way or other, but when I'm already half on to the grass, he stubbornly takes the normal line. If he goes on like that, he'll

never make it. I bounce over the kerbs, we touch, and when the wheels come free again, the Lotus leaps into the air.

Senna slides off the track and can't go on. Mansell's car is damaged, and a little later he is forced to retire. But after the race he visits the Brazilian looking for redress. 'I could tell from the way his eyes were blazing that he hadn't come to apologise. Completely insane.' Mansell even got physical, and the Williams and Lotus mechanics had great difficulty stopping the situation from escalating into a cheap brawl. Mansell and Senna, they were each other's best opponents, neither gave up. Like magnets their cars were drawn together, the collisions and close calls were legion, but they never lost their mutual respect. Why not? Because Mansell and Senna never became team-mates.

In Hungary Mansell confirmed his status as the circus's tragic clown. Five laps before the finish, with a comfortable lead, he's overtaken by his own rear wheel. A wheel nut has come off. 'The wheel drive shaft and the wheel nuts are made of different alloys and when they get hot they can come loose,' explains Williams. 'The chance of something like this happening is one in a hundred. With Mansell evidently a little higher.'

As the battle for the championship intensifies, Piquet pulls his masterstroke. Full of hatred for Mansell and disappointed in Williams – 'Williams recruited me to become world champion, not to demolish myself in a struggle with Mansell' – he signs a contract with Lotus. In itself a lesser team, but more importantly: Piquet is taking the superior Honda engines with him. Suddenly Williams doesn't stand a chance in '88, they don't even have a turbo at their disposal. And Mansell can forget about the 1987 title as well, because Honda is looking ahead and would rather see the 1988 Number 1 on Piquet's Lotus-Honda. Politics. Mansell doesn't have a hope. When he runs short of horsepower in Portugal he is furious, but the Honda engineers just smile politely. And Piquet fans the flames. Asked who's the best, he answers: 'I've won two titles,

Mansell has lost one. Being quick isn't all there is to it. Often just keeping your car on the track is more important . . .'

Finally Mansell eliminates himself, in Japan of all places. Moving at high speed, the Williams goes into a spin, presumably caused by dirty tyres. The rear of the Williams hits a tyre barrier, the car spins around, bounces over the asphalt, then comes to a standstill. No signs of life from Mansell. Everyone in the pits freezes. But Mansell is alive. When they lift him up out of the car, he screams in agony: his back is broken. In hospital he ends up next to a man who calls out and moans all night. The next morning the man is dead. It's all too much for Mansell, who seriously considers giving up racing.

But with thirteen Grands Prix to his name and the ultimate goal within his grasp twice, he talks it over with Rosanne and decides to go on. But without a turbo engine in '88, even Mansell is just another back marker. At the end of the season he goes to Ferrari after all.

The Romantic and the Master of Intrigue

At Ferrari Mansell is perfectly at home. The romantic, the tragic hero, the unrewarded slogger. Chance has it that Mansell is allocated car Number 27, and from the first, the Ferrari fans, the *tifosi*, see him as the new Villeneuve, a man who drives with his heart. The Italians love him, and that's just what Mansell needs.

In Italy the ex-window-cleaner goes from astonishment to astonishment. In the Ferrari factory he expresses his admiration for the Ferrari Testarossa and, a week later, he finds one parked out the front of his house. The same with a Ducati motorbike. After excursions to factories, Mansell has to hire a van to transport all the presents home. But most astonishing of all is his first race for Ferrari.

Practising for the Brazilian Grand Prix, virtually everything that could break down broke down. The semi-automatic gearbox, operated with paddles on the back of the steering wheel, is new and far from fully tested. Berger and Mansell haven't driven five continuous laps between them. Team director Fiorio briefly considers half-filling the cars' fuel tanks, so that they can take the lead heroically before being forced to sadly retire with obscure defects: in other words, empty fuel tanks. The plan is rejected.

Berger and Senna collide in the opening phase of the race. Mansell is third, he gets past Boutsen, and in the fifteenth lap Patrese as well – spectacularly on the outside – and takes the lead. But, of course, victory doesn't come easily or without moments of anxiety. With twenty laps to go, Mansell notices that his steering wheel is coming loose. He has to drive almost a full lap with a loose steering wheel before he is able to pit for a new one. Prost – in the lead after Mansell's pit stop – has problems with his clutch and Mansell wins the race. An exhausted Mansell climbs the podium. In Maranello the bells ring and the Italian fans start painting giant banners: 'Nigel = Gilles'.

But there was a big difference between Mansell and Villeneuve. Both were born racers. Both sold their house to be able to race, both showed phenomenal commitment and a fearless driving style. Definitely. But Mansell was too up-front about it. He made more show of it, song and dance, theatrics. His victories were invariably heroic achievements, courageously wrested from the jaws of physical deprivation, devilish bad luck, tough opponents and unscrupulous team-mates. The exhaustion that Mansell exhibited after each and every race was bad enough, but it went further; Villeneuve never whinged about mechanical defects, intense pain, doubts or cheating. Whether it was cramp, toothache, dehydration or diarrhoea, Mansell had them all at least once. Even after a victory, Austria 1987, he smacked his head on a gantry on the way to the ceremony and appeared at the press conference sporting an enormous bump. And even when he was coasting towards the title in 1992, all the enjoyment was taken out of it by a villain behind the scenes and the torment of a new injury, this time it was his foot: pressing the accelerator was like stepping in glass, just ghastly. But ultimately the greatest difference was this: 'against all odds', Mansell *became* world champion. Villeneuve crashed fatally the moment he smelt treachery.

In 1989 Ferrari had too many problems, Mansell only succeeded in winning in Hungary. There was a sensation in Portugal, where Mansell made one of his infamous blunders. Going in for new tyres, Mansell missed the Ferrari pits. He stopped two garages further, put the car in reverse and did a perfect reverse park between his mechanics. On a circuit, however, traffic is strictly one way and the stewards decided to disqualify Mansell: black flag. But Mansell drove on, and in an unforgiving duel ran both Senna and himself off the track. The FIA suspended Mansell for one race for ignoring the black flag. A deeply indignant Mansell claimed he'd never even seen the flag and threatened to turn his back on Formula One for ever.

But the title beckoned. By 1990 the teething pains were over, the Ferrari 641/2 was a potential winner. Just not for Mansell. The season that had been predestined as *Il Leone*'s time to reap was spoilt by the arrival of Alain Prost. Prost was made for the Byzantine environment of Ferrari and soon had all kinds of top bosses convinced that there was only one way of beating McLaren, Honda and, above all, Senna: by concentrating on one car, *his*, of course. Prost's store of questionable tactics was too much for Mansell. For the second time, Mansell was side-tracked by team politics.

Prost's slyness went so far, relates Mansell, that he surreptitiously had the cars changed for the British Grand Prix after Mansell had done so well in France. Mansell noticed it immediately, and his mechanics grudgingly confessed. Mansell responded by promptly seizing pole position. He then led the race until forced to retire with gearbox problems. Theatrically, he flung his gloves into the crowd and announced that his racing days were over.

The People's Champion

In 1991 Mansell was back in a Formula One racing car. Frank Williams had appeased him with big money and an array of rock-solid guarantees. In 1991 they would lay the groundwork and then, in 1992, it would finally happen. Agreed. At least, that's how Mansell looks back on it in his autobiography. In reality he could have done much better in 1991 if he hadn't bungled in his customary style.

Like in Canada when he stalled while leading in the final lap. A mechanical defect, Mansell insists. A blunder, his many critics claim: Mansell was so busy waving to the crowd that he let the revs drop below a critical level, various systems inside the car stopped functioning properly and the engine seized up. While an enraged Mansell pounded the steering wheel and parked his Williams in the grass, Piquet of all people raced past to claim the race. 'I almost came,' sniggered Piquet afterwards. It was his last victory.

By the end of the season, the Williams was easily the best car on the grid, but by then Senna's lead was too great. In Portugal Mansell squandered his last chance. Leading, he pitted in the thirtieth lap. He did it fast: four new wheels in seven seconds. That was a little too fast because, when he drove off, his right rear wheel went its own way. Helpless on three wheels, the Williams sat there in the pit lane. Williams and wheel nuts. The mechanics whipped out of their pit and quickly mounted a new rear wheel, but repairs outside of the team's own garage zone are forbidden. This time Mansell noticed the black flag.

Mansell went into 1992 with the best cards. The best car, the best engine, the most advanced electronics, even the fuel gave him extra horsepower. Of course, the car still needed steering.

After five races, Mansell had scored a maximum of fifty points. Senna, the only serious contender, was way behind on eight. Prost had left Ferrari after a hell of a row and was absent for a year. No one realised that the master of intrigue was already working on his fourth title behind the scenes.

With Patrese as loyal team-mate, a superior Mansell zeroed in on his well-earned championship. But the temptation to bungle remained irresistible. Like back in Canada, the first time he failed to take an immediate lead. Senna beat him to it. At the end of the fifteenth lap Mansell risked a passing manoeuvre and flew off the track. Mansell insisted that Senna had punted him off, Senna claimed that Mansell had simply braked too late and taken to the gravel of his own accord. Everyone knew that Mansell, in a superior car and with the championship as his only goal, should have known better. Five years after Spa-Francorchamps, nothing had changed.

In Monaco too Mansell showed his best side. For almost the entire race, he led the field without a problem, keeping Senna at a comfortable distance. Then suddenly Mansell was gone, even the TV cameras couldn't find him. Mansell had slipped into the pits with a suspected rear puncture. It turned out to be – what else? – a loose wheel nut. But Senna was past. Six laps left to go. Within a single lap, Mansell was dangling from Senna's gearbox. Five hilarious, fabulous laps followed. Over and over, everywhere, even where it was absolutely impossible, Mansell tried to overtake Senna. But Senna was not going to be tricked out of his fifth Monaco Grand Prix, he knew exactly where to hog the track, which lines to take to keep Mansell behind him. Over and over again, at Mirabeau, at the chicane, before Rascasse, in Rascasse, after Rascasse, Mansell pushed the nose of his Williams left or right, sometimes left *and* right beside the McLaren. 'Sometimes I saw two or three McLarens in front of me.' The only way to get past Senna was by driving over the top of him. Forbidden.

Senna won. It had been Formula One at its best. Once again Senna and Mansell had shown that they were the circus's best and above all most entertaining fighters. Of course, Mansell had to be lifted out of his car after the finish and his knees buckled several times as he made his way to the prince's box. That was our Nigel.

But for the rest of the season, the 'Red Five' cruised relatively easily from pole to victory. The highlight was Silverstone. Mansell qualified on pole, two seconds ahead of Patrese, three before Senna. With his tanks still full, Mansell broke the lap record in just the second lap, and went on to win from his team-mate with a forty-second lead. The British fans stormed the track even before the slowing-down lap was over. At risk of life and limb. Mansell said later that he did actually run over someone, but the man thought it was fantastic. An enormous crowd of fans finally halted the Williams, dragged their hero out of his cockpit and hoisted him up on to their shoulders. The People's Champion. Damon Hill, driving just behind Mansell in his début race, was scared he wouldn't come out of it alive. 'They even cheered me, although I was last by four laps.'

Mansell mania was understandable. Mansell wasn't the only one, his fans had been waiting for ever as well. No one begrudged him his success, but it didn't exactly make for an exciting season.

By Hungary he had already secured the title; never before had the championship been decided so early in the season.

Mansell wasn't given long to enjoy it, however, because in a sense the 1993 championship was decided even faster. To Mansell's detriment.

As early as the second Grand Prix weekend in 1992, Frank Williams had sounded out Mansell as to how he felt about Prost as team-mate for the coming year. Mansell tried to play for time – he remembered Prost from Ferrari. But he didn't know Prost well enough, because what he didn't realise was that Prost had already signed with Williams. For the third time, Mansell was confronted by political machinations. When Williams kept on nagging about Prost, Mansell realised what had happened. He succumbed, but made demands. Now it was Williams's turn to hesitate: obscure games were played, there were rumours of an offer from Senna. With his pride badly wounded, Mansell himself finally cut the knot. Despite last-minute whisperings about Williams accepting all of his conditions, Mansell gave an emotional press conference at Monza announcing his second departure from Formula One.

Mansell crossed the ocean and became – totally unprecedented – Indy car champion of the United States in his first year. Without really raising a sweat, but *with* a more or less broken back, almost fatal crashes and other discomforts – that goes without saying.

And of course he came back. After Senna's crash in 1994, Mansell succumbed to pressure from Ecclestone and drove a few more races for Williams, the man who had treated him so disgracefully just two years earlier.

In Japan Mansell put up another heroic battle. On a wet track, he duelled with Jean Alesi for third place. Lap after lap they raced up to the 130R corner wheel to wheel. Every time Mansell pushed his Williams up next to the Ferrari, but Alesi never blinked, he just braked a little later or a little less and forced Mansell back. Afterwards the two die-hards hugged each other. Now, just when their sport was catching so much flak, they had shown how breathtaking and beautiful it could be. In Adelaide, Mansell even managed to win the last race of the season. Next to him on the podium, Berger could not restrain a disappointed smile: 'So, you old bastard, you back again?'

All the same, Williams didn't want Mansell for another whole season. For the umpteenth time, Mansell's departure seemed imminent. But then McLaren managed to recruit him for 1995. Proudly, Mansell declared that he had now driven for all the great Formula One teams: Lotus, Williams, Ferrari and McLaren. But the McLaren adventure turned into a ridiculous fiasco. When he turned up for testing, Mansell didn't even fit into the cockpit! He was forced to miss two whole races. He could forget about the championship before he'd even started, and in the races that followed the car turned out to be uncontrollable. Mansell looked a fool and chucked it in after just two Grands Prix. For good. Probably.

Prost and Senna: The Best and the Fastest

Here begins the story of Alain Prost and Ayrton Senna. A story without an equal. Neither in the history of motor racing, nor in sporting history in general.

Prost on Senna: 'He has completely destroyed everything. I thought he was one of the human race. I thought he was hard but fair on the track. Forget it. I am not ready to fight against irresponsible people who are not afraid to die.'

Senna on Prost: 'He is always trying to destroy people. He tried to destroy me in the past on different occasions and he hasn't managed. He will not manage, because I know who I am and where I want to go.'

In the words of Gerhard Berger: 'Alain Prost and Ayrton Senna felt a profound and sincere hatred for each other. Leaving aside everything to do with origins, culture and character, the absolute claim to the number-one status alone was enough to generate an excess of emotions.'

It started straight away, in their fifth race together, the 1984 Monaco Grand Prix, the water ballet.

After Mansell slipped on the white lines, Prost resumed the lead. Quick but cautious, Prost picked his way through the rain. He wasn't in a hurry, his lead over Lauda was comfortable. What's more, Prost didn't like the wet. Didier Pironi's 1982 accident at Hockenheim was still fresh in his memory.

Pironi was on the verge of securing the world championship. He already had pole position. Was it just because he was testing new rain tyres that he was driving a good 280 on the straight to the Motordrome that morning? In front of him, Prost's Renault was hidden in the spray from Daly's Williams. Prost felt the crash, he saw Pironi's Ferrari take off 'at least thirty metres high', cartwheel over and over again, bouncing over the asphalt until it finally lay still, totally mangled. Pironi came out of it alive, but it cost him his title and his career. That morning Prost must have set his own internal limit: win, but not at any price.

Senna is completely different. In his first Formula One season and driving a car that is scarcely competitive, he has nothing to lose and wants to win at any price.

Senna is the discovery of the season. This is his first race in Monte Carlo. Overtaking impossible? He pushes his rattling Toleman past Laffitte, Winckelhock, Rosberg; all big-name drivers, but they don't stand a chance. He takes care of Arnoux, leaves Lauda behind like a learner . . . But Prost's lead is still considerable. Never mind. The weather is on his side, it's getting worse by the minute.

Prost feels Senna approaching. He's having problems with his brakes, as he explains later, and one of his wheels is loose. He also thinks that the conditions have become too dangerous. Passing start-finish he gestures repeatedly that the race should be stopped or ended completely.

The official starter in Monaco is Jacky Ickx. As ex-rain master, he knows the score. In his younger years, Ickx sometimes claimed that the risk and the danger were the sport's greatest challenge. But when even Lauda slides off the track in the twenty-third lap, Ickx takes it as a bad omen. 'When people are flying off everywhere, there comes a moment when you have to cut the knot: is a race safe or isn't it? That's a personal judgement of someone with experience, who decides whether or not to stop the race, independently of team managers, drivers and the public.'

Senna is getting closer. He's three to five seconds a lap faster than Prost. Of course, he's taking risks, but Senna knows what he's doing, Monaco suits him. In the twenty-seventh lap the gap is still twenty seconds, a lap later, fifteen, twelve, seven . . .

But then Ickx red-flags the race, in the thirty-first lap. Immediately there is a barrage of criticism. Just one or two laps more and Senna would have been front-runner. Ickx, still driving for Porsche in 1984, is accused of favouring Prost and Porsche. 'Nonsense,' according to Ickx. 'For me, it's crucial for a driver that his career lasts twenty years or more. I'm against voluntary accidents that injure or maybe even kill people.'

Whether or not it was because of Porsche, it's good that Ickx prolonged Prost's and Senna's careers a little longer. Because the incident at Monaco turned out to be the prelude to a ten-year epic, full of controversy, obscure treaties, clear violations, ruthless duels, cunning contracts and merciless crashes – a battle, in other words, that gave Formula One new standing.

Ironically, both drivers drew the short straw in 1984. Ickx's decision handed Prost the victory on a platter, but because he hadn't driven 75 per cent of the normal distance, the points were halved. Instead of nine points, Prost scored just four and a half. At the end of the season he stood on the podium at Estoril in tears. For the third time running, Prost had just missed out on the title: he'd ended up half a point behind his team-mate, Niki Lauda.

Jackie Stewart called Prost and Senna the best and the fastest. But what was the difference? The difference, despite everything to do with origins, culture and character, was that Prost started Formula One four years earlier. Prost had already lost several times and he'd been through the horrors of 1982: Villeneuve, Paletti, Pironi . . . His successes were all achieved against that background.

Senna's triumphs, on the other hand, led almost immediately to an unlimited future. Loss and horror were not part of his vocabulary. It wasn't until 30 April 1994 that he was finally confronted with the ultimate price; one day later it was all over.

Nicknames often reveal the extremes. Prost was generally called 'The Professor'; Senna, 'Magic Senna'. Prost and Senna: more than anything else, it was calculation versus sorcery, reason against ecstasy. The best and the fastest. The difference: death.

Ecclestone's Circus

In the second half of the 1980s, Bernie Ecclestone smoothed out all the bumps. After various failed treaties, his latest deal with FISA held up. Ecclestone's reputation for using aggressive business methods to get his way was established; when all else failed, he simply bought out his adversaries. Whatever his tactics, FOCA's grip on the Grands Prix became more and more apparent. Formula One had changed for ever: from a hotchpotch reeking of motor oil it had become a streamlined customised circus with all conveniences. What's more, FOCA had taken over television direction and rights, a change that turned out to be the key to unparalled financial success.

The efforts in the safety area also bore fruit. The sport's image improved by leaps and bounds. For a long time Riccardo Paletti was the last fatality during a Grand Prix weekend. Elio de Angelis was killed at Paul Ricard in 1986, but that happened during testing, far from the cameras. De Angelis died because there were not enough marshals present to extricate him from his burning wreck. This made organisers finally realise that Formula One practice is not some kind of high-speed soccer training; since then tests have been permitted only under optimal safety conditions.

After De Angelis, Formula One stayed clean for eight years thanks to extremely strict safety regulations, thanks to new equipment that had become standard in motor racing and, above all, thanks to a tremendous run of luck.

But clean? How clean is clean? At Imola in 1987 Piquet cheated death in the Tamburello thanks to the strength of his car. For a few years, almost all chassis had been constructed of carbon fibre, an incredibly expensive synthetic fibre developed for space travel: a third the weight of aluminium and four times as strong. Carbon fibre doesn't dent and only breaks after an extremely hard impact. One problem: now that the cars came out of the collisions undented, the driver's bodies were subject to much greater forces. Piquet: 'The worst thing is that this kind of chassis doesn't get wrecked. You'd be dead long before it breaks – the human body can't cope with such tremendous forces.' After the Tamburello, Piquet was groggy for a half a season, but he lived and even became world champion.

In 1989 Philippe Streiff crashed in Brazil and was left paralysed. And at Imola, again in the Tamburello, Berger was pulled out of his burning Ferrari by fast-moving marshals. Since then fire has been a rarity. The tanks and fuel lines were fitted with valves that close automatically in emergencies. Clean. At Monza in 1990 Derek Warwick turned upside-down coming out of the Parabolica at more than 200 km/h. The Lotus slid over the asphalt on its roll bars – shock in the crowded stands. But Warwick crawled out, crossed the track, ran into the pits, climbed into the spare car and quickly drove another fast lap. Less fortunate was Martin Donnelly who demolished his Lotus at Jerez but was lucky enough to be catapulted out of the wreck along the way. Choking on his own blood, unconscious and with multiple compound fractures of his legs, the driver lay on the asphalt. Briefly regaining consciousness in the medical centre, he asked about his lap time . . .

At Estoril in 1992 Patrese spun through the air at more than 200 km/h and missed the pit wall by a fraction of an inch . . .

The following year Warwick repeated his Monza stunt at Hockenheim. This time he landed upside-down in the gravel. Professor Watkins even removed gravel from his ear canals. Warwick: 'I recognise the gravel. I got it at Monza in 1990.' Also in 1993 Christian Fittipaldi survived a backward somersault at 300 km/h at Monza; and at Spa the sturdiness of his car saved

Alex Zanardi when he smashed into an embankment coming out of Eau Rouge. Carbon fibre. The cockpit of the Lotus was still whole, but everything else had come off. Launched components were clearly going to be the next problem.

But Formula One was safe, wasn't it? If nothing else, the sponsors' names were no longer being blackened by association with a *danse macabre*. Formula One flourished and appeared every two weeks live on more and more TV screens all over the world.

The explosively expanding media universe opened the way to unprecedented advertising possibilities. But now that it had come of age, Formula One made sponsors pay accordingly. The costs sky-rocketed. In the late 1970s, a couple of million was enough to get the sponsor's name plastered all over the car, ten years later the same amount was laid down for the rear wing alone. The teams hardly knew what hit them. In a decade their budgets were multiplied by a factor of fourteen or even twenty. This, of course, brought sweeping changes to motor racing. The small 'racing teams' – out-of-hand hobbies of English lords or uneducated Italian garage owners – had to step aside. Teams that wanted to survive had to become big companies with factories, large numbers of staff, long-term planning and market strategies. Williams and McLaren were the first to catch on and emerged as clear winners. Time-honoured teams like March, Brabham and even Lotus, that had determined the face of the sport for years, missed the boat, fell behind and went to the wall – often after undignified tricks and gambits with anonymous major sponsors. Ferrari saved its skin by selling out to Fiat. Tyrrell lasted the longest, but after more than ten pitiful years, the curtain fell for 'Uncle Ken' as well.

The drivers, at least the top ones, had no regrets. Ecclestone may have been an autocrat, but he was always there for them. 'Thanks to Bernie everything we do, on the track but off it as well, is properly valued, and I'm not just talking about the cash,' says Gerhard Berger. Not just the cash, but it was still nice to see the salaries shooting up.

In 1981 stars like Piquet and Villeneuve made around a million a year. Big money in those days. But Lauda, as astute as ever, was the first to realise that there was much more to be earned. Media-driven Formula One needed stars. Appropriately, Lauda's 1982 comeback cost McLaren's Ron Dennis 5 million dollars a year.

Lauda paved the way, but Piquet followed. In 1987 he received 3.3 million dollars from Williams. With Prost and Senna, the salaries really took off. In 1991, at his peak, Senna received 10 million dollars from McLaren. Two years later Mansell asked Williams for more than twice that amount – he didn't get it. But by 1996 Ferrari was already shelling out 25 million dollars for Michael Schumacher. Even taking inflation into account, salaries have increased by a factor of at least fifteen in as many years. For the stars. Because most drivers still have to put in their own money to get a car to drive.

If you're getting that much money, you don't need garlands. With budgets assuming astronomical proportions, sponsors began objecting to the garland of laurel that had always been hung around the neck of the Grand Prix winner. That unwieldy piece of shrubbery just got in the way of the brand names they'd paid top dollar to display. Ecclestone was sympathetic. Formula One had to move with the times, advertising was more important than ritual: the garlands disappeared.

No one even notices any more. But the last link to Olympus had been broken, the gods of speed had been degraded into money machines.

Who cared? Ecclestone's circus was a success story. Formula One attained an unprecedented degree of perfection and professionalism. But as it grew, the sporting commitment and financial interests became increasingly entangled. The asphalt heroes were swallowed up by sponsors and media, but in the new generation, Ecclestone had found the drivers he needed, the ones who could carry the whole business on their shoulders, phenomenal racers who developed into megastars who were perfectly at home with Formula One's megalomaniac image.

Until the First Corner

In 1985 Prost dominated and won the championship. It was about time, everyone knew he was the best. In 1986 Prost profited from the rivalry between Mansell and Piquet and, for the first time since Jack Brabham in 1959 and 1960, a driver won two consecutive titles. In 1987 the Williams-Honda combination was superior, but Prost had something else to celebrate that year. At Estoril he booked his twenty-eighth Grand Prix victory, breaking the record Jackie Stewart had set in 1973. Stewart was the first to congratulate Prost: 'Alain deserves it. There is no doubt in my mind that he is the best race driver of his generation.'

In 1988 the world championship beckoned again, because Honda had announced its move to McLaren. But part of the deal was that McLaren would also take Senna. Ron Dennis didn't think twice.

'Never put two bulls in one meadow,' warned Frank Williams. He was jealous, of course, but also a wiser man after all the aggravation involving Mansell and Piquet. But Dennis wasn't listening. During the 1987 Italian Grand Prix, Dennis introduced his new team to the press. Both drivers spoke friendly, professional words. Prost: 'I think in the past we at McLaren have shown we could have two equal number-one drivers. I know that Ayrton is very professional and I will help him to integrate in the team. We have to work together, but of course I will do my best to beat him on the track.' And Senna: 'From a personal point of view I am very happy to work with Alain: two top drivers working together can only make a team stronger.'

Moving words and initially Ron Dennis was shown to be right. In 1988 Senna and Prost's McLarens left the competition far behind. They came within a whisker of winning all sixteen Grands Prix, leaving only Italy to Ferrari. A mistake of Senna's: with two laps to go and in a winning position, he crashed into a back marker. Never before had one team been so dominant.

Prost won seven races, normally more than enough to clinch the title, but this time Senna won eight. Prost had still scored more points. In the style of a true champion, he did his sums and finished more often than his team-mate. But this time, doing his sums didn't help him. According to the rules, only the eleven best results counted. Prost was obliged to discard three second places (behind Senna) – eighteen points – and ended up with three points less than Senna. World champion Senna. Speed was rewarded.

Apart from this bizarre scoring system (abolished at the end of 1990), the season seemed perfect. But the duel, the feud, was already smouldering. Prost in retrospect: 'Even before he joined McLaren I knew we were never going to be friends because our personalities were completely unalike. He is a very strange guy.'

Oddly enough it was Ron Dennis himself who fed the flames. In Monaco Senna had given away a sure victory by suddenly driving extremely fast laps ten laps before the finish. That weekend, Monaco had made Senna ecstatic. After a superior qualification he began talking about speed and a higher level of consciousness, the absolute limit and God. But a long, exhausting race was another matter – too human perhaps. Coming out of the Virage du Portier, Senna's high ended with a thud. It was a turning point in his career. The arithmetician slipped past and scored his fourth victory at Monaco, and also his last.

That evening at a gala, the sportsmanlike winner admitted that it had been Senna's race, that Senna had deserved to win, but that it was all part of the game and he, Prost, was very happy with his victory. Dennis rushed up straight away and declared that it must have been a problem with the car: Senna didn't make those kind of mistakes. Prost immediately knew the score: Senna was Dennis's new pet.

Prost was forced on to his back foot, and that was how it would stay, even when he was well ahead in the battle for the title. For example, when he was obliged to explain retiring twenty-five laps into the British Grand Prix: rain. 'You can see nothing and drive by ear, listening for the man in front to change down for a corner, hoping he reduces speed consistently.' Pironi's crash at Hockenheim was clearly on his mind.

The race was won by Senna, rain master yet again. This race at Silverstone was a turning point, the beginning of Senna's unstoppable advance. Prost really was forced on to the defensive. Perhaps explaining that strange manoeuvre at Estoril.

At the start of the Portuguese Grand Prix, Prost clearly deviated from his line, forcing Senna to go off the track with two wheels. Senna was furious, but still took the lead. A lap later Prost came up alongside on the long straight, but now Senna deviated from *his* line, almost forcing Prost into the concrete pit-lane wall. Speed: well over 250 km/h. With the cars almost touching, Prost hit a bump. People dived off the wall in panic. Prost: 'We didn't touch but we could have and then it would have been a disaster. I don't understand manoeuvres like that. If we have to do things like that to win the world championship, frankly I don't care about it.'

But why did he deviate from his line at the start? No answer. And that was what had enraged Senna, because it was Prost himself who had tried several times to arrange a non-aggression pact until the first corner. Or was the agreement only supposed to apply *in* the first corner? Never mind: Prost won in Portugal, Senna took the championship.

But in just the second race of the next season the shit really hit the fan. Definitively. Because where's the first corner at Imola? Is it the Tamburello? Most drivers take that one flat out. The Curva Villeneuve then, named after Gilles, who once had a spectacular crash there. Full speed as well – if you've got the guts. The drivers only really brake for the Tosa, a genuine hairpin, the first real corner, one and a half kilometres into the circuit.

Berger proves that the Tamburello is a real corner by losing it at 280 km/h and hitting the wall almost full on. With Berger unconscious in the cockpit, the car bursts into flame, but lightning-fast, perfectly equipped marshals manage to pull him out of the wreck. He is carted off to the medical centre.

Italy. Chaos. It is touching to see an obviously upset, worried Mansell on his way to the medical centre to enquire about his team-mate. Later it turns out that he only wants to know if it was a mechanical fault, so that he can have his own car checked before the restart. Berger himself is no less cynical: 'In our sport nothing is more important than beating your own team-mate. All that stuff about "the most important thing is that our team wins" is hogwash. You cross your fingers, hoping his engine will blow up or, better still, that he'll fly off, without really hurting himself of course, that really is the limit. It's a fact though that your face is one big smile under your helmet the moment he's stuck in the tyre wall.' Without really hurting himself . . . Berger got off with light burns.

The drivers were still jittery at the restart and then it happened. Prost got away fastest and took the lead, but Senna was behind him in his slipstream: 'I gained speed because of that and I pulled out well before the braking point. My overtaking manoeuvre was thus begun, in my opinion, well before the first corner and as a consequence outside the terms of our agreement.'

Prost disagrees: '. . . Senna said to me, as we'd often done before, "At the first corner let's both of us try and escape the others, neither of us will attack which one of us is in the lead and we'll start the race at the end of the first corner." He took advantage to overtake me since I was in the lead and thus he broke his word.'

Listen to what Senna adds later:

> Long ago Prost had already proposed not getting in each other's way in the first metres. Whoever got off fastest wouldn't be attacked until we were through the first corner. I found it a strange suggestion, not at all consistent with my idea of racing. Each time I answered Prost, 'OK, we'll try it.' Until he did the dirty on me last year at Estoril. Then he suddenly no longer remembered anything about a non-aggression pact. At Imola he

got his own back. I don't see why I should have lifted there. I was faster. That's what Formula One's all about, isn't it?

Comparing Senna's statements, it's unclear whether or not there was an agreement and to which point it applied. This hedging turned out to be typical of Senna. If nothing else, it compromises an impression of fair play.

Prost is a bad loser, often that makes his defence childish and vindictive. Senna must win, often that makes his attacks risky and questionable.

The bulls were on the loose. It was not the first time that Imola had signalled the start of a duel between team-mates, but the hatred between Pironi and Villeneuve only lasted two weeks, Prost and Senna had five years to go, exactly, until Imola 1994.

Ron Dennis tried to calm things down. During testing a few days later he pressured Senna to apologise. In the interest of the team, Senna gave in. The team manager breathed a sigh of relief: 'This stays between us, we won't speak any more about it, OK?' But a week later he read the whole story in *L'Equipe*. Senna's apology had not been enough for Prost: 'I do not wish to drag McLaren into difficulties caused by the behaviour of Senna. McLaren has always been loyal to me. At a level of technical discussion I shall not close the door completely but for the rest I no longer wish to have any business with him. I appreciate honesty and he is not honest.'

Of course Prost is going too far, but he knows that his days with McLaren are numbered. Mud-slinging is the only option he has left. On the eve of Monza, Prost announces that he will drive the next season for Ferrari. The *tifosi* cheer, his victory is celebrated as a victory for Ferrari and, adding insult to injury, Prost throws his trophy to the audience. The hatred runs deep, very deep.

At Estoril Mansell ignores the black flag lap after lap, then crashes with Senna. Mansell is Prost's team-mate for the next year. An out for Senna is just what Prost needs, and with a comfortable lead in the world championship, he departs for Japan, where Senna now has to win to retain a chance at the title.

Suzuka. Drama in Two Acts

Just before the race in Japan, Prost announces that he has kept the door open many times to avoid a crash with Senna, but he does not propose to do it again today.

It is an unforgettable race. Prost takes the lead. Senna messes up his start and has to come from the back of the field. But, by halfway, he's tailing his team-mate again. Man to man, identical cars, no back markers, Mansells or other spoilers in the way, lap after lap. Senna attacks, taking the corners faster and wilder, but every time, the more consistent Prost does a better job of accelerating out of them. The First Corner, the Esses, the Degner, the Hairpin, the Spoon: Senna stalks Prost, but nowhere is there a chance to overtake. The chicane perhaps. In front of the right-left-right chicane, Prost lingers ominously on the left of the track. Maybe, if Senna can get close enough and brakes very late and Prost lingers over on the left, maybe the gap on the right will be big enough.

Before the chicane is the 130R corner, where the cars hurtle over the kerbs at almost full speed. Senna takes it a little wider than Prost, his McLaren jolting over the red-and-white bumps, but he's hanging on to the gearbox of his enemy, who swings left again, left, left, long enough, and Senna dives into the gap on the right. At the same moment Prost slams the door shut. Both drivers brake, skid, hook into each other and fraternally slide off the track. The McLarens stop alongside each other. For a moment the drivers look at each other and Prost raises his hands: is this what you wanted? Of course not, this is what Prost wanted. That was why he dawdled on the left before the chicane and uncharacteristically closed the door when the time came. Even if they crashed, the cars are only doing about 80 there. Prost knew exactly what he was doing. He also knew that Senna had to try, and now they're both out of the race and Prost is world champion.

Senna disagrees. Gesticulating furiously, he convinces the marshals to push him back on to the track. It's forbidden, but Senna has to win. And he does, after repeating the manoeuvre, this time without colliding, and outbraking Nannini in the chicane. As expected, Senna is disqualified. Prost, world champion. But McLaren disagrees and appeals against the disqualification and, with it, Prost's title.

Two weeks later, in Australia, the rain is pelting down. After one lap Prost has had enough. Pironi. Theoretically Senna can still win the title, *if* McLaren's appeal is upheld. But in the spray, Senna doesn't notice Brundle and crashes. Prost, world champion.

Of course, McLaren's protest was rejected. Prost, in retrospect about Suzuka:

> I always thought the race would be decided one of two ways: either he would lead from the start or it would finish like this. I looked in my mirrors, saw where he was and thought he was too far back to try anything. He had been closer than that before and stayed behind. You know Ayrton's problem? He can't accept not winning and because of that he can't accept someone resisting his overtaking manoeuvres. Too many times he tries to intimidate people out of his way. A lot of times I have had to open the door . . . He is unbelievably quick but for me he is driving too hard and if you have two drivers like this in Formula One then you have an accident in every race. I'm very sorry to see it end like this.

A year later they're back. At Suzuka. Senna on pole in a McLaren. And this time he's leading the world championship. Next to him on the front row: Prost, Ferrari. Today it's Prost who needs to win to retain a chance at the title. You feel it coming. The year has been full of conflict: six wins for Senna, five for Prost. But more than anything, there has been conflict off the track. Their rivalry completely dominates Formula One and everyone has done their best to fan the flames. Over and over, journalists have asked them to shake hands, not to bury the hatchet of course, just for the camera. Prost is willing, but not Senna. Only at Monza does he agree, uneasy, sullen: 'We have the same profession, the same passion, but beyond that we have nothing in common. I'm willing to shake hands with him, but don't go drawing any conclusions. It's a comma in a fat dictionary.'

And now Suzuka. You feel it coming. Even before qualifying, Senna has complained to the organisers: pole position is on the right of the track, a good position for the run at the first corner, but bad for the start. There's too much dust and grit on the track on the right, the grip is not optimal; left is at an advantage. The organisers agree to switch positions, Senna clocks up the fastest time and hears later that he has to start on the right after all. You feel it coming.

It's one o'clock in the afternoon in Japan. Five in the morning in Holland. In the nick of time but already wide-awake, I sit down in front of the telly. My heart pounds as the adversaries complete the warm-up lap and take position alongside each other. The absolute claim to number-one status: the lights go red, then green, and it's Prost. On the cleaner asphalt, he has the best start and shoots at the first corner in front of Senna. He starts on the right-hander a length in front. But he's still left a gap. Enough? Too little? Without hesitating, Senna dives in on the inside. A fraction of a second later both cars are spinning through the gravel. Finished. Senna, world champion.

It lasted fifteen seconds. Across the globe the viewers shuck off a great tension. Then comes the disappointment, the emptiness. He just rammed him, you think, before falling asleep again.

Later the insiders agree. Senna deliberately crashed into Prost, paying him back for Suzuka 1989. Except while Prost played his game at 80 km/h, Senna did it at over 200.

Still, some wondered why Prost hadn't closed the door all the way, he hesitated before taking the racing line, there was a gap, even if it was never big enough, and Senna was behind. Stupid of Prost, in the eyes of Watson and Stewart. Wrong of Senna, according to Rosberg and Arnoux. 'Who was inside, who was outside?' grinned Lauda.

The wisest words came from Jacky Ickx, once Clerk of the Course at Monaco.

> Suzuka Part Two is the result of Suzuka Part One. In Part One it was obvious Prost knew he was going to be overtaken at the chicane and he completely changed his line compared with the forty-five laps he had done before; and Part Two is the logical answer to Part One, even if it was a desperate attempt to overtake. These things would never have happened twenty years ago. You were on your line and somebody was going to overtake you if he was faster but you never changed your line even *half a metre*. Now you block people to stop them overtaking. It is not only not behaving like a gentleman, it is also awfully dangerous and if you don't stop the drivers doing these kinds of actions it is going to be very . . . difficult. One of these days we are going to have a terrible crash.

Ickx was right: Stewart and Fittipaldi, Lauda and Hunt, Villeneuve and Pironi, even Mansell and Piquet, hadn't run each other off the track. Senna and Prost may have been the greatest of all time, phenomenal and unparalleled, superstars – their drama in two acts still went beyond the pale and permanently blemished motor racing. Because in that regard, too, Ickx was right: Suzuka created a precedent. In the years that followed, numerous championships were decided by a deliberate crash. The trend seems irreversible, fewer and fewer drivers have a real chance at the title, there's too much at stake.

Prost was furious: 'What Senna did is disgusting. I am not ready to fight against irresponsible people who are not afraid to die. Anyone who understands motor racing does not have to ask what happened. He did it because he saw that I had a good start, that my car was better and he had no chance to win. So he just pushed me out.' And then he really let loose. The hatred went deep. And Prost is not a good loser, that went deep as well, the fact that he brought up the subject himself tells volumes. 'I have no problems about losing the world championship, I have lost many but not this way. I do not like people who do not tell the truth, people who show one thing but are different inside. Senna has shown his real face. He has completely destroyed everything. I thought he was one of the human race. I thought he was hard but fair on the track. Not like this. For him it is much more important to win the championship than it is for me. It is the only thing he has in life.' Then he started ranting: 'In Islam, for someone who is about to die, death is a game. The problem here is that we have seen Senna ready to take all the risks to win the championship. I am not ready to play this game.'

Senna reacted coolly. 'I was going faster. In the first corner, when you have cold tyres, low pressure, the car heavy, you normally brake earlier and if you try hard you can try to overtake. It is difficult, it is risky, but in my position I had to try. Prost should have known that. I think he made a big mistake to close the door on me because he took a chance that went wrong.'

You can feel Senna's discomfort. A year later he put a new spin on it: 'The 1990 World Championship was decided in a stupid way. I contributed to it, I admit that, but I wasn't responsible. Jean-Marie Balestre was.' The French president of FISA had dictated from Paris that the pole position at Suzuka was to remain on the right. 'I told myself, "Okay, you try and work clean – and then you get screwed by stupid people." Right then, I knew that Prost would be better off not deviating from his line at the start. In that case I wouldn't do anything to avoid a crash. And the unavoidable happened. A shame for the sport, but Balestre asked for it.'

Twisting, twisting. Senna had to win, that's why he had no qualms about going too far.

The Proviso

If only it had stopped at Suzuka. Because the duel and the bitterness continued undiminished. Even in 1991, when Senna dominated the championship and the only resistance came from Mansell and Williams. In his Ferrari, Prost was clearly outclassed. But the two rivals were still at each other's throats at every opportunity. Like at Hockenheim, for example, where they fought it out for third place behind the peerless Williamses. Lap after lap Prost tried to stab past Senna, but Senna never gave an inch. Finally, during an all-or-nothing attempt in the Ost Kurve, Senna forced him off the track. Again Prost was furious: 'A few times I had to go over the grass at 320 km/h. Now and then he braked early, which really is cheating. I did what I could, if he tries something like that again I'll take him on the inside and push him off the track.' The FISA reacted with shock. Both drivers were given a warning and Prost even received a suspended punishment: running adversaries off the track was *not* something one discussed in public.

Two weeks later in Hungary, things seemed to have settled. Senna needed to call a halt to Mansell's rise; at Ferrari Prost had his hands full with political infighting and the anger of the Italian sports press about the team's mediocre performance. For the first time since 1980 Prost failed to win a single Grand Prix. Finally he took his frustration out on the Ferrari itself, comparing the car to a truck: blasphemy. For the second time in his career, Prost was unceremoniously dumped.

'But I'm not stopping. I'll take a year's sabbatical,' the Professor declared cleverly. Prost had realised that the Williams-Renault combination was leaving McLaren-Honda behind, and Renault was a French engine . . . He didn't succeed in securing a seat for 1992, but by March of that year he already had a contract for 1993. With Mansell cruising easily to his first title in 1992, Prost knew that he would be able to win his fourth title just as easily in the year that followed. Thanks to a wily proviso, the political animal already had his adversaries beaten.

This proviso led to an undignified game of bluff poker, with everyone involved losing face. It began with Mansell resisting Prost's arrival. Better than anyone else, he knew that the arch-conspirator would have the team eating out of his hand and disadvantage his team-mate in all kinds of ways. He'd seen it happen at Ferrari. It was only after realising that Prost already had a contract that Mansell resigned himself to the inevitable and began making his own demands, including financial ones. Williams hesitated. There were, after all, rumours of another offer: Senna wanted to drive for Williams as well, and for much less money, free of charge if necessary.

In one fell swoop the three stars were transformed into whining brats. Spoilt by big money and their many victories, they were only willing to race in a car that could give them the title: a Williams.

Mansell was the first to drop out. The indignant, freshly crowned champion had no patience for Williams's foot-dragging, and once again Mansell made a great show of leaving Formula One. But Senna too came out empty-handed. Because now Prost's secret proviso was revealed. It emerged that he had a right to veto his team-mate. In other words: anyone except Ayrton Senna. Childish, of course. Prost himself called it a 'question of mental comfort'. During the press conference after the Portuguese Grand Prix, Senna was scathing. Prost was a coward. He wanted the title on a platter. That was bad for the sport. 'Prost is scared of fighting with equal weapons. It's like a hundred metres race and he wants running shoes and everyone else to be in lead boots.' Beside him Mansell, the new world champion, despondently nodded his agreement.

The 1993 season was decided before a single race had been held; Prost wins thanks to behind-the-scenes gamesmanship. But occasionally on the track he is still out-classed by a dogged but superior Senna. Like at Donington, in the wet. Short downpours, sun and a track that dried quickly made for dicey conditions. Navigating cautiously, thinking of Pironi, Prost pitted a record seven times to change his wet-weather tyres for slicks and vice versa. The cloudbursts scarcely seemed to bother Senna. In the very first lap, with zero visibility, Senna overtook four competitors: Schumacher, Wendlinger, Hill and, lastly, Prost. Senna in the lead. Later in the race, during another cloudburst, a cold-blooded Senna roared on down the dangerous, narrow track on slicks, overtaking left and right. Since Monaco 1984, nothing had changed: Prost did his sums, Senna provided the magic. Afterwards Prost complained about the handling of his car, whereupon Senna generously offered to swap.

In late 1993 Prost retired – bought out by Senna according to rumour – and their rivalry seemed over. After their last race together, in Adelaide, Senna made a conciliatory gesture, putting an arm around Prost's shoulder on the podium. He was relieved that it was all over and he knew that he could finally move to Williams, the team that made winning the championship so easy. Of course, that kid Schumacher had appeared in the mean time, and drastic changes in the rules had been announced, but still, there was now one clear favourite for the title: Senna.

In 1994 Prost was co-commentator for the French TV channel TF1. When Senna provided commentary from his car for a few laps for that same channel, he greeted his arch-rival: 'I would like to say welcome to my old friend, Alain Prost. Tell him we miss him very much.' It was the warm-up for the San Marino Grand Prix, Imola, 1 May 1994.

Ayrton Senna: The Ultimate Conclusion

> There was something supernatural about him. An aura, as if he came from another planet and therefore had more insight, more brain cells, more power, more energy.
>
> Gerhard Berger

Sunday afternoon. It doesn't matter when. Let's say it's Spa-Francorchamps. The fag end of summer. Sometimes it's still warm, hot even; then it's party time and flags are fluttering all the way downhill to Eau Rouge, shimmering in the bowl at Poulhon. Sometimes the warm days are over and it's raining, incessantly, phantoms at Blanchimont, awash at the Bus Stop. But usually you get a bit of everything at Spa, changing all the time and everywhere. And once again, it doesn't really matter what kind of weather it is this particular Sunday afternoon.

It's over. Get up. Sway down the hall in a daze, past coats smelling of rain, hungry, but above all, thirsty. Two hours in front of the telly without a break, no matter how boring it was. Now you pay the price, everything's hazy in front of you, here come the first bars of that much too familiar national anthem.

A cold beer in the fridge. Badly needed. Forage around for some bread. The fag end of summer. Ah, that whole *cérémonie protocolaire*, the champagne, Beethoven's *Freude schöne Götterfunken* . . . What's the matter with you? Why do you need to see it all? What difference would it make if you missed some of it? It's not as if you don't know exactly what's going to happen anyway.

Outside, from the minuscule lawn (the sun must be shining after all), comes a voice. She's reading a book, *she* at least is doing something useful: 'Who won?'

Dull, as always, the answer: 'Senna.'

The Ultimate Racer

The team manager: 'He was certainly the first driver since Ronnie Peterson to have people excited about some of the things he could do with a race car – you know, things you just couldn't believe.' (Peter Warr)

The biographer: 'Ordinary people simply could not relate to one man with a total obsession, it was utterly unfamiliar to them, they instinctively distrusted it.' (Christopher Hilton)

The colleague: 'Everything was subject to the Senna factor. If he ran 15 kilometres, the newspapers would say the next day: "Senna ran 35 kilometres on sand in the scorching heat." The truth was impressive enough.' (Gerhard Berger)

I was no fan of Senna's. A good Catholic isn't fixated on God, he's more moved by all those stubborn, dramatically martyred saints that surround Him. God is too straight, just like Senna. From the very beginning, Senna was too superior to appeal to me.

In an impressive portrait of his friend, Gerhard Berger writes: 'The years and decades of success made him grow ever stronger: go-karts, Formula Ford, Formula Three, Formula One. You had this constant growth of a mental strength that had been spot on from the beginning.' It's the only time Berger sounds jealous.

Senna won, everywhere and from the start. He drove his first kart race in July 1973 as a thirteen-year-old and won. In 1978 he came to England and won virtually everything there was to race in. Thanks to these results, and the press releases he distributed himself

– press releases from Formula Ford, unheard of! – his name was soon known to everyone who was anyone in Formula One.

And yet even Senna had trouble graduating to the highest class. Although, *trouble* . . . Everyone wanted him, they were standing in line. But Lotus's sponsor insisted on keeping Mansell because of his publicity value in Britain; at Brabham, Nelson Piquet resisted Senna's enlistment, and Piquet was world champion and, more importantly, assured of the support of a major Italian sponsor . . . The contact with Williams never really got off the ground – 'a mistake', Frank Williams admitted later. And Senna himself had rejected an offer from McLaren because of the many contractual restrictions. (It really is true: a driver who hasn't driven a metre of Formula One rejects an offer from McLaren!) As a result Senna had to start at the bottom in 1984 with Toleman. In a car that was more or less completely non-competitive, he came in sixth in just his second race. Once, because of a dispute with the tyre supplier, he failed to qualify, at Imola. A month later, on different tyres, he almost won Monaco. Lotus manager Peter Warr was never in doubt: 'It's not a question of whether Senna will become world champion, it's a question of when.'

And who with, Warr should have added. In any case not with Lotus, Senna's team for the next three years. This was his apprenticeship. Lotus was no longer one of the top teams, and Senna had nothing to lose and everything to win. In just his second race for Lotus, in pouring rain at Estoril, Senna was first to cross the line.

This was the big difference between Senna and the other drivers of his generation. His main adversaries had all known struggle, drama and defeat. Prost missed out on three world-championship titles, two in the last race, before finally seizing the crown. Mansell lost two championships, then spent years in the doldrums. The other winners in the Senna epoch – there aren't that many: Patrese, Boutsen, Nannini – had to conquer themselves to win. They were quick, but too human, too friendly, too good-natured. They didn't have the killer instinct. The same applied to Berger, who started at

Benetton and Ferrari and seemed to be headed straight for the top, until he signed with McLaren as Senna's team-mate and became aware of nothing but his own shortcomings.

After two seasons of driving around behind Senna, Berger finally won another race: Suzuka 1991. A bitter victory: presented to him as the most humiliating kind of gift. After having left Berger far behind, Senna blatantly lifted off in sight of the finishing line and let Berger past.

But Senna had no choice. Senna had to win. Giving away victory went against his very nature. It had already been like that in the lower classes. One of his opponents in Formula Ford 2000 told Christopher Hilton: 'He personally felt he was head and shoulders above everyone else, as if he was in a different league to everyone else. When it came to "I may get beaten today" he didn't know how to handle it. He'd maybe put you off the track or crash trying to overtake you.'

Berger agrees: 'Being slower because of an inferior car didn't occur to him. There was just Senna, the rest belonged behind him.'

Senna's own words are legendary. When Nigel Mansell won the world championship in Hungary in 1992, Senna told him: 'Well done, Nigel. It's a nice feeling, isn't it? Now you know why I'm such a bastard. I have to have that feeling, no one else.'

Of course all Formula One drivers are headstrong egotists who always want to win, otherwise they would never have reached the highest class. But Senna had more; his will to win was not only greater, his obsession also manifested itself in an abundance of insight and technical knowledge.

'Perhaps it is a professional tic,' he said himself, 'but I can't do anything without thinking of technical things. Mere speed, or even victory, have little meaning to me in themselves.'

Even victory? I think that technology, speed and victory were virtually one and the same for Senna, inseparable components of a single obsession.

Berger: 'Niki Lauda was the first to realise that the only way to defeat superbly talented drivers like Peterson was by using your brain. That was why he became interested in the interconnections between things. Prost was Lauda's first apprentice, and when the time came, Senna profited with McLaren in 1988 from the most important transfer of knowledge in Formula One history.'

It's all true, but Senna's tremendous dedication and analytical capacity had been evident even with Lotus. Bernard Dudot, boss of Renault, at the time Lotus's engine supplier:

> Ayrton was especially demanding for everyone who worked with him. He never missed a thing. If there was something he didn't understand, he'd ask for an explanation, two, three, four times, sometimes until it was no fun any more. I remember talking to him at Spa, the day before his second Grand Prix victory, for three-quarters of an hour. I had to explain exactly how the engine reacted to each corner of the circuit, going in, in the middle and coming out. I was amazed by his ability to relate exactly what he'd felt at such and such a spot. Everything he said corresponded precisely with the data from the computer. Senna was tiresome, but what a memory!

The computer. More or less together with Senna, advanced electronics had appeared in Formula One. Lotus was the first team to use active suspension, a system that not only reacted to the bumps on the track, but was, because of the tremendous speed of the computer, also able to anticipate them, significantly improving adhesion.

But Senna did not place his faith in electronics alone. The relationship was not that one-sided. Steve Nichols of McLaren related that, for hours after a race, Senna was still able to cite the fuel economy for each lap to three decimal places. Senna himself: 'Everything has to be in your head, it's a kind of mental radiographic control.'

Electronics and particularly the study of computer-registered data, telemetry, set off a true revolution in Formula One. And Senna immediately took it to the ultimate conclusion. With the computer printout in his hand, he was able completely to unravel every facet of the car. Berger saw it at first hand:

> After training at Ferrari I used to tell my engineer, 'Listen, my car has a little understeer here, a little oversteer there, and it's a bit too stiff as well.' Then I'd pat him on the back and say, 'Now it's your turn, and first thing tomorrow, no more understeer or oversteer.' Then I'd be out of there with some excuse or other. But with Senna, a day on the circuit suddenly meant working from early in the morning to seven o'clock at night, endless analysis of computer data, endless discussions with the engineers. Senna knew the torque of every screw. He just had to know everything, and be involved in every decision. He'd turn a stabiliser around ten times to look at it from every direction, before he'd let them use it.

For Senna computer data was no abstraction. He knew how to translate it into physical technology and the car's performance on the circuit. Even when it came to the smallest of details, Senna knew what he was doing. Gerard Ducarouge, technical mastermind at Lotus: 'Ayrton had a perfect sense of the boundaries of the achievable. If he said, "This afternoon I missed eight-tenths of a second," you could count on him going out the next day and making it good. Eight-tenths: no more, no less.'

It is remarkable how much of the praise, not forgetting the Senna factor of course, is related to practice, to setting up the car and clocking ultra-fast lap times. In this discipline Senna had no peers. His record number of pole positions is incomparable: 65. Equal second with 35 are Jim Clark and, who else, Alain Prost. Senna's 65 is almost double the score of his greatest rival, no Senna factor here. The statistic shows unambiguously that Senna was the fastest driver of all time.

In qualifying, Senna pushed the limits, in races he was much more vulnerable. In direct confrontations his obsessiveness often shipwrecked on the cunning calculation or indomitability of his opponents. That is why the Professor comes out on top in all other statistics, such as the number of fastest lap times, victories and world championships. Prost himself was the first to realise that his fame would lie in the statistics: 'Once I've stopped, people will remember me for breaking all the records, not because of my personality, that's not my strongest point.'

Although his true personality remained a mystery to many, Senna will be remembered for his speed, his single-mindedness, his urge to perfection, his craving for victory. He will be remembered as the ultimate racer, maybe even the encapsulation of everything that matters in Formula One, including death.

God

Senna's personality. Since his death, there has been an overwhelming interest in Senna's character. Friends, girlfriends, biographers, fellow drivers and journalists do their best to show the other side of the genius, the man behind the racing-car driver.

Never speak ill of the dead. And of course, the Senna factor has done its work here too. Admittedly, he had trouble showing it, it didn't really suit his image, but you only had to get to know him a little better, at first hand, to discover Senna's boundless warmth, charm, charity, helpfulness and benevolence. His humility too. And his sense of humour. And Senna even believed in God as well.

Human-interest stories are a natural response to a cold, meaningless and indifferent world. But the intellectual laziness and smugness that permeate them only generate greater indifference. This kind of human interest obscures any sense of real motivation, of what people do, what they want to achieve, why they live.

Ayrton Senna was a racer. Everything in his life served motor racing, speed, perfection and victory. Senna had no flip-side, that's what's so extraordinary about him. No matter how hard his admirers try, they will never be able to turn him into a tragic hero. There was nothing tragic about him: he knew who he was, what he was doing and what he wanted to achieve.

Of course, Senna was human, he had his weaknesses, his shortcomings, his fears and his jokes. Once he handed out sweets in the Lotus pit and seconds later the whole crew was walking around with blue tongues. A real scream.

Senna was a Formula One star, that was why he was constantly followed, watched, spied upon and admired. He should be judged on his achievements, style and behaviour as a driver. Senna himself liked to cultivate a monastic image, but his dedication and obsession were deadly serious. Senna lived for Formula One. On that, friend and foe agree. 'It is the only thing he has in life,' Alain Prost observed scathingly. But Senna's friends confirmed Prost's verdict, they too described a lonely perfectionist who concentrated on racing twenty-four hours a day. Martin Brundle, once Senna's greatest adversary in Formula Three, tried to explain the process: 'He has been completely converted to Formula One. We have two lives, he only has one.'

Converted. Brundle could not have chosen a more apt word. Senna himself saw his total dedication to Formula One as a religious, almost mystical affair. Senna was a pious man. In his view, religion and Formula One were inseparable. It is a quintessential characteristic of Senna, Senna the Formula One driver.

Berger, who followed him closely for years and analysed him carefully, finally came up against Senna's faith: 'Of course, I watched him and constantly wondered what his secret might be and what a clever Tyrolean lad needed to do to emulate him. In the end there was nothing except his religiousness, but that was no use to me.'

It wasn't easy. Senna himself only spoke of it reluctantly, too often he'd seen his words twisted:

> I have been questioned many times about religion and often I was misquoted or misinterpreted. Sometimes it was by accident, sometimes to do me damage, but I think it is worth talking about because in this godless world there are lots and lots of people looking for religion. They are desperate for it. I am only being truthful. I am saying what I believe and what I feel. You offer religion to those who want it. If you don't do that, they will not have the opportunity to look and see. Some people may not understand you and do not have a clear opinion, some will understand because they are open enough to understand what you are talking about. It is for them that it is worth it.

But the things that Senna did say about religion, and especially about religion in relation to motor racing, were anything but unambiguous. Often he himself was still trying to find the right words.

'I am just at the beginning. I am like a baby in this respect. You have to work on it. It is a difficult thing. You can be logical or stupid but you are not in control of everything that is happening with your life.'

Senna, who mastered and controlled everything down to the finest details, always knowing exactly what he was doing all the way down the line, admitted to not having everything under control. Could this be the 'extra helping of insanity' that Lauda considered essential for a fast qualifying time?

Senna:

> You can have it if you want. It is a question of believing it and having faith, of wanting it and being open to the experience. I think there is an area where logic applies and another where it does not. No matter how far down the road you are in understanding and experiencing religion, there are certain things which we cannot logically explain. We tend always to understand what we can see: the colours, the touch and the smell. If it is outside

> that, is it crazy? I had the opportunity to experience something beyond that. Once you have experienced it, you know it is there, and that is why you have to tell people.

Beyond logic. Is that also beyond the third decimal place of the fuel economy, beyond the torque of the screws in a McLaren? What does religion have to do with motor racing? 'Everything,' according to Senna. Many times, at the peak of his achievement, Senna fell back on religion as a way of explaining his experiences. Not just for moments of euphoria, but also for moments of deep disillusionment.

Starting with the latter. Monaco, 15 May 1988. Senna, after a weekend of euphoric driving, is leading, with Prost far behind in second place. Towards the end of the race, Senna starts driving one record lap after another. Over the radio, Ron Dennis warns him to take it easy, but it's already too late. Senna takes the Virage du Portier too fast and slams into the armco. Immediately he leaves the circuit for his nearby apartment. When his engineer finally gets him on the telephone hours later, Senna is still sobbing.

'It had nothing to do with the car or the equipment. I was feeling easy in front. It was a hundred per cent perfect weekend. Suddenly I lost concentration, made a stupid mistake and threw everything away. The mistake I made changed me psychologically and mentally. It gave me the strength and the power to fight in critical moments. It was the biggest step in my career as a professional, a racing driver and a man. It brought me closer to God than I have ever been. It has changed my life.'

Later that year, in Japan, where Senna won his first world title after a fantastic chase, the mood was different. Senna's euphoria even led to a vision: 'In the last corner I suddenly saw an image of Jesus.' Again, Senna was in tears until late at night.

These high-flown reactions unavoidably evoked astonishment, ridicule and even hurtful distortion of Senna's words. One of the cruellest misinterpretations is credited to – who else? – Alain Prost.

A year later, again at Suzuka, but now in the chicane, Prost saw Senna's faith in a completely different light: 'Ayrton has a small problem. He thinks he can't kill himself because he believes in God and I think that's very dangerous for the other drivers.'

'Not true at all,' Senna retorted later. 'Those are his words, his conclusions.' All the same, Senna *could* be quite trite in his invocations of the Almighty; for example, in Portugal in 1989, after all the problems with Prost had led to his departure. 'If you have God on your side everything becomes clear: white becomes white again, and black becomes black, and you realise what is really important in life.' Of course, banalities like this were begging for misunderstanding, especially since Senna seemed to say exactly the opposite at other times: 'I want to learn and know everything that faith can bring me, and to make other people understand it in the same way. Many people don't succeed in finding contentment because, in the world in which we live, what's white is white and what's black is black.'

In the wake of his crash at Imola, more and more implausible stories have surfaced about Senna's devotion: Senna was engaged in charity, his business empire only ever benefited the poor of Brazil, Senna pushed little old grannies around in wheelchairs, Senna had a long and very stimulating conversation with a bishop (momentarily forgetting that Jesus preferred the company of prostitutes and sinners); or the most beautiful story of all – the one about the miraculous healing. At Imola, years earlier during testing, someone asked Senna to speak a message on to a tape for one of his fans who had been left in a coma after a motorbike crash. The good fellow does it. The parents of the sixteen-year-old boy play the tape regularly and, sure enough, the youth awakens. Still paralysed, it's true, but able to communicate again, even with Senna himself, who visits the boy and talks to him whenever he has free time in Imola. Behold, the first miracle.

I wouldn't be at all surprised to hear that there is already a group lobbying for Senna's canonisation. But let's be clear about this: a saint does not run opponents off the track, not even heathens like Alain Prost, who arrogantly declared that he owed everything in his life to himself, because God had better things to do than help *him* to score victories.

No doubt Senna, as a civilised man, did his best to live up to a morality of charity and good works, but when it came to racing, his religion was based on personal mystical experience. He consistently emphasised that experience, and never cited any moral code that went along with it.

Let us return again to that magical weekend in May 1988, Monaco. During the last qualifying session, Senna was dazzling. Faster and faster, better and better, at and beyond the limit, he flew through the maze of armco, leaving the world of Formula One flabbergasted behind him. But Senna had left himself behind as well and admitted as much in an interview with Canadian journalist Gerald Donaldson:

> Sometimes I think I know some of the reasons why I do the things the way I do in a car and sometimes I think I don't know why. There are some moments that seem to be the natural instinct that is in me. Whether I have been born with it or whether this feeling has grown in me more than other people, I don't know, but it is inside me and it takes over with a great amount of space and intensity.
>
> When I am competing against the watch and against the other competitors, the feeling of expectation, of getting it done and doing the best I can, gives me a kind of power that some moments when I am driving actually detaches me completely from anything else as I am doing it . . . corner after corner, lap after lap. I can give you a true example.
>
> Monte Carlo '88, the last qualifying session. I was already on pole and I was going faster and faster. One lap after the other, quicker and quicker and quicker. I was at one stage just on pole, then by half a second and then one second and I

kept going. Suddenly I was nearly two seconds faster than anybody else, including my team-mate with the same car. And I suddenly realised I was no longer driving the car consciously.

I was kind of driving it by instinct, only I was in a different dimension. It was like I was in a tunnel. Not only the tunnel under the hotel but the whole circuit was a tunnel.

I was just going and going, more and more and more and more. I was way over the limit but still able to find even more. Then suddenly something just kicked me. I kind of woke up and realised that I was in a different atmosphere than you normally are. My immediate reaction was to back off, to slow down. I drove back slowly to the pits and I didn't want to go out any more that day. It frightened me because I realised I was well beyond my conscious understanding. It happens rarely but I keep these experiences very much alive in me because it is something that is important for self-preservation.

Here Senna doesn't even mention God. He is trying to describe the ecstasy of speed and perfection, things that are beyond logic. In his attempt he appeals to mysticism, and for Senna, mysticism led automatically to God:

I am permanently seeking perfection. I want to improve in every respect. I spend my time pushing back limits. I want to constantly go further, to solve problems. I want to be capable of doing better than other people. At the same time I feel that I possess a kind of strength that brings me nearer to God. It is difficult to explain, but it is what I feel. And I am lucky to have found this route to such a state of harmony. I would like to provide concrete proof that we can really push back our limits, that this strength we find in ourselves does enable us to improve constantly.

This has nothing to do with Christian charity. What matters is Senna's belief in the possibility of expanding human perception and other mental capacities. In Monaco he felt this at first hand.

Senna was no saint, no prophet, no religious fanatic. 'I've never said that God would make me invincible or immortal. I feel a personal bond with Him, but I have my own moral code.'

Senna experienced God in a wholly personal way, at moments of perfection and ecstasy, moments that were beyond comprehension even for him, with his immense powers of concentration. To approach some kind of understanding he reached out for God. Perhaps he might just as well have resorted to poetry; listen to the lyricism of John Watson, Brands Hatch 1985:

> In qualifying I was coming down from Westfield bend and I was on an in lap – going to come in to the pits. Round Dingle Dell dip into Dingle Dell I saw this car coming very quickly behind me. Just at the bottom of the dip Ayrton came through on the inside – I'd left him room. I witnessed visibly and audibly something I had not seen anyone do before in a racing car. It was as if he had four hands and four legs. He was braking, changing down, steering, pumping the throttle and the car appeared to be on that knife edge of being in control and being out of control. It lasted maybe two seconds. Once he had checked the speed of the car and he'd got the right gear, what he was trying to do was maintain boost pressure. On a turbo you lift off and the power goes away very fast. He got to the point of the track where he wanted to make his commitment to the corner. Then – hard on the throttle and the thing was driving through the corner. I mean it was a master controlling a machine. I had never seen a turbo car driven like that. The ability of the brain to separate each component and put them back together with that rhythm and co-ordination – for me it was a remarkable experience, it was a privilege to see.
>
> I was so moved that I went down to the Lotus pit and I said to

Peter Warr and Gerard Ducarouge, 'I've just seen something,' and they said, 'Yes, yes, we know.'

Including Death

'This will be a dangerous season,' was Senna's bleak prognosis in early 1994, 'we'll be lucky to get through it without severe crashes.' This was not a sudden premonition and Senna had not lost his nerve, he was talking about the FIA ban on a number of electronic support systems as of 1994. Pre-programming and even long-distance control over the racing cars had got out of hand. More and more often computers were anticipating and correcting drivers, cars and engines. Technology seemed about to completely overshadow human input, heroism and romanticism.

But it wasn't just a question of romanticism. It was also a matter of the costs involved: they were rapidly rising far beyond the means of the smaller teams. It was also about safety. Electronic aids such as traction control, ABS and active suspension might have made driving more comfortable and, in the first instance, safer as well, but they also made the cars faster, especially cornering. What's more, the danger of handing control over to computers had been demonstrated the year before at Estoril.

Estoril, 1993, about halfway through the race. After a quick wheel change, Berger leaves the pits – the pit-lane speed limit has yet to be instated and coming out on to the track he must be doing at least 200 km/h. Suddenly the Ferrari swerves left and shoots out of control straight across the track, right between two cars that are both doing some 300 km/h. Berger doesn't even see them. It's only that evening, watching the video, that he feels sick to his stomach: 'The chance that this would not lead to an annihilating explosive crash cannot be expressed in figures of probability. You'd need a NASA computer to calculate that.'

After the initial shock has passed, all of Formula One is baffled:

how could an experienced pro like Berger spin on cold tyres coming out of the pit lane? No, Berger explained later, it wasn't the tyres, it was the computer. The computerised active suspension anticipated all kinds of bumps on the circuit, except the ones in the pit lane; the specialists had forgotten to program those ones in. The computer mistakenly assumed that the car was on the smooth asphalt of the start-finish section and simply bounced the car over the pit-lane bumps, that was why the Ferrari shot out on to the track out of control.

The disappearance of driver aids meant a big step backwards. Especially for Williams. Thanks to Williams's advanced computer technology, Mansell and Prost had hauled their titles in easily. Now that Senna's turn had finally come, that advantage was gone.

Once, at Donington in July 1983, Senna had driven his first metres of Formula One in a Williams. Frank Williams remembers that 'he got into the rhythm very speedily. He'd never driven anything as quick as a Formula One car but you'd never have thought so. In the end he stopped with some excuse about the engine. He was simply in danger of going too fast.' But the early contact with Williams had never led to a contract. There had been negotiations, but they had probably only been intended to push up the price for McLaren. Senna was ready in 1993, but came up against Prost's veto. But, for 1994, Senna managed to supplant Prost; finally his day had come. This was the dream team: the fastest driver in the best car, a loyal team-mate who wasn't a danger, Damon Hill – serious Formula One experts wondered what would stop Senna from winning all sixteen this year. Senna himself tried to temper the overheated expectations; the Williams FW 16 was jumpy, temperamental, it would be a dangerous season . . .

As it turned out, he didn't win the first two races. Even worse, he didn't score a single point. Sure enough, he had started twice from pole position, and had thus unarguably been the fastest, but in the races themselves he'd flown off the track twice. Both races were won easily by Michael Schumacher, the new super-talent. And as if that wasn't bad enough, Senna had spun off the track at home in Brazil trying to keep up with that snotty-nosed kid; it was the kind of thing that hardly ever happened to him any more. Senna admitted it himself: it was his own fault, he'd gone over the limit.

Senna was under pressure. Something he hadn't been for a long time. Either he'd dominated, or else he'd had nothing to lose and had demonstrated his superiority. But now, with the best car and all the expectations, he was in danger of simply being beaten. Even in Formula Ford, that kind of thing had been unbearable for him: 'When it came to "I may get beaten today" he didn't know how to handle it. He'd either put you off the track or maybe crash trying to overtake you.'

At Aida Senna got mixed up in a crash at the first corner. Mika Hakkinen knocked him off the track, there was nothing he could do about it. But thanks to a lightning start that devilish Schumacher came through unscathed.

Schumacher's superb starts gave rise to rumours that Benetton was surreptitiously using electronic aids. Traction control suppressed wheel spinning at the start, optimising grip and making the car shoot off. Of course, Benetton denied it all. It was true that the requisite software was still in the on-board computer, but the team wasn't using it – honest injun.

Meanwhile Ecclestone's circus set off for Imola, where the season would really start. It would be the race of truth, the fast circuit that would finally prove whether Schumacher really was good enough to beat Senna and Williams. No one was that worried, except Senna himself: 'Maybe,' he sighed to girlfriend Adriane Galisteu, 'I've come to Williams too late.'

Friday, 29 April. Afternoon

The first qualifying sessions. Schumacher clocks 1 minute 22.564 seconds. Senna answers with 1 minute 22.430 seconds. And then the red flag is out. Training session stopped. Just before driving into the pits, Senna sees an upside-down Jordan.

It's Barrichello, a young driver who has grown up with high-tech devices. He missed the line in the fast right-left combination just before the pits, the car launched off the kerbstones, bounced on the tyre barrier in front of the fence and landed in the grass. It looked frightening. Track marshals turned the car over, Barrichello was sitting motionless in the cockpit.

Senna climbed out of his cockpit and hurried to the medical centre to see Barrichello. The injuries were much less severe than expected: Barrichello had broken his nose, and a helicopter was about to take him to Bologna's Maggiore Hospital for further examination. None the less, Barrichello remembers seeing tears in Senna's eyes. There was something strange about it; hadn't it been a crash like so many others in the past few years: scary because of the speed, but with a happy ending thanks to the excellent facilities? Barrichello was even joking with the Italian nurses.

After twenty-five minutes, practice resumed. But Senna couldn't really concentrate any more, as he explained at the end of the day. None the less he still recorded the fastest time, half a second ahead of Schumacher.

Saturday, 30 April. Morning

A grinning Barrichello is back in the pits. Nodding his head while a worried, almost paternal Senna talks to him. Free practice proceeds without problems, slowly the nerves settle. Qualifying starts at one o'clock.

Saturday Afternoon

As usual the lesser teams go out on the track first. That gives them a chance to attract some much-needed publicity. The big boys wait, watching to see what the others do. Senna too is standing beside his car in the pits watching a TV monitor.

Suddenly the picture cuts to a wildly spinning car. Parts fly off the wreck as it bounces over the grass between Villeneuve Corner and the Tosa. It's a Simtek, Roland Ratzenberger's, and now, sliding slowly backwards, it comes to a halt beside a big blue-and-white ad for Magneti Marelli. Dead. You can tell immediately. It's back again. Eight years, twelve years, it's been gone and now it's back again, here, unmistakable, that sickening feeling, the terrible . . .

The driver is slumped in his car like a dummy, head down. The left side of the car has been torn open, through the hole you can see the lifeless body in its immaculate white overalls.

Red flag. Marshals come running, ambulances on the circuit. On TV they're showing a replay, of the collision as well this time – fortunately the cameras just miss the horrific impact – and then the wreck spinning like a top for hundreds of metres until it stops. There's blood on the helmet, near the visor.

The driver is lifted out of his car and laid down on the ground near the blue-and-white advertising. He's surrounded by doctors – resuscitation, heart massage, ambulance – they rush him off. His condition is hopeless.

Another replay. In slow motion a detail is revealed: just before Villeneuve Corner the Simtek loses one of its front wings and becomes unsteerable, stabbing straight ahead. Later the telemetry shows that Ratzenberger hit the wall at 308 km/h, the shock of the impact was too much for his body, he died immediately.

But no one knows that yet. In Formula One there is a tacit world-wide agreement that drivers never die on the circuit in Italy. The Italian authorities would close the circuit for a thorough Italian investigation and the resulting chaos would be incalculable.

Another picture on television. Senna watching the monitor in the pits, seeing the crash and turning away with a mixture of disgust and disbelief. It touches him. Deeply.

Ratzenberger was no celebrity, he was no superstar. It took him a long time to get into Formula One, too long to be convincing. In early 1994 he was overjoyed to sign with the foot soldiers of Simtek. In Brazil he failed to qualify. At Aida he finished eleventh. Imola would have been his second Grand Prix.

Next image. A course car stops at Villeneuve Corner. Senna gets out, is shown various things. What's he doing there? What does he want to know?

Professor Watkins relates that Senna then asked to be driven to the medical centre. He wanted to see Ratzenberger. Why? He was sent away, but climbed over a rear fence. Only Watkins can stop him. He thinks it would be irresponsible to confront a sensitive person with Intensive Care. At Senna's insistence, he admits that there is no hope left for Ratzenberger, and suddenly Senna is crying on his shoulder. The professor responds by asking Senna why he doesn't just stop. 'What else do you need to do? You have been world champion three times, you are obviously the quickest driver. Give it up and let's go fishing.' At once, Senna is calm. 'Sid, there are certain things over which we have no control. I cannot quit. I have to go on.'

Not far away, Berger is still trembling in the Ferrari motorhome.

> For the first time I was confronted with someone dying in a racing car. In all of my time in Formula One there had not been a single fatal accident. I could only see two options: go straight home and forget the whole sport, or flick a switch and somehow convince myself to go on. By saying things like, 'If you die like Roland, then at least it will be doing the thing you love most in the whole world.' Thoughts like that ran through my mind and I had to decide quickly. I went outside, climbed into the car and drove a fast lap, out of self-protection.

Practice was indeed resumed while Ratzenberger was being flown to Bologna in a helicopter. Officially he died eight minutes after arrival at Maggiore Hospital.

Senna too needed to make a choice. Frank Williams left it to him. Senna did not take up the opportunity to continue training. Damon Hill called it a day as well, and, a little later, Benetton and Schumacher closed up shop too.

And so the next day, Senna started from pole position for the sixty-fifth time. It was his 161st Grand Prix, but his first race with death. Like Berger, Senna had never before experienced a fatal accident on a Grand Prix weekend.

Ironically enough, he was at Zolder on 8 May 1982, but at the time he had other things on his mind – he wanted to meet Piquet and came back furious: 'He just snubbed me. I'll beat the bastard one day!' Not a word about Villeneuve.

And yet Senna was aware of the risk. Berger was emphatic about that: 'He didn't have the mad, absolute fearlessness of someone like Gilles Villeneuve. He came up to me many times with a computer printout of a corner I'd taken flat out, and told me that I was crazy. "If you go off there, you've had it . . ." No, absolute fearlessness was not his strong point.'

Ratzenberger's death affected Senna tremendously, but wasn't his reaction disproportionate? People who were there would later explain that even before arriving at Imola, Senna was over-sensitive and over-tired – depressed, even. But on the eve of death, everything takes on a different meaning. On Saturday night he called Adriane in tears, he didn't want to go on. That was something he'd never said before.

Why didn't he just stop? He'd been with Adriane for more than a year and seemed to have found true love. The contours of a second life were beginning to emerge, and at the end of 1993 he had even hinted at his departure from the sport: 'Sometimes I think that nothing will ever give me the same kick as Formula One. But maybe I've got it all wrong. As you get older, you appraise things differently. Being a father must be something very special.' But there are certain things over which you have no control, Senna had to go on . . .

Sunday, 1 May. Morning

'Welcome to my old friend, Alain Prost. We miss him very much.' During the warm-up Senna spoke these memorable words inside his Williams, near start-finish and headed for the Tamburello. On the eve of death, everything takes on a different meaning. But Senna really did miss Prost. He missed the secure world in which they had been at odds with each other for ten years. Once at Imola, between Villeneuve Corner and the Tosa, their epic brawl had begun. Now everything had changed. The balance was lost. Prost had been his equal and his opposite, fortunately. Losing to Prost was terrible, winning was the best thing that could happen to you, but whatever happened, they both came out of it with their heads held high. With this Schumacher guy he wasn't so sure . . . And then death. Prost had experienced it: Villeneuve, Paletti, Pironi almost . . . Prost had learnt to live with it, all those wet races in which he had resolutely retired. Prost, four times world champion, the best; him, Senna, three times world champion, the fastest. But now his obsession, his compulsion, was pushing him to face up to the ultimate conclusion, the absolute limit. And that in a car that was so different, so nervous, hard to steer, maybe even risky.

The drivers' briefing was interrupted for a one-minute silence. Professor Watkins thought it irresponsible to dwell upon the terrible risk so soon before the race. The drivers stood up well, only Senna let his tears flow freely. Afterwards they came to the issue of the Safety Car, the car that was used to keep the field under control when the race was neutralised, after accidents for example. The drivers were worried that the Safety Car was too slow, behind it the tyre temperature dropped enormously and with it the handling. In other words, it only made things more dangerous. At Aida they had used the Safety Car during the warm-up lap as well, at Imola this practice was discontinued at the drivers' insistence. Afterwards Senna spoke briefly to Schumacher, Berger and Alboreto about re-forming the GPDA, the Grand Prix Drivers' Association, to make the drivers' lobby more effective on issues such as safety. It was remarkable, as eyewitnesses later reported, how many of the drivers walked past Senna and patted him on the shoulder or arm on the way out.

Sunday Afternoon

Without a Safety Car, twenty-five cars begin their warm-up lap for the San Marino Grand Prix on the Imola circuit. All over the world, millions of viewers sit down in front of their televisions. On Saturday evening Italian TV has been heavily criticised for its extensive, up-close coverage of the crash, particularly the footage of the desperate attempts to resuscitate Ratzenberger. But death is a drawcard. Ratzenberger's accident has attracted millions of extra viewers this Sunday afternoon. And they get value for money. From the word go.

J.J. Lehto, in the third row on the grid, does not budge at the start. Immediate tension, cars shoot past left and right at full throttle, ever faster. Only Pedro Lamy, coming from the rear, spots the danger too late and sideswipes the Benetton. The cars are torn in two length-wise, a wheel sails into the stand at high speed, injuring nine people. Lehto's Benetton slides forward a few metres, but Lamy's Lotus shoots diagonally across the track like an unguided missile, finally coming to rest against the barrier hundreds of metres down the track. Yellow flags, pieces of wreckage everywhere, the stewards send out the Safety Car. Meanwhile the rest of the field is storming up at the end of the first lap: Senna in front, ahead of Schumacher and Berger. Warned by all the yellow flags, they slow down, carefully picking their way between the dangerous shards of carbon fibre, lining up neatly one after the other behind the Safety Car.

The driver, Max Angelelli, one of the best Italian drivers in the lower formulas, breaks out in a cold sweat: 'It was an absolute nightmare.'

The brakes of the Opel Vectra were not designed for those kind of forces, what's more the car didn't have the power to go fast enough uphill. Angelelli: 'I was really worried. I wanted to go faster, but the danger of slipping was way too high. Senna was up front and he came up beside me a few times, whenever I had to go uphill after the Aqua Minerale. He gestured furiously that I had to drive faster. I could see that he was angry and nervous, but there was nothing I could do about it!'

Senna was indeed angry. Over the radio he complained about the speed of the Safety Car and his falling tyre temperature. Because along with the temperature, the pressure in the tyres was also falling and with it the car's ride height. Senna had already set up his Williams extremely low so that he could keep ahead of Schumacher. The chance of the Williams bottoming at bumps became ever greater, Senna knew that, and a bouncing Formula One car is virtually unsteerable.

Behind the Safety Car, the nerve-wracking procession lasted five laps. Just before the sixth lap the flashing lights went off and the harried Opel fled into the pits. On the start-finish section the pack put their feet down and disappeared left, left, into the Tamburello. Senna takes the fastest line, slightly left of the middle, where the asphalt is uneven. Senna knows that. Earlier that same year he had complained about it. The circuit management had promised to solve the problem before the next season. But in 1995 the Tamburello is gone completely. Schumacher sees the Williams skip and hit the asphalt, sparks fly out from under the car. For a moment Schumacher even lifts off, afraid that Senna is going to lose it, but miraculously Senna keeps his car under control. The magician leads the dance and the rest are where they belong: behind him.

For a whole lap Senna stays in the lead. Slowly tyre pressure rises, but not enough, the car is still extremely low. Across start-finish, again left, left, and again he chooses the line just to the left of the middle.

At that moment the director cuts to a grand panorama coming out of the corner. The dark handsome trees, a gigantic ad for Kronenbourg, and the majestic curving asphalt with the field fanning out behind Senna, perfectly taut, flat out. It is one of those places where Formula One tears right through your gut. But within two seconds this place of ecstatic beauty has changed into a hell.

Because in that same moment millions of viewers see the Williams deviate from its line by veering right, they see it go off the track at high speed, cross a narrow strip of grass and a concrete run-off area, then slam full into a concrete wall.

I'm standing in the middle of the room, in front of the television, screaming his name. The car flies back like a ricocheting bullet, across the run-off area, over the grass, almost back on to the track, finally stopping back-to-front on the run-off area. My partner runs into the room with our five-month-old son in her arms. Senna is still. Twice a shudder passes through his body, his head twitches, the yellow helmet moves, for a moment I think he's alive, but then he droops, like Ratzenberger, hanging like a lifeless dummy in the wreck. It's back again . . .

Meanwhile the whole field has thundered past, yellow flags, sprinting marshals. The right side of the car has been obliterated, all kinds of parts, wheels, fragments of suspension and pieces of upholstery lie scattered over the track. What a disgusting sport this is. What vile nonsense.

The red flag is out. Race stopped. The television shows a replay. Again, that strange deviation from his line, so sudden, resolute, then the smash, the parts flying, it's too terrible to watch.

The cameras keep a respectful distance, but the images are the same as yesterday's. Senna is lifted out of the car and surrounded by doctors and security men. Just like yesterday, all the engines are silenced, an ominous quiet, it doesn't reassure anyone. The rest of the field is back on the grid and waiting to see what happens. There is no news.

A helicopter lands in the Tamburello. It takes a little while, then Senna is carried to the chopper on a grey inflatable stretcher. You can tell from the way they're walking, from the gestures of the marshals: it's serious, critical. When the helicopter takes off and disappears over the trees, everyone knows that it's taking the soul of Formula One away with it.

The soul of Formula One? There is no news. One hundred and

twenty thousand people alongside the track and millions of TV viewers sit and wait. Waiting for news, but also waiting for the resumption of the race. The drivers, still in their cars, don't have a clue. Someone tells Berger that Senna is conscious. Bernie Ecclestone fails to reach Professor Watkins.

The professor is sitting in the medical centre, despondent behind a big desk. He has Senna's helmet in front of him. There is a hole in the visor. The first official news from the FIA: 'head injury'.

After more than half an hour, the race is restarted. At the same moment the helicopter lands at Bologna's Maggiore Hospital. Senna's heart has stopped and he is resuscitated for the second time.

The *tifosi* cheer as Berger takes the lead. Behind the pits, Ecclestone has apparently confused the words 'head' and 'dead'. Senna's brother Leonardo is distraught, he wants the truth, the rumours are building. The panic and despair surrounding the death of a hero, a god.

Berger stops for new tyres, but feels something strange about the car afterwards. When he stops again, Ferrari team director Jean Todt orders him out of the car. 'And suddenly I felt that everything was very quiet, despite the roar of the race, and I knew, even if I can't explain how, that Ayrton Senna was dying.'

Berger immediately arranges a helicopter to Bologna. He's one of the last people let in to see Senna, but even he is not entirely sure whether Senna was alive or dead at that moment: 'Ayrton was covered with a green cloth that left part of the wound on his forehead visible. To me the hand and the foot I could see looked like a dead man's. Two or three doctors were working on the head wound and we weren't sure whether or not he was alive.'

Meanwhile the race at Imola has been won by Schumacher, but only after five mechanics have been seriously injured in the pits by a wheel coming off Alboreto's Minardi. The Italians cheer Larini, who has come in second in his Ferrari, Hakkinen is third. The ceremony is restrained. At the press conference, Ecclestone's circus goes on: Hakkinen expresses his satisfaction with his third place, 'the race was *good fun*'. It will take him a long time to live down those words.

At 7:35 p.m. a fax reaches Imola: 'At 18:40 all cardiac activity stopped, we confirm his death.' No name, but by then the whole world knows *who* it is about. Ayrton Senna is dead.

The cause of death was the head wound. Senna had been tremendously unlucky. The smash into the wall had been hard – the telemetry showed that the Williams hit the wall at 215 km/h – but the angle was relatively favourable. The carbon-fibre chassis was still intact. Senna would have survived the crash virtually unharmed if a part of the suspension hadn't been launched through his visor into his helmet and head. It was a question of centimetres.

The reason for the accident remains unclear. The Italian prosecutor made a great song and dance about launching a court case and finally produced a weighty report blaming it all on a broken steering column. Williams slated the technical side of the investigation and insisted that they received telemetric data up to the moment of impact, data that could not possibly have been transmitted if the steering wheel had broken off. Ultimately, nothing could be proven. In December 1997 all defendants, including Frank Williams and his designers, were found not guilty.

On the eve of death everything takes on another meaning. Was the hectic weekend at Imola a Grand Prix weekend like so many others? Or were there really too many things worrying Senna, pushing him beyond the limit, where nothing awaited him except Formula One's ultimate conclusion?

I was no fan of Senna's. But whether they like it or not, real Catholics can't do without God. Whether I liked it or not, for almost ten years Senna had been the centre point of countless Sundays, countless Saturdays, even Fridays. Together with Prost and Mansell, he had determined the image of Formula One; but, unlike them, he had always been the man to beat. You hadn't won unless you'd beaten Senna. No matter how unbearable his dominance might have been, his single-mindedness had embodied the essence of the sport, he had taken Formula One to its ultimate conclusions, including death.

In Brazil millions of people paid their last respects. All over the world his funeral was broadcast live on television.

'The funeral in São Paulo had nothing in common with an ordinary funeral,' related Berger later, 'it was as over the top as everything else about Senna. From each red carpet to each plane flying overhead and his mother's white dress, it was all typical Senna, as if he were directing the whole thing from on high.'

Monaco, 15 May 1994

A few minutes before the start of the fifty-second Monaco Grand Prix: the cars are already on the grid; mechanics, team chiefs, sponsors, footballers, film stars and other big shots swarm around.

A strange silence falls amid this hectic activity as the drivers gather around the first position on the grid. This time there is no car on pole. The spot has been left empty in honour of Ayrton Senna. He should have been there, he would definitely have been there. Monaco was his domain; ten years ago he almost seized his first victory here, in the wet . . .

Two weeks have passed since Imola. The drivers are silent. Their expressions are serious. Barrichello and Fittipaldi, in the middle, unroll a flag. It is a Brazilian flag with a picture of Senna in the yellow diamond, his inseparable blue cap on his head, behind him the shape of the circuit at Imola, like a crumpled nimbus. In the green, two words: *Adeus* Ayrton.

Many Formula One fans will faithfully take this flag with them for years, to every Grand Prix, to every race they visit.

'*Formula Morte*', the headline of an Italian newspaper had blared two weeks earlier. The sport – sport? How can you call Formula One a sport? – is being criticised everywhere. Especially now that Monaco seems to have claimed a third victim. Last Thursday Karl Wendlinger came out of the tunnel weaving strangely. Far beyond its braking point, his Sauber turned sideways at over 200 km/h. At the head of the chicane it slammed into the plastic water tanks covering the barrier. Severe brain contusions. Coma. Wendlinger's condition is critical.

There they stand, the others. The GPDA has been refounded. A number of drivers will survey the circuits in search of dangerous corners where speeds, decelerations and G-forces are irresponsibly high. There need to be more gravel traps, more tyre barriers. The FIA is quick to point out that Formula One is no more dangerous than it was three weeks earlier, but puts together a long list of technical improvements anyway: the attachment of the suspension components needs improving, more head protection for drivers, more spacious cockpits, changes to the bottom of the cars. None of it's going to help Senna, and the constructors grumble. Flavio Briatore, Benetton team boss, finds it all overhasty: 'Formula One mustn't become some kind of Formula 3000, speeds of 300 km/h must remain possible.' Of course, Briatore has an ace up his sleeve with Schumacher, but he's still right – no matter how unpopular his words might be.

Even Bernie Ecclestone is worried. The superstars are gone. Only four Grand Prix winners are there on the grid in Monaco; of them Berger has won the most: eight. Ecclestone looks around for his cell phone to call Nigel Mansell. Maybe the aggrieved hero, now a champion again and incredibly popular in America, would like to be the star attraction for a few Grands Prix. He can name his price.

The drivers' faces are serious. But behind them their cars are unmoved, shining, powerful. Beaming girls hold up the numbers. With laptops, the systems are checked and then rechecked, the tyre warmers are zipped up around the wheels. Five more minutes. There is no alternative.

Intermezzo: The Nature of Speed

'One reason I race,' says Eddie Irvine, 'is to get away from real life. I live life to the full because you're a long time dead. What's the fucking point of having 50 million dollars in the bank if you live like a pig and sit in front of the TV?' Gerhard Berger explains that throughout his career he has been driven by an impatient desire for the beautiful, fantastic, thrilling side of life: 'You'll be old soon enough and you won't have experienced anything.'

But why Formula One? Why risk your life doing it? What's so damn beautiful, fantastic and thrilling about speed?

Racing drivers often came to speed very young. Berger tells of daredevil stunts on frozen lakes and icy roads: 'I was fascinated by speed, nothing else.' And what about Jacques Villeneuve, as a boy virtually the only one who dared sit beside Gilles on the front seat of a road car, even encouraging him – 'Faster, Daddy!' – as he tore through the streets of Monte Carlo like a madman. Extremely talented drivers like Senna, Schumacher and Hakkinen all climbed into go-karts before they were old enough to go to school. And Damon Hill relates that: 'From the very first time I rode a motorbike as a kid, I knew: this was the best thing I'd ever done, and that sense of excitement and determination has never left me. There is a clear link between that childhood experience and racing: exhilaration through acceleration. That simple formula has served me for more than three decades.'

'The speed is the most overwhelming thing about Formula One,' says Mika Hakkinen. Maybe, but what exactly is speed? What happens inside your head, your heart or your gut at 320 km/h? What is the kick, what is the nature of speed?

Michael Schumacher, fastest of them all, doesn't really know: 'The kick of pure speed is totally foreign to me.' Berger, the most experienced, just sighs. He's been asked a thousand times, but his answers never really helped anyone. The feelings, 'which emerge naturally from the essential turn-on of driving fast', are still there, but they are submerged in the work – the sublime and banal carnival of a Grand Prix weekend. 'Speed has become so routine that I only see the difference between 120 and 320 km/h as a peak in the telemetric printout. Speed is my working environment, as normal as a desk for a civil servant.'

Speed. The highest speed in a motor car – well, in something resembling a motor car – was achieved on 15 October 1997 in America's Black Rock Desert. Driving a Thrust SSC with dual jet-engine propulsion, Andy Green reached a speed of more than 1,230 km/h, faster than the speed of sound. Congratulations! Motorised humanity had accelerated from 100 km/h – this limit, considered impossible at the time, was first broken by the Belgian Camille Jenatzy in his electric car La Jamais Contente in 1899 – to break the sound barrier less than a century later.

But the equally heroic as insane tradition of the land speed record was now confronted with a serious dilemma: what was left to break? Even a cursory view of the history of record breaking shows that almost all record attempts have been related to limits, clear milestones: 100 km/h, 100 mph, 200, 300, 500, 1,000 . . .

It is only by crossing these lines that speed appeals to the imagination, otherwise it remains a relatively pointless, arithmetic abstraction. You need something to measure it by, something that makes it visible.

Formula One is no exception. Schumacher: 'Three or five

hundred an hour, to me it's all the same. Racing doesn't really get interesting until the corners come, that's where the magic starts.' After an extremely fast lap at Zeltweg in 1982 – maximum 316 km/h, average 244 – Nelson Piquet just shrugged his shoulders: 'Ah, at Zeltweg I never really feel that fast, much slower than in Monaco. The landscape is much further away.'

You need to be able to see speed, you have to be able to experience it. It needs to be located in an environment. That's why the circuit of Magny-Cours will never develop any real ambience, no matter how superb the surface – there's nothing next to it. That's why circuits like Monza, Spa and Hockenheim are so stunning: 300, 350 between the trees, straight through a park, past historical monuments; only on circuits like these does speed really become visible.

Visible speed. That's the secret of Monaco as well. Of course, Monaco has its tradition, its grandeur and its glamorous image. Long ago: an elderly baroness stops Phil Hill (Formula One world champion 1961, no relation) on the steps of the Hôtel de Paris in his oil- and sweat-stained overalls: 'Are you one of the young gentlemen who are making such a ghastly racket here?' 'Yes, ma'am.' 'Why are you doing that?' 'We're practising, ma'am.' Whereupon the baroness shakes her parasol at him: 'Can't you go practise somewhere else?' Thirty years later it wouldn't happen to Schumacher. Neither drivers nor baronesses wander around aimlessly any more; every square centimetre of Monaco has been sold, rented out, fenced off or placed under guard. The interest in the Grand Prix is relentless. In the principality itself, but globally as well. Only the first and the decisive race of the season can count on more attention. Everyone agrees that Monaco is the race of the year: the best, the most beautiful theatre of speed.

Theatre, definitely, listen to Berger:

> Everything comes together here, driving, Monte Carlo, the commotion and the craziness, the show and a place where you're

> judged, not only for your lap times, but also for the beauty of the execution. Who puts his foot down first, who shaves the barriers the most tenderly, who's the sexiest leaping down toward the Tip-Top Bar? In decisive moments you don't think about that jury and the grades they'll give you, any more than you think about the engineers who'll point out some peak on the telemetry and say 'What a maniac!' but somehow the accumulated madness is pre-programmed. It's inside you.

Theatre. But speed? Monaco is by far the slowest circuit on the calendar. Top speed, coming out of the tunnel: 280 km/h. In the Loews hairpin it can easily drop to 45, and the average speed is around 150, some 50 km/h less than most circuits and 100 less than the fastest.

But 280 or 350, what does it matter? Speed only becomes speed when there's a limit, surroundings. And nowhere are the surroundings as immediate as in Monaco.

The Monaco Grand Prix was first held in 1929 and since then the circuit has remained essentially unchanged. The swimming-pool section has been slightly altered, the tunnel has been lengthened and the lighting has been improved, the infamous Gasometer has been replaced by the now even more infamous Rascasse, but for the rest, the circuit is the same as it was seventy years ago. The reason is simple: you can't just relocate streets and boulevards, and you can't knock down the Hôtel de Paris or the Casino to make room for a few gravel traps. Those who are anti-Monaco, among them some drivers, see the circuit as a fossil, an anachronism, totally unsuited to Formula One. Nelson Piquet described it as 'flying a helicopter in your own living room'.

Niki Lauda considered himself 'too much of a purist to be able to enjoy a race in Monaco'. Lauda called Monaco 'perverse, a trench between buildings'. No one can deny that the circuit is too small, too narrow, madness really – overtaking is impossible, the race often degenerates into a procession. 'A true feeling of claustrophobia,' writes Hill. 'There's nowhere to move, there's hardly enough space for the car.' And yet: 'Winning in Monaco is every driver's goal,' according to Mika Hakkinen.

Madness. Since Hakkinen stunned millions of television viewers by delaying braking by deliberately scraping his McLaren along the barrier in the short straight before Mirabeau, brushing the barriers has been the absolute trend in Monaco. They're only slight caresses, assures Damon Hill, because a few millimetres more and you've demolished your suspension. Any driver is proud if he manages to rub out the white logos on his tyres without crashing. Mansell: 'You have to skim the barriers at a couple of points when you're really flying at Monaco, it's the only way to be really quick.'

The theatricality of touching the barriers shows yet again how tangible the limits are at Monaco.

But it's not just the barriers, it's the whole environment. The buildings, the neoclassic façades, the lampposts, the traffic lights, the signs, the street names, trees, zebra crossings and direction arrows. Speed in Monaco is no abstraction, it's concrete, you can put a name to it, it's a reality.

Listen to Damon Hill:

> Monaco is just an awesome place to drive around. We race at waist height and, because of that, there are some odd things that a driver can see from his car. Parts of the circuit are very slow and don't have any barriers. When people are standing there, taking pictures or spectating, you can see them clearly. At some places, a lot of photographers will congregate and hang over the barriers and I've found I can see their faces and actually recognise them, even while I'm driving the car. For example on one lap I was going round Loews hairpin and caught sight of a girl there, taking a picture. She was wearing quite a short skirt and was kneeling down on one knee, and I could see a lot more than I think she intended me to!

This reveals more than a somewhat voyeuristic tendency. Being able to steer a Formula One car through a labyrinth and still find the time to look up girls' skirts says something about the total concentration of a Formula One driver. Back to Hill: 'When I'm driving the car my mind is taking everything in, every little thing. It is wide open, looking for all the things it needs to know and to recognise; it is completely impressionable and doesn't really miss anything.'

According to Hill, this hypersensitive state is what makes racing so thrilling: 'You feel very intense, completely locked into the job. And that, of course, is the buzz. It is total concentration.'

Berger: 'It's incredible the speed at which your brains process everything in one of those laps. Afterwards I'm so shattered, I have to lie down and sleep . . .'

Concentration, compression, intensification, that is the nature of speed. It is exactly what Senna was seeking with his craving for perfection. It was no coincidence that his most intense mystical racing experiences came to him in Monaco, and it was no coincidence that he won the race six times. Nowhere else does concentration build up to produce such an unfathomable mixture of madness and ecstasy.

The same applies to the spectators. In those claustrophobic surroundings, Formula One drives right through your internal organs, your soul. Nowhere else are speed and limits so immediate, so tangible. Between the barriers, façades, balconies and springtime trees, Formula One reveals itself from an unexpected, clear, lucid, almost intimate perspective. And then there's the noise . . . Everywhere the tumult of shrieking engines echoes off buildings – the principality literally trembles to its foundations. It makes the thrill instantaneous, brutal, almost frightening. You realise immediately that this old, stylish labyrinth is home to a terrible Minotaur.

More show than speed, Monaco's adversaries will continue to claim. But as always, fiction provides a much better insight into inner truths, the nature of things. And even Formula One seems to need a shot of that each year.

PART 3: WHIZ KIDS

Michael Schumacher: A Boyhood Dream

Silverstone 1994. Warm-up lap. The parade lap, as they call it in England. We're halfway through the 1994 season and Schumacher is the new star. Up till now he's won every race except Spain, where he came second. His lead over the closest contender, Damon Hill, is devastating: 66 to 29. The title is as good as his.

But Hill is getting things figured. Williams is recovering from Imola. In France Hill took pole, and here, in front of a home audience, after a nerve-wracking duel with Schumacher, he has proven fastest again. A difference of three thousandths of a second. 'If I'd eaten another couple of spoonfuls of pasta at lunch, I wouldn't have made it,' says Hill. The jubilant British newspapers declare that the season has reached a turning point.

The lights turn green. The warm-up lap begins. When it's finished, the cars will take position for the start. The Safety Car has been scrapped. The man on pole now leads the parade, he sets the pace and the other drivers follow in neat starting order. The cars creep over the track, now and then weaving wildly to further warm up their tyres. Then something strange happens: Schumacher overtakes Hill, drives in front of him for a few hundred metres, then lets him retake the lead. A mistake most probably. These things happen, albeit rarely: a driver accelerates too hard, accidentally passes the man in front of him, then lets him by again at the next opportunity. But it's unprecedented to see something like that at the front of the field. Peculiar, but as the cars resume position the incident seems forgotten: Hill, Schumacher, Berger, Alesi, Hakkinen, Barrichello, Coulthard and so on until everyone is in their correct position and a green flag is being waved at the rear. Except the green flag doesn't come. Instead, yellow flags are waved near Coulthard. Senna's replacement has stalled. Start procedure interrupted.

Mechanics run out on to the track. Tyre blankets around the tyres, new checks, five minutes to restart, start the engines again, new warm-up lap. According to the rules, Coulthard stays where he is and joins the parade at the rear. Drivers who interrupt the start go to the back of the grid for the restart. And then it happens again: Schumacher overtakes Hill. This time he stays in front for quite a long time, this can't be a mistake, this is deliberate. The officials scratch their heads. Does it say anything about this in the rules? On the grid everyone gets back into place. Green flag. The red lights go on one by one and all turn off together: start. Hill gets off best, Schumacher second.

Meanwhile, feverish consultation behind the pits. What about that warm-up lap? The regulations turn out to be unambiguous: Schumacher should have been relegated to the back of the grid. Only no one was ready with article number whatever, buried deep in that thick rulebook. What's more, it had only been a few hundred metres and maybe not even deliberate. But what about the second time, then?

The race roars on. Hill leading, Schumacher second. The Brits cheer. But like so many times before, Schumacher has a much better pit stop. After changing wheels, he's out in front, Hill second. And then the stewards finally agree: Schumacher gets a stop-go penalty. Not for the customary ten seconds, only for five: the offence was not that serious. Schumacher has to come into the pits and remain stationary for five seconds during which no work may be done on the car, after that he can resume racing. With the pit-lane speed limit that has been in force since Imola, it will cost him approximately twenty seconds. With Hill on his heels, that will almost certainly cost him the race.

The decision is put down in writing and handed to the Benetton team leadership. They are given five laps to call Schumacher in to sit out his punishment. But now the haggling begins. The stewards have forgotten to mention that it is a stop-go penalty. Uproar on the pit wall. Everyone has seen the monitors where the stewards' decisions are announced publicly, everyone knows that Schumacher has to come in for a stop-go – everyone, that is, except Benetton. 'It doesn't say so on the form,' insists Briatore. The five laps pass. The snubbed stewards immediately pull out their biggest gun: the black flag. You don't accept their authority? Then expect no mercy: Schumacher is out of the race. Lap after lap, he is shown the black flag in combination with his number: 5. Schumacher claims later that he didn't see it. He saw the number next to it, but thought it referred to the five-second penalty. Radio? Never heard of it.

Meanwhile Briatore is debating with the officials. The others gnash their teeth and look on. And finally Schumacher comes in . . . to sit out his stop-go penalty after all! It costs him the race. Schumacher comes in second behind Hill. But the incident will cost him much more, nothing can stop the protests now, the FIA launches an investigation, no one can be allowed to ignore the black flag, suspension threatens. The season has reached a turning point.

The incident at Silverstone is more than just an incident. In some ways it is typical of Schumacher as a Formula One driver.

The most important question, which everyone forgot about afterwards, is why he drove past Hill in the warm-up lap. 'He was going a bit slow,' was Schumacher's explanation. Not particularly convincing. There was probably another reason. Schumacher overtook Hill to show off, to belittle Hill in front of his home audience: 'You belong behind me.' Trying to intimidate his opponents, that's typical Schumacher.

But what he does on the circuits really is intimidating. Schumacher is without a doubt the most gifted driver of his generation. Just take the one race he *didn't* win in the first half of 1994. In Spain Schumacher ended second because his gearbox was jammed in fifth gear for two-thirds of the race. But even with a jammed gearbox, he was still able to follow Hill: the silhouette of the Benetton was a constant threat. Afterwards journalists refused to believe it until they'd actually seen Benetton's telemetry. Impressive.

He would probably have won the race at Silverstone easily as well because he was the first to see the importance of choosing the right pit-stop strategy, then executing it impeccably. Unfortunately Silverstone also turned out to be the start of something else that has dogged Schumacher throughout his career: controversy. Over and over, especially when he is in a winning position, Schumacher is the focus of incidents and scandals. Not least of all because of his somewhat peculiar driving style in races that are decisive for the world championship. But also because of his – let's say, natural – tendency to try to intimidate others. Arrogance is never endearing. Perhaps the unfortunate timing of his accession has also played a role. Many people had difficulty accepting that a new star was already rising even before Senna's grave had been properly covered over.

The Rise

Few careers have developed as quickly as Schumacher's. Whether it was go-karts, Formel König, Formula Three or sports cars, everything he turned his hand to immediately drove a second or so faster.

Five days before his first Grand Prix, Schumacher tried out a Formula One car for the first time. On 20 August 1991 he test-drove a Jordan at Silverstone. 'The first three laps were quite impressive,' he explained later, 'in the impression they made on me – then it was normal. Sure it was something special, but not over-special.'

Berger knew why everything went so smoothly for Schumacher: 'He started in karts when he was only four years old. In those things you use your senses just like in the big-time, and the kids develop a sense of detail. Even before they've ever dragged themselves off to school, they're already playing around with hundredths of millibars of air pressure to get the optimal set-up for their karts. This kart generation automatically has a computer-like approach to a sport that is now dominated by computers. No child of nature will ever beat these kids with speed alone.' In Schumacher, Berger also recognised a mental strength like Senna's, one that was solid to start with and just grew and grew. This time he really was jealous.

Eddie Jordan had hooked a big fish and was up on the pit wall waving contracts around. Schumacher signed a letter of intent, the definitive arrangements would be completed after Spa.

In the Ardennes Schumacher was very impressive. He'd never driven there before, let alone in a Formula One car, but it was a circuit for born racers and it suited him down to the ground. Years later he looked back lovingly on his introduction to the Eau Rouge: 'I had my most sensational experience there. The car's grip was simply perfect and there was so much downforce that it was sitting full on the titanium blocks attached under the floor plate. I felt like the wheels were hanging in the air and that I was actually driving on the titanium blocks. Crazy of course, but I really felt that at the time. And I realised: you can actually do a lot more than you thought. That really was an exhilarating moment . . .' During practice he qualified as eighth, during the warm-up session he was fourth fastest. Schumacher was impressive. Journalists were full of his charisma, the way he stalked down the pit lane – there goes a new world champion. The race hadn't even started.

When it did, Schumacher didn't get very far. Even before La Source, the first corner, he'd burnt out his clutch: race over.

But Schumacher had shown enough; the haggling could begin. With the contracts waiting on his desk, Jordan watched his deadlines elapse. Competitors were afoot. Whereas Mercedes had to pay for the seat with Jordan, Schumacher could drive with Benetton for free. Briatore knew what he was doing and he could afford to do it. The first controversy. Schumacher had only signed a letter of intent, hadn't he? Lawyers, court cases. Later, years later, Schumacher's manager Willi Weber placated the still-angry Jordan with a substantial pay-off. The championships had been won long before.

Schumacher drove the next race for Benetton and immediately came in fifth, in front of team-mate and triple world champion Piquet. The path to the summit lay open before him.

A year after his debut Schumacher won his first Grand Prix, at Spa. In the usual, highly variable weather conditions, Schumacher displayed his superior circuit judgement by swapping his rain tyres for slicks at exactly the right moment. He was immediately eight seconds faster than Mansell, who was still touring around on wet-weather tyres. Eight seconds! Schumacher and Spa, he would go on to win there often. Only the many controversies have stopped him from long ago dethroning the kings of Spa, Jim Clark and Ayrton Senna, both of whom won the race four times in a row.

Senna. It was inevitable that the old and the new champions should clash.

As early as Brazil 1992, Schumacher felt justified in lecturing Senna about irresponsible driving. Engine cut-out, was Senna's defence. In France, Schumacher punted Senna off the track in the first corner after an all-too-optimistic attempt to overtake. 'My mistake,' Schumacher admitted, 'today I learnt that races aren't won in the first corner.' Testing at Hockenheim, Schumacher and Senna got in each other's way again. Back in the pits, an angry Senna jumped out of his McLaren, rushed over to the Benetton pits and collared Schumacher. His mechanics dragged him away. Where had we seen that before?

A magnificent duel between the two great talents was in the air. It was postponed in 1993, the year Prost declared his veto over the title, but 1994 was going to make up for everything. With the Schumacher–Benetton combination going from strength to strength, Senna moved to Williams. The promised duel never eventuated. Or was the conflict so harsh and unforgiving that it could never have lasted longer than those first two races?

Schumacher won the opening races. Easily, with Senna spinning off the track in the first race and getting mixed up in an accident at the start of the second. Schumacher seemed invincible. But how could that be possible all of a sudden? Controversy. Rumours spread that the Benettons were in contravention. That the team was still using banned driver aids. Senna too vented his suspicions. Just before Imola. Then it was all over. For Senna. And many Formula One fans with him.

But Schumacher kept on winning. At Imola, in Monaco. Before the eyes of the mourning prince, Schumacher danced a victory dance with Briatore. At Senna's funeral, Schumacher was conspicuous by his absence. Scared of being assassinated, he explained later. Not as exaggerated as it may sound. Of course, no one in their right mind would claim that Schumacher and Benetton were responsible for Senna's death, but the rumours about illicit software refused to lie down. The FIA launched an investigation and Benetton needed to clear their name of the suspicion of cheating. They began by dragging their feet and not providing the requested information. A fine of 100,000 dollars was imposed. Briatore paid. Then it turned out that the suspect programs were present in the on-board computer, but that the program to use them was absent. Really, honestly, Benetton hadn't broken any rules. Nothing could be proven.

And Schumacher won. In Canada, in France. The title was as good as his, until Schumacher decided that he belonged in front of Damon Hill on the warm-up lap at Silverstone.

All hell broke loose. Benetton caught flak from all directions and no one felt sorry for them. After all, Benetton were the beneficiaries of the drama at Imola. Benetton were rolling in money and Benetton didn't have a real racing tradition. Just take that guy Briatore, plucked out of the world of pullovers to run a Formula One team. Berger, who experienced Briatore a few years later, was scathing: 'Briatore brushed over everything with unimaginable superficiality. He held forth on technical matters, but meanwhile you got the uneasy feeling that he couldn't tell the difference between a back wheel and a steering wheel. Racing wasn't in his blood at all. He only lived for marketing, especially his own.' Money and market strategies. Briatore had already bought Ligier's team as well, what was he up to? And the way he'd nagged at the stewards at Silverstone. Just because he wore his cap backwards, he thought he could get away with anything, even ignoring the black flag . . .

The FIA struck hard. The last person to ignore the black flag, Nigel Mansell, Estoril 1989, had been suspended for a single race; Schumacher was relegated to spectator status for two races. But Benetton didn't take it lying down, they launched an appeal to ensure that Schumacher could start in his home races at Hockenheim and Spa. The only thing was, those two races just made things worse.

In Hockenheim it wasn't Schumacher himself who was the centre of commotion. During the pit stop of his team-mate Jos Verstappen – four new wheels and a full tank in eleven seconds – fuel suddenly sprayed out over driver and car. The refuelling system had failed and within seconds the Benetton was on fire. The mechanics recoiled, Jos rushed to climb out of the inferno, and a few cold-blooded team members doused the flames. Formula One had only just escaped another disaster. Jos and a few of the mechanics suffered light burns.

Controversy. Benetton were accused of tinkering with the refuelling system: a filter had been removed from the mouth of the hose. Formula One shook to its foundations. Benetton's series of victories were partly due to their lightning pit stops. Rumours: Benetton would be excluded for the whole season. And the next season as well. No mercy. The team reeled. Even Schumacher voiced doubts: 'If it is established that the team have been doing things behind my back which are forbidden by the rules, I would not accept that. By that I mean that I could move to another team.'

It turned out that Benetton had already explained that the filter was superfluous because they filtered the fuel themselves at an earlier stage. An official from the FIA itself had even given permission for its removal. But that emerged later, in the board-room: what stuck in people's minds was the fireball at Hockenheim and the bad smell that just wouldn't go away.

In Germany Schumacher retired for the first time in 1994, but went on to convincingly win the next two races. But at Spa there was a new uproar after the race. Sure, they were out to get him, but unresolved suspicions are like dominoes. The stewards who check all the cars after the race found that Schumacher's Benetton did not conform to regulations.

One of the changes introduced in the aftermath of Imola had been to the bottom of the cars. To guarantee a minimum ride height, everyone had been driving since Hockenheim with a wooden plank affixed to the bottom of the car. This plank had to be ten millimetres thick. If the car was set too low, it might go faster, but it would also wear away the plank faster. After the race a maximum of one millimetre was allowed to be missing – not a half a millimetre more. The thickness of the plank under the Benetton in the *parc fermé* at Spa was 7.4 mm. Disqualified. Benetton appealed. Appeal rejected. On top of that, the appeal against the Silverstone suspension was also rejected: Schumacher had to grit his teeth in Italy and Portugal while Hill caught up in the world championship – Schumacher 76: Hill 75. Three races to go.

Schumacher made his return at Jerez and immediately struck home. Victory, Hill was second. But in Japan Hill proved that he could stand the pace. In the wet Schumacher just couldn't get past him: score 92–91 in Schumacher's favour. The decision will come in Adelaide.

Adelaide 1994. During qualifying on Friday, Mansell – he's back again – clocks the fastest time. In an ultimate attempt to better it, Schumacher flies off the track – in the Senna chicane of all places.

Hard. The pressure is on. And under pressure, it seems, Schumacher makes mistakes. That's probably why he tries to intimidate his opponents. And it's probably why he slated Hill mercilessly long before the race:

> I don't think we would have been in this situation if Ayrton Senna had been in the car. Ayrton would have been driving circles around me. That shows what I think of Damon as a driver. He has been thrown into the number-one driver position but he never really was a number-one driver. With David Coulthard driving quicker than him after three races, it proves he is not a number-one driver. So the respect is certainly not as much as I have for other drivers. You always start to know people when you are in trouble and he has not been very helpful when I was in big trouble. Every time we proved we did not cheat they found a way to turn it around and say 'yes, but there was something else'. This has made me more determined to win the championship. I always get stronger when I am in trouble. I am certainly more determined because there is one point between us and if I win the title I will have done it in 12 races, not 16. If I don't win the championship, I think everyone will know why.

Hill refused to rise to the bait: 'I'd rather not drag the championship down by trying to diminish the reputation of the opposition. I think that's sad. Formula One has been in that situation for too long, with the two protagonists seemingly hating each other's guts.' Hill was not alone in thinking back on the days of Prost and Senna.

Saturday qualifying was washed out, leaving Mansell on pole in front of Schumacher. Asked whether he would resort to unethical methods if that meant deciding the championship in favour of his team-mate, the Lion roared: 'That is a disgusting question. I'm above that.'

The streets of Adelaide are bumpy with lots of tricky, ninety-degree corners. Overtaking is difficult, the start is crucial.

Mansell gets off to a bad start. Schumacher immediately draws up alongside. Wheels spinning, Mansell lets his Williams drift to the middle of the track, but Schumacher is already past. Hill passes on the other side. After just one hundred metres the rivals are together in the lead.

For a moment it seems as if Schumacher is getting away, but Hill hangs on. Lap after lap, they fly over the track, one behind the other. Now and then Schumacher edges a few metres ahead, then Hill hauls him in, metres, centimetres at a time. Everyone is amazed at Schumacher's inability to shake Hill. The Benetton even goes sideways a few times. Schumacher is under pressure. In the Benetton pits they're holding their breath. All year long, they've been faster. Of course, they've missed races, but Hill has come back strongly: the title that seemed so assured halfway through the season could slip away just like that . . .

The difference remains minimal, Hill even comes close to running into the back of the Benetton. Hill seems quicker, but where can he get past the Benetton?

Then they start overtaking the slower cars. All year Schumacher has been faster at overtaking the back markers and he shoots past them again now, but this time Hill follows, not losing an inch of ground. Eighteenth lap: pit stops. Schumacher, fastest in the pits the whole year, comes out first, but Hill follows, not losing a second. When Schumacher roars out on to the track the Williams is hanging under his wing.

The whole world is glued to the screen. The fact that Hill still has to overtake is almost forgotten. Sometimes he seems about to mount the challenge, deviating from his line on the Brabham Straight, but he's never close enough. For thirty-six nerve-wracking laps, the chase goes on. Then Schumacher makes a decisive error.

In Flinders Street, a fast ninety-degree left-hander, Schumacher hits a bump. The Benetton is thrown sideways. It jolts over the multi-coloured kerbing, slides over the narrow strip of grass and hits the wall with both right wheels. Dust and grass whirl through the air as the Benetton bounces back on to the track. At just that moment Hill comes around the corner.

Millions of TV viewers have seen it, but for Hill it was hidden around the corner: he doesn't know that Schumacher hit the wall.

Hill sees that his rival has gone over the grass and lost speed and he doesn't hesitate for a second: the moment has come. Maybe he can get by on the left. But the Benetton is crossing the track diagonally. In doing so, it's opened a gap on the right at the start of the next corner, a right-hander. Hill steers into it. At the same moment, Schumacher regains some control over his car and swings sharply to the right, in front of the wheels of the Williams. Hill goes over the kerbs on the inside, but can no longer avoid a shunt.

The wheels touch, the Benetton has been hit, the right side of the car flies up. Hill sees the bottom of Schumacher's car. The Benetton slides across in front of him on the sides of its left tyres, heading for the tyre barrier and the wall on the other side. The car almost tips over, drops back on to four wheels, damaged: race over. Hill drives on and disappears into the distance off screen.

A disillusioned Schumacher climbs out of his car, jumps over the wall and disappears through a hole in the fence. He scarcely dares hope, the waiting begins. Has Hill's car been damaged as well, or will he come past again shortly, whistling on his way to the championship? Hill has driven into the pits. Slowly – his left front wheel is locking. The team is waiting. When Hill stops, the damage is immediately obvious, the left front suspension is bent, almost broken. The mechanics look, feel. The seconds tick away. Someone tugs desperately at the metal. Hill watches from the cockpit and shakes his head.

On the circuit Schumacher sees a Williams approaching but this time it's Mansell, who has taken the lead. A nervous Schumacher leans against the wire fence. He can't make out the announcement coming over the loudspeaker, is Hill in the pits? When Mansell comes past again, and again, and the marshals start to congratulate him, Schumacher knows that he has won. World champion, with a one-point lead. In the pits Hill has climbed out. At Benetton the mechanics, bosses, managers and camera teams are all over each other.

Again the world championship has been decided by a dubious collision. Was it deliberate? Was the Benetton already damaged after hitting the wall? Only Schumacher knows. Shortly after the race, his engineer claimed it had been. Schumacher disagreed first, then changed his mind later. What's more, he hadn't seen Hill, and besides, he was in front of him and according to regulations, that put him in the right, and he was the one who had earned the title anyway.

At the press conference after the race, Schumacher took back his earlier comments about Hill: 'I said I didn't have much respect for him, then, but I was wrong. He has done a fantastic job in the last two races, a proper and fantastic job. He has been a great rival.'

The title is Schumacher's.

Somewhere in the back of the Williams pit, Hill almost falls off his chair when he sees the TV footage: 'If I'd known that he'd hit the wall, I never would have dived into that gap . . .'

Confirmation

The 1994 season was finally over. The thriller in Adelaide had pushed the nightmare of Imola and the controversy surrounding Benetton into the background. It seemed as though the team would start 1995 with a clean slate.

But then, at the opening race in Brazil, it was back again, an uproar around Schumacher and Benetton. 1994 hadn't been forgotten after all . . .

As of 1995, the FIA had banned the teams from mixing all kinds of different fuels in their cauldrons. The fuel in a Formula One tank should be the same as what's available at an ordinary petrol station. But the fuel samples taken from Benetton and Williams after the race were irregular. Schumacher and Coulthard, the race's numbers one and two, were disqualified and Berger and Ferrari were declared winner. Two weeks later the decision was reversed. Apparently there had been some kind of error sampling the fuel, and the penalty was limited to fines for both teams. Niki Lauda, now an adviser with Ferrari, was furious: 'If this is the new rule, you can build an illegal car and let the team pay for victory. The whole thing is only commercial and has nothing to do with sport any more. The FIA cannot govern the sport any longer.'

Even more dubious was Schumacher's weight at the official weigh-in on the Thursday before the race. Schumacher scaled in at 77 kilograms and according to regulations Benetton could deduct this figure from the car's minimum weight for the rest of the season. But on Sunday after the race, Schumacher only weighed 71.5. Sure, they were out to get him. The team and all his personal staff exhausted themselves providing explanations: well, of course, everyone knows how much Schumacher loves good food, French cuisine, so you understand . . . and he hadn't really been to the toilet properly yet, he'd had a lot to drink and he didn't have his helmet with him . . . Patrick Head, Williams's chief engineer, made a neat calculation showing that a difference of 5.5 kilos translated to an advantage of 14 seconds per race.

The FIA regretted the course of events, but nothing could be proven.

With all these scandals, Schumacher was under pressure. And he made mistakes. At Imola he crashed hard into the tyres on the Piratella corner. The *tifosi* cheered, the Damon Hill fans cheered, the Senna fans cheered. No sympathy: 1994 was far from forgotten.

Hill won at Imola. An emotional victory. And Hill saw that Schumacher was under pressure. In 1994 he'd always held back, but now he felt that it was time to rub it in: 'I know he has a certain amount of arrogance, but I don't believe he is impervious to criticism. At the weigh-in in Brazil he was pushing the regulations, and effectively stuck two fingers up at them. That is not the sort of behaviour you expect from a champion. He has been making mistakes too, which is the sign of someone over-driving.'

But Schumacher hit back. With victories. Lots of victories. 1995 became his best season. Benetton now had the same Renault engine at their disposal as Williams, and although Hill consistently demonstrated at practice that he had the quicker car, Schumacher showed him up in race after race. With perfect races, with sublime and sometimes surprising pit-stop strategies. Schumacher was consistently impressive and, perhaps even more important, there were no controversies.

All the pressure was reserved for Hill. And it was too much for him.

At both Silverstone and Monza he knocked Schumacher and himself off the track. In Italy Schumacher almost physically attacked him, but restrained himself: no new scandals.

At Spa Schumacher imitated one of Senna's legendary masterstrokes. When it started to rain, sending everyone else in for wet-weather tyres, Schumacher stayed out on slicks. Hill, much faster on rain tyres, caught up with him, but was, for a long time, unable to get past. Lap after lap Schumacher stayed in front of Hill on the slippery track. Weaving over the Kemmel at almost 300 km/h, braking late, puddles everywhere and not a millimetre of tread. Hill lost valuable seconds. By the time he finally slipped past it was too late. The track dried and they all had to go back into the pits to change back to slicks. Except Schumacher. A brilliant victory.

On the Nürburgring Schumacher virtually clinched the title. While Hill piled mistake upon mistake, Schumacher drove like a star. After a fantastic chase, he passed Alesi in the third-to-last lap with an impeccable manoeuvre in the Veedol chicane. Schumacher braked exceptionally late, the Benetton glided alongside Alesi, who was about to turn in. The wheels banged. Alesi, who was on the outside, lifted, and Schumacher was past. And there in front of a home audience, on the podium . . . No, not yet.

Ferrari

After two consecutive titles, Schumacher had nothing left to prove with Benetton. It was time for a greater challenge. In late 1995 Schumacher announced a move to Ferrari. It was a logical choice, they were paying 25 million dollars, and besides, he might succeed where even Prost had failed: pulling Ferrari out of its doldrums and bringing the title back to Maranello after almost twenty years.

But it was a golden opportunity for other reasons as well. Ferrari liberated Schumacher from the black page of 1994 and the Benetton scandals.

Flavio Briatore immediately announced that Benetton could now demonstrate that they hadn't owed their two world championships to Schumacher alone. And Briatore didn't settle for second-rate drivers either: with Schumacher on his way, Alesi *and* Berger traded Ferrari for Benetton. But during the first tests both Alesi and Berger slammed into the barriers. Berger: 'The car simply swerved away, just like that. I didn't even have time to look.' A thorough investigation, on Berger's orders, revealed that the nervous Benetton responded very badly to bumps in high-speed corners. All of Schumacher's team-mates had complained about the car's handling, but Berger was overcome by admiration: 'My last doubts about Schumacher fell aside, anyone who could so easily keep this car under control at the limit was absolutely in a class of his own.'

Berger and Alesi were now under pressure with Benetton and Briatore, but at Ferrari the pressure was off Schumacher.

He was still impressive. Only this time in a new way. Schumacher succeeded in tempering the Italians' perennially high expectations. In the past, Ferrari had often been the winter champion: the fastest in all kinds of tests. The press and the *tifosi* expected nothing but victories, and then the first Grands Prix came and the red cars fell short yet again or simply broke down. But Schumacher managed to adopt the right tone, the necessary reserve. 1996 would be an apprenticeship, essential to getting the team back on track. If they won one or two races, he would be more than satisfied. And the *tifosi* swallowed it.

Even if they continued to view Schumacher with reserve. Their hearts still belonged to Alesi – spirited, reckless, tragic Alesi.

Once Alesi had stormed into Formula One as the coming man. In one of his very first races, Phoenix 1991, he had badgered the great Senna with his modest Tyrrell. It was the same race in which Tyrrell introduced the 'shark nose'. Instead of hovering just above the asphalt, the nose of the car was several decimetres higher. Later this nose became standard in Formula One. Alesi refused to be intimidated and led the race lap after lap, giving Senna a lot of trouble. The first time Senna passed him, Alesi immediately returned the favour. Formula One was flabbergasted; this guy Alesi was someone to watch! But Alesi didn't live up to his potential. His spectacular, aggressive-looking driving style – lots of going sideways, lots of slips, lots of show – won him plenty of fans. Especially once he'd inherited Ferrari's Number 27. And there is a bit of Villeneuve in Alesi. But ten years after Gilles, that won't get you very far. Berger: 'There's a chasm between a superb talent and the *basics* of motor racing. Alesi has never become a world champion because he's too impatient, he's not interested in technology and avoids working on the finer points.' Keke Rosberg, himself a renowned daredevil and still a world champion, is much harsher: 'Alesi drives just like he did in Phoenix in 1991. He hasn't learnt a thing.' What remains is visual spectacle with an unhappy ending. In Italy that can be enough.

But Alesi did not go entirely unrewarded. In his last year with Ferrari he scored his first and only Grand Prix victory. Appropriately enough, it was on the Gilles Villeneuve circuit in Canada. Alesi toured around in second place for almost the entire race, far behind the unapproachable Schumacher. Then, in the final phase, Schumacher went into the pits: gearbox problems. A laptop is plugged in, keys pressed: reset. Alesi reaped the benefit. Overcome by emotion, he stalled in the slowing-down lap and, still ecstatic, stood up in his Ferrari. Schumacher, who had ended fifth, gave him a ride. Perched on the Benetton's air box, Alesi waved to the moved crowd. No one begrudged him his victory. A year later, Alesi is with Benetton and Schumacher with Ferrari.

And while Alesi rolls to a halt in the first race of 1996 because he forgets to refuel, Schumacher seems to win the hearts of the *tifosi.* At any rate, he brings success and euphoria, he has them cheering *Forza Ferrari*.

At Imola Schumacher takes pole, but the race is even more beautiful. He only comes in second, but does it by dragging his car through the last lap with a completely locked front wheel. The fans go wild, it's just what Gilles would have done. And Schumacher wins, in Spain, a phenomenal, wet race. A 45-second lead over the number two, Alesi. Then Ferrari goes through a period of serious problems. The races in Canada, France and England are all lost at an early stage because of mechanical problems. In France, Schumacher even blows up the engine during the warm-up lap. But Schumacher impresses again. He tames the crisis and keeps everyone's head pointed in the same direction, a miracle in Maranello. And he wins again. At Spa, thanks to a clever pit stop while the race is neutralised. Overjoyed scenes on the podium, where . . . No, one more race: Monza.

Because Schumacher wins at Monza as well. With the requisite luck. Because while Hill fails to safeguard his title after a crash into the tyres in the first chicane, Schumacher hits the same tyres and is able to drive on to victory. Luck? No, Schumacher can even intimidate a pile of tyres.

On the podium Schumacher leaps so high he makes a mockery of the laws of gravity; he's overjoyed, radiating happiness. Winning in a Ferrari on the holy ground of Monza, a dream come true.

But Schumacher is happy with every victory. Genuinely happy. When Senna or Prost stood on the podium, they always stood there as if that was where they belonged, they were calm and in their rightful place. Schumacher rushes every podium, every time he places, he has fulfilled his boyhood dreams. This is the last and nicest characteristic of the greatest driver of the last decade: he's such a big kid.

There's a photo of Schumacher as a spotty fifteen-year-old: dressed in tacky, shiny-black racing overalls, kneeling beside his helmet, one arm ostensibly relaxed on a knee, a wristwatch that's way too big . . . You can see the shoddy, background paper of the photo studio, you can imagine Mum or Dad quickly tidying up his hair. German Junior Karting Champion.

Somehow Schumacher always remains that boy. An adolescent, with his flaws, his stubborn rudeness, but also with the joy, the pride of the child who sees his dream become a reality. Those who persist in calling Schumacher cold and arrogant have never looked closely when he ascends that highest podium. It's not too late, Schumacher still wins often enough.

Damon Hill: His Father's Son

Hockenheim 1993. At last Damon Hill is poised to win his first Grand Prix. Unchallenged, the Williams Number 0 is in the lead. Lap after lap, a majestic Hill zooms through the curves of the motordrome, the stadium section of the circuit where 120,000 Formula One fans are watching the race from the immense 1930s stands. Here he comes again. Through the Agip right-hander into the motordrome, hitting the brakes for the hairpin Sachs Kurve, a bit of throttle, slight bend to the left with the track climbing slightly, and then right, right, Süd Kurve, into the start-finish straight. Ducking and weaving, the deep-blue helmet with white stripes follows the turns of the wheel.

That helmet . . . It's his father's helmet. The deep blue – almost black – and the eight white stripes are the colours of the London Rowing Club; Graham Hill was once a respected member.

I saw Graham Hill race once himself, the deep-blue helmet with white stripes on his head. He was at the back of the field, but I remember it well because he was at the wheel of the red-and-white Embassy-Shadow DN1, one of the most beautiful cars on the circuit. Graham Hill was already in the autumn of his career. But in his heyday he had driven up front. The 1962 and 1968 Formula One world champion. Five-time winner on the Monaco street circuit, for a long time an absolute record. 'When I was a kid,' relates Damon, 'I thought winning the race in Monaco was my father's job.' And Hill senior is still the only driver to have won the Indianapolis 500, the Le Mans Grand Prix d'Endurance *and* the Formula One world championship. With his enormous sideboards, his moustache and his slicked-back hair, he was a gentleman driver through and through . . . Graham Hill went back to the days when racing-car drivers wore open helmets, goggles and a white dust mask.

For years he was a living fossil. Long after his contemporaries Brabham, Surtees, Clark, Stewart and Rindt had retired or been killed in accidents, Hill was still active – with Brabham, with Shadow, with Lola and finally with his own team, Embassy-Hill. In 1975, after failing to qualify for the Monaco Grand Prix, he got the message. He was forty-six years old and stopped racing. He said goodbye to his fans with a lap of honour at Silverstone. I have a photo of it somewhere: Graham Hill in shirtsleeves at the wheel of his Hill GH1, gruff, emotional, waving to the crowd. Two weeks ago I meant to have another look at that photo on the morning that would see his son Damon starting in the front row of the British Grand Prix, the race Dad never won.

Things have come full circle. Damon Hill's helmet is not just a crash helmet; through those colours his father drives with him, and so does Zandvoort 1973, and so do Stewart, Peterson, Lauda – everything. No, this isn't nostalgia, it isn't a longing for days gone by, it really is a living present. But it's a connected present, rooted in the past, a past that has left its mark. Suddenly everything seems right: the unity, the continuity, the fullness of life, of my life. A phase has been completed.

Damon Hill did not choose his helmet lightly. That alone makes him my hero: he drives Formula One the way I watch it, with a sense of the past. He's not the kind of hero who comes out of nowhere. We're almost the same age, we have a common history. 'Our childhood,' says his sister Brigitte, 'was an ordinary sixties childhood: school, *Dr Who*, piano lessons, a dog called Honey and playing outside in the summer.' Damon Hill is where Formula One and I come together; Hill's style, behaviour and image coincide almost inevitably with the way I see myself.

Two weeks ago at Silverstone he didn't win. He was leading – ahead of Alain Prost, who showed no signs of wanting to deprive his loyal team-mate of a historic home victory – until his engine failed. A rare thing for a Renault. Blue smoke at Bridge signalled the end, Prost slipped past: race over. Hill climbed out, gestured that there was nothing he could do about it either, and waved to his fans. I thought of the photograph I had neglected to find.

But today victory cannot elude him. He leaves the motordrome by way of the Nord Kurve and disappears into the woods. Two more laps to go. I want to shout through the window: 'Come and watch! He's going to win!' But my sweetheart is sitting outside in the sun with a pregnant belly. Two weeks ago I made her come running as well, and there had been all those other races too . . . I decide to wait until the last lap.

Hill flies down the straight before the first chicane, 300, 310, braking in time, no more risks, into the corner, right-left-right, stepping on it once again. An insane circuit really. Again I suppress a desire to call out, and then it happens, slowing down for the third chicane, at a speed of about 200 km/h, it's as if something snaps inside the Williams, the rear end collapses, the nose goes up, the car is almost out of control. The cause is immediately apparent: a blowout in the rear left. The rubber shreds, sparks fly up from the magnesium rims, the car shudders left and right. I shout, I scream that this can't be true, it isn't fair. Hill struggles to keep the Williams under control, brakes and brakes, takes the corner, left-right, the rubber flies from the rim and bounces mindlessly over the asphalt and through the grass while Hill wrestles the car around the left-hander. He slithers into the motordrome on three wheels, taking the corners cautiously, desperately, realising the race is lost . . . Prost passes, then Schumacher. Driving into the pits, the Williams Number 0 turns half circle. Sympathetic marshals come running, but Hill is pounding his helmet, that deep-blue helmet with white stripes. He can't believe it either. The rest of the field comes by: Blundell, Senna, Patrese, Berger. One and a half laps . . . It really is unbelievable.

But things like this always happen. That's another reason he's my hero. You don't believe in a Hill victory until he has crossed the line with all four wheels, gearbox and wing. Until that moment, you're wracked by a horrible mixture of fear and doubt.

The Doubt

The seed of all doubting was laid on the evening of 29 November 1975. In the Hill family home the table is set for a pleasant dinner; Dad is due back from tests in France. But suddenly, worrying reports come over the radio. A plane has crashed at nearby Elstree Airfield. The family's fears are soon confirmed: in bad weather Graham Hill has crashed his private jet into trees. Almost the entire Embassy-Hill racing team was on board, including the talented driver Tony Brise. No survivors. It's unbelievable: less than six months after finally giving up racing – with its strange, unpredictable menace of death – your father dies in a plane crash.

Damon Hill is fifteen. By comparison: at the age of fifteen, Michael Schumacher was already sending his first autographed photos to fans.

The disaster is complete when it turns out that Graham Hill had neglected to extend his pilot's licence; the insurance company refuses to pay. Besides withdrawing the children from their public schools, Bette Hill is also obliged to sell their country home, all kinds of memorabilia and even trophies to cover the damages claims.

Is it strange that Hill's teenage son vents his frustrations in a thrash band called Sex, Hitler and the Hormones? That he drops out, works part-time delivering fast food in London, and dedicates his weekends to England's low-budget motorbike-racing circuit, where he regularly tumbles from his bike with exhaustion and cold?

His helmet protects him in many an accident. The deep-blue helmet with white stripes. 'With that helmet on,' explains Bette, 'he looks exactly like Graham, the way he does things as well.' It is Bette who finally convinces Damon to make the change to four wheels: 'He was very good on the bikes, you know, but they were so dangerous. They scared me. I thought he would be safer in a car.'

On four wheels Damon soon discovers the advantages and disadvantages of his surname. Sponsors lend a more willing ear. The name Hill generates instant publicity. But fellow drivers, managers and journalists are doubly critical, sometimes even prejudiced. In late '83 'the son of' makes his first appearance in motor racing. The comment of a team manager: 'I feel sorry for the lad, but he isn't wanted here.'

Unlike Senna or Schumacher, Hill is no all-conquering hero. Sporadic wins in Formula Ford 1600, followed by just four wins in three years of Formula Three. Despite these hardly inspiring results, Hill moves up to Formula 3000. Here, too, he fails to make a name for himself: three years without a single victory. Normally his career would have been over.

But just as a penniless Graham once made it into the Lotus team through the back door, a promising perspective now opens up for Damon as well. Mark Blundell gives up his job as a Williams test driver in order to drive a whole Grand Prix season for Brabham. Hill is asked to succeed him. He is deeply impressed by his first metres in Formula One: 'The first time I got behind the wheel of an FW14, I felt like a kid in Santa's basement. It took a while for me to come back down to earth. I had to tell myself, stop dreaming of being the budding world champion, just get in the car and do your job.' The team is very impressed by Hill's discipline, his concentration and his feel for the vehicle. It's the time when the dominance of Formula One is just passing from McLaren-Honda to Williams-Renault, and test driver Hill shares in Nigel Mansell's triumphs.

In 1992 Brabham asks Hill to replace the disappointing Giovanna

Amati. Cleverer than Blundell, Hill manages to combine his test-driving commitment to Williams with racing for Brabham. None the less, he hardly gets to race at all. Hill too starts off by failing to qualify. He doesn't crack it until his sixth attempt: at Silverstone, the circuit where Graham made his farewell seventeen years earlier. Hill finishes an inglorious sixteenth, four laps behind the victorious Mansell.

But 1992 brings more. The jockeying for the second seat with Williams. After Prost sidelines Senna, and Senna Mansell, Williams is left with little choice, and Hill is promoted to second driver of the leading Formula One team.

His competitors from the lower formulas can hardly believe it. An embittered Blundell deeply regrets his own test-driver contract with Williams: 'I don't want to cast any aspersions on Damon and his achievements, but there's no need for any of us to have any qualms about looking back on what he'd done before getting in with Williams. We all know the figures. Damon does too.'

Since Mansell is not defending his world title, the Number 1, traditionally reserved for the world champion, is not allocated in 1993. Prost opts for Number 2. Hill is given Number 0. In his first years with Williams it becomes his trademark. The almost non-existent number seems to suit him down to the ground.

In South Africa, his third Grand Prix and his first for Williams, even Hill can barely believe what happens. He comes out of the start second behind Ayrton Senna and gets so close that his car loses all adhesion in the first corner and spins off the track. Hill: 'It was just too much of a good thing.'

In Monaco historical sentiment rears up now that the son of 'Mr Monaco' is in with a chance of victory. But Senna wins as usual. It's his sixth victory in Monaco, breaking Graham Hill's record. Damon comes in second. During the press conference afterwards he does the honours: 'It is thirty years since my father first won here, and I am sure that he would have been the first to congratulate Ayrton on breaking his record. It is a tribute that it took someone of Senna's calibre to do it.'

Although Williams never issues team orders, Hill clearly plays second fiddle to Prost in 1993. Hill adopts a loyal attitude, and Prost does not need to resort to non-aggression pacts or other tricks. With the title in Prost's sights halfway through the season, Hill too seems ready for a victory. But at Silverstone his engine explodes, then the blowout at Hockenheim . . .

Still, a win is only a matter of time. When Prost stalls in Hungary and is penalised by being sent to the back of the grid for the restart, Hill has a clear run to his first victory. All the same, no one dares hope, no one dares start cheering until he's made it all the way over that line. Hill doesn't either. A full minute in front of Patrese, Hill goes through nerve-wracking final laps: 'I kept on telling myself that it wasn't over until the chequered flag, and I thought of Dad and what he would have said to keep my mind on the job at hand. And if you knew him, you'd know that just the idea of him speaking to me was enough to keep me concentrated.'

Hill won. The jinx seemed to have been broken, and at Spa and Monza, Hill won the following two races as well. Three in a row, and it could have been five, but still the doubts lingered: was Hill only in that Williams because he was 'the son of'? Forgetting that Graham had been dead for almost twenty years and that his accident had had a very bitter aftermath. Only Jackie Stewart remembered everything: 'I am truly moved by Damon's success. Because I know what he's been through. And I've known him since he was in short trousers, ever since I started driving with BRM with Graham as their top driver. Sure, he got the best car in the world, but you still have to drive it.'

The doubts only grew when Williams announced in 1994 that Prost would be leaving to make way for Senna. For the second time running, Williams was showing a world champion the door. Hill was again allocated the Number 0 and again he was very clearly second fiddle. Ron Dennis went so far as to predict: 'Now Damon's really in for it. Senna is no Prost. If he gets the chance, he'll crush his team-mate.'

Hill's reaction was cool: 'I know that he sets the standard for all Formula One drivers, but I also know that there are a few others who can beat him. I'm starting this season with a chance at the title.' Hill did get his chance at the title, but not the way he had expected, and the doubts about his capabilities only grew.

After Imola, Hill is suddenly Williams's only and therefore their first driver. A beaten team, distraught and grieving. And again there is a remarkable echo of the past. In 1968 the death of Jim Clark, who stood much higher in everyone's estimation, made Graham the only and thus the first driver in the Lotus team. Damon: 'I remember Dad coming home quiet, very quiet, one day, and I saw Jim Clark's death on the news, but I didn't really understand what it all meant. I was only eight.' In 1968 Graham managed to get the team back on its feet, and in the last race he even won the world title. Can Damon do the same?

Not a soul believes it possible. Not Frank Williams, not Renault, not Bernie Ecclestone, no one in the whole world of Formula One. Even his fans don't really believe it, but that's the very thing that makes them his fans. Does Hill believe it himself?

Williams, Renault and Ecclestone convince Nigel Mansell to return to Formula One. For three races and a fat pay cheque. He earns more per race than Hill does in the whole season.

But Mansell is a superstar. Frank Williams sees Hill as nothing more than a reliable number-two driver. Like Patrese. Hill isn't a brilliant bastard, he's not an impossible character, and Williams refuses to settle for anything less. Hill is too nice, he's too friendly. There's no denying his talent, but he's too much of a gentleman, he lacks that extra one per cent, the killer instinct that gives drivers like Schumacher their edge.

Schumacher. Schumacher is Hill's undoing. Because whenever Hill fails to dominate, Schumacher is there. And the more Schumacher impresses, the more condescending the world of Formula One is about Hill. The two drivers are in perfect harmony. Unfortunately for Hill. Because Hill only wins when Schumacher breaks down, is penalised, or even disqualified. Like at Silverstone.

Yes, in 1994 Hill won the British Grand Prix, the race Dad never won. 'A great day for the family,' declared Hill, but nobody was listening, everyone was concentrating on the incidents involving Schumacher.

Of course, Hill profited from all the controversies Schumacher and Benetton brought upon themselves in 1994. Hill won at Spa because the plank under Schumacher's car was 1.6 millimetres too thin, and he caught up in the world championship at Estoril and Monza because Schumacher was suspended. The fact that he left twenty-five others behind to do so was irrelevant.

In Jerez Schumacher won again. But Hill won in Japan, after a phenomenal race in pouring rain. Opinions about Hill remained divided. Niki Lauda, who had given up his chances at the title under similar circumstances eighteen years earlier, was impressed: 'Honestly, I'd have shat myself. If I had needed to fight for the world championship under conditions like that, I'd have said, forget about it. What Hill did there was incredible, and I know what I'm talking about.'

Ron Dennis's analysis went a step further: 'The fact that he didn't make a single mistake says volumes about Hill's character. But that doesn't come over after he's left his car, and I think that's making him pretty frustrated. He's longing for recognition. His peace-loving character isn't in keeping with his results. If he were a more outgoing, exuberant kind of person, he would probably be held in much higher regard.'

A turbulent, dramatic season was drawing to a close. One point behind, Hill travelled to Australia. As cold as ice, Patrick Head, chief designer and Frank Williams's right-hand man, declared: 'If I were a betting man and I had 100,000 dollars, I'd be putting it on Schumacher.'

* * *

For Hill fans, Adelaide 1994 was an absolute nightmare.

Distraught and hugging the tube, I saw straight away that Hill was only driving at a snail's pace after his collision with Schumacher. I had seen Schumacher hit the wall and realised that the title was Hill's for the taking, but before it had time to sink in, all hopes were shattered.

In the pit Hill stayed in the cockpit for a long time with the seconds ticking away, then he shook his head, climbed out and took off his helmet. It was over.

But then. Between the images of a jubilant Benetton crew and a happy but restrained Schumacher, comes the occasional shot of Hill sitting on a toolbox in the back of the Williams pit. He rubs his face, looks up at the heavens and clenches his fists. There is no doubt in anyone's mind, this is a disappointed man. It's 99 per cent true. But I immediately recognise that one per cent that is embarrassingly theatrical, trying to hide the fact that he never really believed it himself.

A Last Chance

After the race in Adelaide, Hill showed that he was a good loser: 'At least I made him do the running, even forced him to make a mistake. Of course, if I had seen him clip the wall I would never have dived into that gap. But it's over, accidents like that are part and parcel of racing. You won't hear me saying that it's Michael's fault. I won't hold it against him. Better next year.'

But 'better next year' proved an idle hope. Schumacher obliterated Hill in '95. Adelaide 1994 might have made him a celebrated Formula One driver – 'from zero to hero' as the British press blared – but in 1995 there was precious little to show for it.

As Schumacher went from triumph to impressive triumph, Hill's response became increasingly frantic. Turning point: Silverstone. During a desperate, impossible attempt to pass, Hill pushed both Schumacher and himself off the track. In one swoop the unrewarded hero changed into a frustrated villain.

Naturally the first person to vent his anger was Michael Schumacher himself: 'What Damon did was completely unnecessary. I don't understand that kind of thing at all. Even driving for a home crowd, you still have to keep your nerves under control, otherwise you're a road hazard.' Schumacher even dared to draw comparisons to Adelaide: 'It was the same situation as in Adelaide, trying to overtake on the inside when there wasn't room. Unbelievable.'

Things went wrong in Hockenheim as well. In the lead, Hill skidded off the track after just one lap. Schumacher had no trouble providing an explanation: 'Hill made a big mistake. He should have known that there was all kinds of crap on the track there. I knew it would be slippery, everyone loses some oil during the first lap, so I braked early. When I saw him skidding I couldn't believe my eyes, he hit the wall and I thought, good, that's taken care of.' Thank you, Michael, you can sit down now.

But it was true, Hill simply wasn't a match for Schumacher. At Monza he again knocked his rival and himself off the track. 'The big problem with Damon is that he doesn't have control over things while overtaking. He makes these half-hearted attempts that get him into trouble and then he can't go back.'

And while Schumacher finished off the job on the Nürburgring, Hill went wrong again. In the starting phase he overtook Schumacher, but one corner later he spun sideways and had to let his rival past. Later he was too optimistic taking on Alesi, was forced over the grass, lost the nose of his car, mounted a desperate pursuit, and ended up in the gravel in front of a stadium full of jubilant German fans.

It was an all-time low. According to Hill's wife Georgie: 'In late 1995 Damon was seriously considering quitting racing. He didn't feel like anyone was supporting him. I could hardly bear it. He had always been so enthusiastic, and now all the fun had gone out of it.'

Meanwhile Williams and Ecclestone had put their heads together. For 1996 they decided to bring Jacques Villeneuve to Formula One. Jacques was another son of. The son of Gilles, the legend. That alone made him a great attraction, but there was more. Jacques was a real winner: he had won the Indycar championship in just his second season, and he had also won the Indianapolis 500. Ecclestone was convinced that Villeneuve was the only one who could take on Schumacher. A conviction that grew when Schumacher announced that he would be driving for Ferrari in 1996.

Hill himself said that his main goal in 1996 was to regain his racing pleasure. The prospects were better than ever. Schumacher finding his feet with Ferrari, Villeneuve without Formula One experience. All the same, the pressure was on because 1996 – and Hill realised this as well – was not only his best, but also his last, shot at the title.

Hill favourite. It was tempting the gods. I was already keyed up with that horrible mixture of fear and doubt. And I wasn't the only one. Crystal-gazers everywhere had declared that Hill needed to score heavily at the start of the season, because there was a good chance of Schumacher and Villeneuve coming back strongly at the end.

But Hill did what he had to do. He won the first three races, Australia, Brazil and Argentina, although Villeneuve almost beat him to it in the first one.

And Hill kept on scoring. Only the most sentimental race, the Monaco Grand Prix, eluded him. After Schumacher smashed into the barrier in the first lap, Hill led the field for half the race. But coming out of the tunnel in the forty-second lap the engine started gushing, all the oil overboard. The glue on a screw in the oil pump had melted. Hill was doing 280 and just succeeded in parking the Williams in the escape road at the chicane. He climbed out and thumped the barrier in disappointment. It was the very spot where Graham had lost a wheel during his Monaco debut in 1958.

At Imola Hill won thanks to a cunning pit-stop strategy, in Canada he beat Villeneuve in a tense race, in France he reigned supreme. Hill dominated. Halfway through the season he had a comfortable lead of 21 points over Villeneuve and 27 over Schumacher, who had been more or less eliminated as a title candidate after a series of remarkable retirements. Still . . .

Silverstone had been the turning point before. Now too it signalled the beginning of a bizarre second half of the season. Starting at pole, Hill made a mess of the start, spent a long time behind Hakkinen and spun off the track at Copse Corner in the twenty-seventh lap. The whole world accused Hill of making mistakes under pressure, but in reality the bearings in the front left-hand wheel had cracked because of an incorrectly attached wheel nut. Another Williams wheel nut.

At Hockenheim, Hill started badly again. Both Berger and Alesi were too fast for him. He passed Alesi halfway through the race during the pit stops, but couldn't catch Berger. With the same engine in the back, Hill couldn't power past in the straights, and in the chicanes he couldn't get close enough without losing adhesion and control. Hill was visibly faster, but where to pass? Berger didn't flinch, he knew that with the championship in his sights, Hill would not be taking any unnecessary risks.

Then, in the forty-third lap, coming out of the Clark chicane, ominous sounds could be heard coming from one of the engines. The cars were so close that both drivers went through a moment of hope and fear until an enormous cloud of oil and smoke billowed up from the Benetton. Hill was already past. Three laps to go. No tyre blew, the engine didn't explode, the wheel nuts were on tight, and Hill won. At Hockenheim. Hadn't there been a saying in Dad's day that the winner of the German Grand Prix would also win the title?

But the damage had already been done. On the Thursday before the race, the authoritative British magazine *Autosport* reported that Williams planned to dump Hill. Worse still: Heinz-Harald Frentzen had reputedly been signed for 1997. Hill spent the whole weekend telling himself that sensationalist stories always popped up on the Thursday before a Grand Prix.

But the seeds of doubt had been sown in fertile ground. Just imagine that it was true. Besides, Frank Williams had a tradition to keep up. Hill would not be the first world champion Frank had shown the door, although Williams himself had admitted that his sponsors had emphatically advised him not to do it again. But Hill wasn't world champion yet. With just five races left, he still had a lead of twenty-one points, but imagine that it *was* true, and the team preferred to carry on with Villeneuve as champion . . .

An ominous pattern began to emerge in the following races. In both Hungary and Belgium there were communication problems involving Hill's pit stops. Villeneuve profited and the margin shrunk to thirteen points. Schumacher, winner at Spa, praised Villeneuve to high heaven, and Frank Williams made the gloomy prediction: 'If the Ferraris hold together next season, we won't see the back of Schumacher.'

Of course, everything could now be interpreted to Hill's detriment. But, as Hill relates in his book about that season, Frank Williams phoned him just a few days after the Belgian Grand Prix: 'Damon, we won't be asking you to drive for us next year. It is not about money. I can't tell you much more, but I have to think about the future of the company as we'll be losing our Renault engines at the end of 1997, and I must consider how I'm going to get replacements – and I am not going to change my mind.' Later, years later, it seems that Williams was using Frentzen in a play for BMW engines.

Hill asked Williams when he had made the decision.

'An hour ago.' That was doubtful. Rumour had it that Williams had signed Frentzen in late 1995 in the expectation that Hill would not win out over Villeneuve.

For Hill too, Williams's news cannot have come as a surprise. But it was still a hard blow. 'All the euphoria of being in the lead in the championship, the thrill of the race wins, suddenly seemed for nothing.'

The lead in the world championship: thirteen points. If Hill won at Monza, and Villeneuve failed to do better than fourth, then the contest would be decided.

Hill is convinced that 'at Monza the key to a fast lap is the way you take the chicanes'. But in 1996 the chicanes were not up to scratch. They had been adapted for motorbike races earlier in the year, and now the Formula One racing cars just tear up the kerbs, sending stones and clumps of grass flying. On the insistence of Hill, Villeneuve and Berger, stacks of tyres are bolted down in the chicanes like black sentinels to stop anyone from taking it into his head to drive over the grass or the kerbs.

Despite the commotion over his dismissal – 'No, I haven't been fired, I'm just not driving for Williams in 1997' – Hill takes pole. Beside him: Villeneuve.

And finally, Hill has another good start. He beats Villeneuve in the sprint to the chicane. But not Alesi. Alesi in front of Hill. Villeneuve has to go over the grass, behind the tyres, and is third. Alesi takes the first Lesmo too wide. Hill sees it and reacts immediately. He puts the Williams next to the Benetton and passes Alesi before the second Lesmo. In the first lap! But Alesi doesn't give up. Like a shadow, he follows Hill over the Serraglio, sticks to him under the old track, and pops up next to him again as he swings into the Ascari. 'I saw his front wheels next to me. I could hardly believe it and thought: Christ, Jean, please, for once, back off!' Despite the risk, Hill keeps it up and beats off the attack. He comes through the Parabolica in the lead and flies up the long straight – I knew it all along – in true champion style.

Behind him Villeneuve is in trouble. His brief excursion in the chicane has damaged his car, it is no longer willing to do exactly what its driver wants it to, and Villeneuve can see his championship hopes fading.

After a few laps Hill notices Villeneuve falling behind. With a comfortable lead on Alesi he decides to relax with victory in his sights and just drive home. And then he hits the tyres.

Coming out of the first chicane, Hill clips the pile of tyres, hard enough to immediately spin around backwards. The steering is damaged, the engine stalls. The car is a weird sight sitting there crossways on the track at the start of the Curva Grande. You can hardly believe your eyes. Is it any wonder that Williams wants to fire this dolt? Fifty metres further along, Hill is leaning over the barrier. 'I just wanted to die.'

But Hill is in luck. Villeneuve just misses out on the points. Schumacher wins, after his own scrape with the tyres. 'Never before had I been so happy with a Schumacher win,' Hill confesses.

And things get even worse. At Estoril, Hill lets another won race slip through his fingers. While he wastes oceans of time lapping the back markers, Villeneuve shows the manoeuvre of the year: he overtakes Schumacher on the outside in the sweeping final corner. Formula One is in a tumult. What's all this about overtaking being impossible? Villeneuve is the man. He wins the race in front of Hill. No one is surprised. What a stunt it would be if Villeneuve grabbed the title in his first year – perfect publicity for Williams, Renault and the rest.

Schumacher rubs some extra salt into the wounds. 'When Damon wins, some people, myself included, ask themselves, "How good is he really?" Moving to another team gives him a chance to show that he's better than some people think he is.' Vicious. Because which teams are left for Hill to choose from? With a certain malicious pleasure, Flavio Briatore comments: 'Benetton's full up, McLaren's full up, Ferrari's full up. Damon doesn't have much choice. It would be different if he was bringing the Number 1 with him, but that isn't looking too good either.'

Before Suzuka, Hill announces that he will be driving for Arrows in 1997. For years Tom Walkinshaw's team has been stuck at the back of the grid. 'Tom and I are going to turn Arrows into a winning team,' declares Hill over a glass of champagne. But you can tell from his gestures, the way he's standing and the look in his eye that it's a put-up job. Lauda's comment says enough: 'Just as he consistently ensures every year that he won't win the world championship, he is now going to a team with which he will never win again. Is there any hope left for him?'

World Champion

Then comes Suzuka, 13 October 1996. Again the world championship will be decided in the last race. Villeneuve is nine points behind. The winner gets ten points. Villeneuve needs to win and Hill mustn't get a single point; in other words, he can't finish sixth or higher. With an equal score, the number of wins decides: seven to four in Hill's favour. Villeneuve has a small, theoretical chance. Insiders would normally view the struggle as decided, but not this time . . .

Before all those other races I was able to sleep, no matter how exciting the struggle in Suzuka or Adelaide promised to be. But not this time. All kinds of doom scenarios flit through my mind. Long before it's time for the race to start – one p.m. in Japan, five a.m. here in Holland – I'm wandering through the house. On tiptoe, partner and child are sleeping the sleep of the righteous.

I spread the Damon Hill T-shirt I bought at the last Marlboro Masters out on the sofa. Childish insanity, I know, but this time there is so much at risk. Damon Hill's racing has taught me how important it is to maintain a unity in your life, and how important it is to remain true – not blindly, but respectfully – to the child you were, the child with all its expectations and longings. And nowhere has that child remained so well preserved within me as in Formula One. The race in Japan is not only decisive for the 1996 world championship, it is decisive for me as well.

Hill left for the Far East over a week ago to make sure he got over the jetlag in time: 'It was the strangest feeling leaving home on Thursday. When I returned I would either be world champion or the "other thing", the unthinkable alternative. One thing was sure, though, my children probably wouldn't give a hoot either way. I saw them off to school and left for my appointment with destiny.'

On the circuit you can feel the tension. 'From the moment I arrived at the track, I could see that this race would be different. I could see it in the looks on the faces of so many other people, their faces betraying their emotions. The last race of the season usually has an "end-of-term" feel to it, and, for that reason, everyone sports a big smile because they know there's just one more to go. But this time the smiles were few and far between. I could see another look on their faces. They were thinking, "How does he look? How's he coping?" '

The Williams team goes to great lengths to avoid any semblance of bias. They have even brought two spare cars, one for each driver. Hill's mechanics are wearing caps in the family colours, blue with eight white stripes.

As the two Williamses take up position in the front row during qualifying, Villeneuve first and then Hill, no one mentions Suzuka '89 or '90. No one. And not a word about Adelaide '94 either. It simply doesn't occur to anyone. It is not appropriate to a gentleman driver.

Hill can't get to sleep before the race either: 'It was my last night with all this championship thing going through my head, and I knew that when I woke up on Sunday morning it was going to be the conclusive day of the year. After all those nights of not being able to relax properly, it was great to know, when it came, that this was it – the final day.'

By the time the cars are on the grid the tension is unbearable. Interviewed by the BBC, Hill says that he is very conscious of all the tired, sleepy and nervous people glued to the television back home. 'But I know it is going to be worth it. I feel confident.'

We don't.

I can't sit still during the warm-up lap, but with the cars stopped on the grid, Coulthard stalls. Restart.

Briefly, very briefly, the tension is gone. Restart. The cars are motionless, one after another the red lights go on, then all off at once. It is irreversible and Hill, Hill takes off first! Villeneuve blows his start.

I mustn't scream, it's quarter past five in the morning, and a flawless Hill sweeps into the first corner. In front of Berger, Hakkinen and Schumacher. Thinking of Monza, of Estoril, and probably of so many other races, he decides: 'This time I'm staying here.' Later he explained: 'I tried to drive with as much exuberance as I could, but I could not rely on my instincts and detach myself from what was going on.'

Berger in pursuit. Since he has left with very little petrol in his tank, he is the only one who can keep up with Hill. But that's not enough. He needs to overtake Hill if his strategy is to succeed. Accordingly, he launches his attack at the end of the third lap. Taking the necessary risks, he goes into the 130R at top speed and tries to pass before the chicane. Senna–Prost 1989. But Berger is coming from too far back. He's mad. I curse him and all his wonderful Formula One stories into the third generation! But Hill doesn't give an inch. The front wing of the Benetton is five, maybe six, centimetres away from cutting Hill's right rear tyre to shreds. What a disaster that would be: just past the pit entrance, tyre blown, spin, gravel, and Villeneuve suddenly smelling blood. It's only after seeing the videos later that Hill realises how close it was, but not an angry word about Berger: 'I shut the door on him and the next time I looked he was a long way back. He took avoiding action, hit the kerb – not me – and that was it.' Berger, the fantastic old hand.

Meanwhile Villeneuve is sixth. If Berger drops back he'll be fifth. It is obviously not his race. But still . . . There is not a moment's relief. After the Esses, a steep climb to the Dunlop Curve, treacherous descent to the Degner Curve, ninety degrees and immediately under the bridge. Hill is a class apart today, but will he make it? Will the car hold up? Show us something else, director. Switch back if something happens, show us Hakkinen and Schumacher now, then the laps will pass so much easier, so much faster.

Pit stops. Wheel nuts. Hill flies back on to the track, keeping the lead, first corner, second, nothing falls off the car, but I don't trust

Williams. Villeneuve has already made his stop and is still fifth, fourth even, waiting his chance . . .

In the pit the Williams crew watches the TV screens anxiously, Georgie in the middle. Up front, a blank-faced Frank Williams stares at a monitor, no signs of tension, no emotion.

The next series of pit stops. Schumacher first, immediately followed by Hakkinen and then Villeneuve. They all get away well. So does Hill, who follows two laps later. Berger is back at fourth. And then the picture switches to a Williams jolting through the sand. Villeneuve, I see it at once. A rear wheel overtakes him, the fans understand straight away: a wheel nut. The car comes to a halt in front of a stack of tyres. The dust settles and Villeneuve jumps out.

I'm already on my feet dancing around the room. The title! World champion!

Somewhere in England a telephone rings, daughter calling mother: 'Mum, can you believe it? He's done it!' Bette Hill is in tears.

On the screen the cameras are back on Hill. What is he thinking inside that helmet, that deep blue helmet with white stripes? Hill hears the news over his radio: 'Jacques is out, Damon! Jacques is out.'

> That was it. Championship decided. I had done it! I was world champion! All I could think was that I must have had an angel looking over me that day. It all went my way: absolutely everything was too good to be true, and to cap it all I could clinch the race victory as well. For two laps I drove like a zombie, watching the road fly beneath me, unable to work out if it was real. I realised I could just stop the car if I wanted to, climb out and walk away and the result would be the same. The car could break down, and it wouldn't matter one bit. At one point I thought I could crash, end up in hospital with a leg in plaster and still be the champion, which would have been somewhat

> unusual! Then my mind switched to all my friends and supporters. What must they be doing now?

Dancing, of course, screaming, fists clenched and yelping for joy. World champion.

My child, my son, wakes up. Through a chink in the curtains, I see that it is already light outside. It's six thirty. My little boy. Almost three. Through a fanlight he sees the flickering of the television, he hears idiotic stamping and smothered cheers from the living room. 'Daddy!'

I quickly get him out of bed. Within minutes he's sitting on my lap in his sleepers, staring with big eyes at the nonsense flashing past on the screen.

'Suddenly driving my car became a task so simple I was able to reel off the remaining laps and think about what I was going to say in the press conference directly after the race. It was as if the car was driving itself.' Sixteen enraptured laps to drive.

By the time Hill starts on his last lap – no, nothing can go wrong now, he has the title and he's going to win this race as well – my partner has arrived in the living room. Even BBC commentator Murray Walker is choked with emotion: 'History is being made. For the first time we are seeing the son of a father who was world champion becoming world champion himself. Damon Hill, here he comes over the line.'

The entire Williams team is up on the pit wall. Georgie is holding a big sign saying 'Damon Hill World Champion 1996'. A clenched fist raised from the cockpit.

> The whole pit wall was like the Hanging Gardens of Babylon. I slowed down and tried to pass right under the sign so I could see all the faces of the Williams crew. After passing the pits I knew I had only the slowing-down lap to be alone, to allow all the tension of the race, the weekend, the months – even the years – to escape. It is one of the unusual features of our sport that

> because our faces are hidden away in crash helmets and, by necessity, we have to complete a slowing-down lap, our most triumphant and ecstatic moments are almost totally private. But I don't mind sharing the experience in these pages, and admitting that I cried with joy and relief all the way back to the pit lane.

Relief.

When Hill drives into the *parc fermé*, his whole crew is crowded up against the railings. Hill sits there for a count of ten. It's over. There are tears in my eyes. He climbs out of the car. Schumacher and Hakkinen are the first to congratulate him. Hill forces a path between all the gesticulating officials and organisers, reaches Georgie and hugs her, still wearing his helmet. Deep blue with eight white stripes. I'm crying in front of the TV.

Hill, my hero, the slogger no one believed in, who didn't really believe in himself, who drove his races with so much more significance, memories, meaning, the totality of a whole life – who drove the way I watch the races – has finally, finally become world champion. In style, that too is important. My tears are tears of relief. Relief that he was able to do it after all.

In a daze I sit through the ceremony and even the press conference. I don't hear Hill's elaborate praise and thanks for the team that's dumping him, neither do I hear Schumacher's snide aside about how long Damon has had to wait for his title.

When it's all over, I get on my bicycle. My son in front of me in his child seat. It's still early, a sunny, golden morning in October. We ride through the woods. Now and then, I can't restrain myself and raise a clenched fist. I'm happy. For the first time in all the years that I've been following Formula One, I feel a bit like a world champion myself.

Jacques Villeneuve: Mr Cool

Magny-Cours 1996. Qualifying. Jacques Villeneuve is chasing Damon Hill's lap time. He has to. He either stays in front of Hill or gives up all hope of the world title. It's Villeneuve's first year in Formula One, but he already has his sights on the championship. Nothing less will do: 'I know I can be quick, so that means I can fight with the quickest. That's my personality. You're in there because you are a competitive person in anything you do. You want to win and you want to beat everybody.'

Villeneuve gets ready for a fast lap. Cutting aggressively over the kerbs in the chicane, then into that horrible, right-angled Lycée corner, where you exit a hair's breadth away from scraping the pit wall. It happened to Jos Verstappen in '94, taking out McLaren's monitors in the process. Then over start-finish, the clock starts ticking. The director cuts to the on-board camera: we're driving the fast lap with Villeneuve. Through the Grand Courbe, left, full-speed in fifth. Then down to fourth for a long sweeping right-hander, uphill, the Estoril corner. It's fast, the lateral G-forces are enormous, drivers need strong neck muscles. Cars are drawn inexorably to the outside of the curve. Villeneuve's too, he slides left, left, he keeps his foot down, left, and suddenly he's gone too far.

On board, the unsuspecting TV viewer gets the fright of his life. The Williams slides over the kerbs, on to the grass. Villeneuve tries to correct, but doesn't lift off at all! The car bounces, ploughs through the soil and finally slams sideways into the tyre barrier. For a moment the screen goes white, then comes snow, then a blue confusion of tumbling tyres. The car, you see that at once, has turned half circle and is now rolling backwards on to the track. Where it stops. Later it turns out that David Coulthard only just managed to avoid the Williams as it rolled backwards on to the circuit.

For a second Villeneuve sits stunned in the car, the left side has been mangled, yellow flags, then he jumps out of the wreck and runs to safety. Formula One has escaped a disaster.

In the pits everyone is looking a little pale. Villeneuve too. It's his first big shunt in Formula One. Hill, his team-mate, describes Villeneuve's first reaction: 'Obviously, Jacques didn't mean to do it, but he seemed quite impressed by his shunt. He had a kind of bravado, a bit of a gung-ho attitude which was a little bit unconvincing. He pulled about 10-G and said, "That's not much, is it?" It's understandable to try and brush it off, but he was a lucky guy.'

Villeneuve's version of the crash is cool:

> Coming out of one of the fastest corners on the circuit at about 220 km/h, the car went a little bit wide, but not wanting to lose the lap, I chose not to lift off. The car went over a kerb for a moment and the wheels were off the ground. When they touched down, it was on wet grass, which made braking useless and steering difficult. Any hope of regaining control was lost when a dip in the ground launched the car into the air just before it ploughed into a tyre barrier. The angle of the car at the point of impact was not particularly severe, but, instead of sliding along the barrier, the tyres grabbed the car with great force, stopping it dead, then bouncing it back on to the track. The car was wrecked and my helmet hit either the steering wheel or the windscreen and there were also paint marks on it from hitting the tyres.
>
> Still, it could have been worse. Throughout the accident I

> kept my hands on the steering wheel which, I'm convinced, helped absorb some of the impact. Normally it is thought that drivers should take their hands off the wheel in these situations, but keeping my hands on the steering wheel has helped me in a couple of heavy crashes in Indycar racing. All that force has to go somewhere and if you don't deflect it by gripping the wheel, a lot of it will be transferred into your shoulder straps, which could break a collarbone or even your neck.

Fourteen years earlier, on Belgium's Zolder circuit, Gilles Villeneuve broke his neck because he didn't want to surrender his fast lap.

'No,' Jacques sighed, bored and irritated about being asked the same question for the thousandth time: 'I'm not racing because my father left too early and I have to carry the name and the tradition. I don't really care about tradition. I'm racing because I have fun and I enjoy it.'

The Son of a Legend

'I'm sorry to disappoint you, but I never think about my father when I race. I have always been different, always my own person. I know what people would like to hear, but I don't say it. People have told my mother: "What is wrong with your son, have you heard what he is saying about his father?" Well, I am super-proud to be his son, but I am racing for myself.'

His father. Like Damon Hill, Jacques Villeneuve is 'the son of'. But unlike Hill, the son of a double world-champion gentleman driver whom everyone recalled with a fond smile, Jacques is the son of a legend, a daredevil speed maniac, a Ferrari hero whose memory still brings tears to the eyes of the true fans. It's not the same thing.

'No matter what I do in Formula One,' Jacques is reported as saying, 'it will never surpass what my father meant to fans around the world.' No wonder he is always trying to escape that shadow, that ghost, and of course, it always comes back.

Until the age of eleven, Jacques toured the European circuits in a mobile home with his family. And yet he remembers little of all those races: 'I was playing with my small cars when he was on the track, so I didn't care!'

Of course, Jacques forgets to mention that he was totally absorbed by his games and that the cars he was playing with were all racing cars his father had given to him!

No, of course he didn't care . . . When people asked him what he wanted to be when he grew up, he invariably answered: 'A racing driver – just like my dad.'

'Most of what I know,' Jacques explains after he has become a driver, 'comes from the few videos I've seen. Like Dijon with Arnoux and stuff like that. It looked pretty good.'

Has he also seen a video of Saturday afternoon, 8 May 1982? Flying to the funeral, eleven-year-old Jacques wrote poems about his father and drew pictures of him in his Ferrari Number 27.

At fifteen . . . Schumacher was fifteen when he sent his first autographs off into the world, Hill was fifteen when his father fell out of the sky, at fifteen Jacques Villeneuve was tucked away safely in a Swiss boarding school. Switzerland, the only sensible country in Europe, where all forms of motor racing have been banned since the horrors of Le Mans 1955 (a Mercedes flies into the crowd: 81 dead, 100 injured). Skiing was still allowed; Jacques enjoyed that. Just like his father before him. Otherwise, Jacques was totally obsessed by computer games. 'He'll be world champion in computer games one day,' laughed his mother Joann.

But car racing was still there, waiting. At fifteen, Jacques climbed into a race car for the first time. On holiday in Canada he attended a three-day racing course at the Jim Russell racing school on the Mont Tremblant circuit. Just like his father.

'I always thought I would do it one day,' Jacques explains later. 'Even when he was racing. Since I can remember, I wanted to do it myself . . .' His mother wasn't really pleased, although Jacques wasn't sure why not. 'I don't think she was scared that I'd get injured or anything. After all, for her it was a normal world. I think it's more that she was afraid I wouldn't succeed and the pressure would be too much.

'That I'd get injured or anything . . .' Mr Cool has a way with understatement.

And the pressure to succeed was there from the first. The racing school had promised to keep things secret, but a few days later a picture of Jacques in a racing car was plastered over the front pages of all the Canadian dailies.

The legend. Jacques used it well. He went to Italy where the name Villeneuve immediately opened doors and chequebooks. And in 1988, without any preparation at all, Villeneuve started in Formula Three with PreMa. He didn't even know how to use the gears! And on the track he was far too cautious. He was worried that the other drivers would think he was arrogant because of his name and whenever he saw another car coming up behind him, he'd pull over to let it past.

The fear of getting in the way of faster drivers; there is no doubt that a video of Zolder 1982 was somewhere in the back of Villeneuve's mind. Tellingly, the only time he dropped his extreme politeness and made a big fuss was when he himself was hampered during practice by an opponent who was cruising around the circuit.

His fellow drivers did not rate him highly and the pressure grew. He wasn't winning and his father's fame began to work against him. After three mediocre seasons, Villeneuve left for Japan.

Japanese Formula Three brought peace of mind, better guidance and his first victories. In the relative solitude of Japanese racing, where Gilles wasn't even a legend, let alone a god, Jacques matured.

After Japan he began to ascend the heights. In 1993, aided by his father's former sponsor, Villeneuve changed over to Formula Atlantic, where his father had excelled in the mid-seventies. A year later, Jacques was already driving Indycars. In 1994 he was

Rookie of the Year, and in 1995 he won the championship, with a victory in the Indianapolis 500 as icing on the cake.

While he was going from success to success in America, some guy called Ecclestone called from Europe, asking whether Villeneuve would like to try a Formula One car, a Williams. Straight into the best car in the paddock. But Ecclestone was determined to have Villeneuve. With Senna dead, Schumacher was threatening to gobble up all of Formula One. Ecclestone needed someone who could stand up to him. Villeneuve was the man.

At Silverstone on 15 August, Jacques Villeneuve drove his first laps in a Formula One car. Just like his father. And he was impressive. Just like his father. But in front of the massed press, Villeneuve parried all comparisons and sentimentality:

> My ambition has always been to be a professional race-car driver and to win races and, if possible, championships; not to be in Formula One at any cost. But if I go to Formula One, it won't be because my father was there and I want to do everything he did. I'm really proud to be his son, and he will always be a legend. He will always be up there whatever I accomplish. But the reason I'm racing is not because he died and, for example, he didn't win a championship so I have to do it instead of him. No, that has nothing to do with it. The reason I'm racing is because I want to.

Ecclestone winked at Frank Williams again, and Villeneuve made his Formula One debut in the 1996 Australian Grand Prix.

And what a debut: pole, fastest lap and within an inch of victory. Suddenly the whole world knew who Jacques Villeneuve was.

After years of being the season's traditional finale, the race in Australia was switched to become the opener in 1996. It had also been moved from Adelaide to Melbourne. Taking pole in his first race was an absolute sensation. The only drivers to have done it before were Carlos Reutemann, Argentina 1972; Mario Andretti at Watkins Glen 1968; and Guiseppe Farina at Reims in 1950, in the very first world-championship Grand Prix. But the comparisons did not stop there. John Watson compared Villeneuve to Senna: 'The way he drives and his tremendous confidence . . .' A beaming Ecclestone went a step further: 'He will do whatever he has to do to get the result. He is like Senna as a person and Prost as a driver.'

In the race too, Villeneuve is sensational. Not once, but twice – a restart is necessary after Martin Brundle plunges into the gravel on Turn 3 – Villeneuve beats Damon Hill at the start. Hill sticks closely to his new team-mate, biding his time, menacing, but Villeneuve stays in front, cool.

Thanks to a faster pit stop, Hill takes the lead, briefly, but in the first chicane Villeneuve outbrakes him brilliantly, knowing that, on cold tyres, Hill has no reply.

In the thirty-fifth lap, Villeneuve makes a minor mistake. He over-brakes in front of the chicane, skids over the grass and the kerbs and, luckily for him, bounces back on to the track just in front of Hill. Hill hesitates, left, right, there's not much room. But this very hesitation gives Villeneuve the time he needs to get his car back under control and coolly block Hill. Everyone is amazed: yes, this Villeneuve has racing in his blood, he's his father's son . . .

But the excursion in the chicane still costs Villeneuve the race. An oil pipe has been damaged and his gearbox starts losing oil. It's clearly visible – in the laps that follow the spray of oil gradually paints Hill's car a golden yellow.

In the pits they're worried, the telemetry shows that the gearbox can't last much longer. They signal Villeneuve to slow down and, with four laps to go, he lets Hill overtake. Villeneuve finishes second.

Villeneuve has made an impression. He's got more than just racing in his blood. Because Gilles would have kept on pushing. Slow down? Not in his vocabulary. He would have done everything possible to keep Hill behind him, even if it meant flying off the track with a seized-up gearbox. But Jacques is cool. Six points are important for the championship.

In the course of the season it becomes even clearer. Jacques has a different view of all those circuits where his father lived like a Gypsy: 'I am here to work, so I work. If I have nothing to do, I go. The race track is more or less my office. If everything is clear and finished, I go. Somebody doesn't stay in the office when his work is finished.'

And Villeneuve scores lots of seconds; thirds if he can't do better. In his fourth Grand Prix, on the Nürburgring, he comes in first after resisting pressure from Schumacher lap after lap. That too is cool.

At Spa-Francorchamps, Villeneuve is delighted by the Eau Rouge, at last a challenge that stands up to comparison with the American ovals. He already knows the long circuit like the back of his hand, he says, after endless practice on the computer. 'Simulations like that look very realistic, they immediately give you a good idea of the lay of the circuit.' All cool.

In the second half of the season Hill begins to falter in sight of the title, and Jacques's carefully gleaned points become invaluable. Not only that: thanks to a few victories, Villeneuve maintains a chance at the title until the last race.

At Estoril he has everyone up on the benches again. In the Senna corner, a long fast sweeper before start-finish, he overtakes Schumacher on the outside, as if they were on an oval. Villeneuve: 'I told the team beforehand that it was possible, but they didn't believe me. "Go ahead," they said, "after the race we'll scrape you off the barrier." But it was possible.'

Even Schumacher is impressed: 'No, I hadn't counted on it at all. It really was on the edge. The wheels hooked into each other, if I'd lifted off even a fraction, he would have flown off . . .'

In Japan, during the last race of the season, Hill turns the tide just in time. Villeneuve isn't in the running and finally falls victim to an old Williams tradition, a defective wheel nut. Villeneuve remains calm and realistic: 'I'm very happy because when I came across here, everyone was telling me that you can't overtake and that Formula One is boring. That's not true. I've had fun this year. It's not only in the last race that you have to look at the championship, Damon did a better season than we did. But I have learnt a lot, driven aggressively, and it should be better next year.'

It all sounds so reasonable, so controlled; even John Watson is sceptical. According to Watson, Villeneuve is sitting on a time bomb and knows it: 'Maybe he's scared of carrying his father inside him. He might be capping it because he has had an education and an upbringing which has given him a better intellect to cope with the situation.'

The Rebel

In 1997, after Hill's departure for Arrows, Villeneuve has the best cards, but still has to deal with Schumacher, who's had his year to get established at Ferrari and no longer has any excuses. He too will be going for the title.

Favourite for the world championship in your second year. And no one is surprised. Cool. But Villeneuve still isn't satisfied. When the FIA announces a number of drastic safety measures, among them compulsory grooved tyres to reduce grip and speed, Villeneuve is incensed: 'When you look at all the changes that are being made to the rules and the tyres, it's becoming scary to see how low Formula One can go just to make it more spectacular. But it's a false, manipulated way of making it more spectacular. It would become more a circus than a sport. Formula One doesn't feel fast enough already, so I don't see the point of making it slower.' And this is only a warning shot.

The season doesn't start as well as the year before. The Williamses of Villeneuve and Frentzen are far superior during practice in Australia, but in the race itself, Villeneuve crashes with Irvine and Herbert in the very first corner. Coulthard dominates from beginning to end; McLaren is looking like a contender.

But in Argentina and Brazil, Villeneuve sets things to right; he dominates and wins. In Brazil he even takes on Schumacher and defeats him in a direct battle. With Imola on its way, Villeneuve gives another interview. His words cause an uproar: 'What I said about safety has been interpreted as if I was saying that people have to die and we want crashes. That's not what I was saying, but you do need that small element of danger that tells you where the edge is, so you have to push yourself to reach it. If you take that edge away, it's easy for anyone to be quick because if you spin off, you go in a sand trap and that's it.'

Villeneuve has no doubts about why so many people are pleading for safety in Formula One:

> Ayrton Senna died and it got many people on their backs, because it's not right any more to hurt yourself on TV. But I'm not afraid of death. It's natural. You're born and then you die. Death is part of the wheel of life, although there is no point in making it come quicker on purpose. Racing is dangerous. There's that risk and this edge of pushing yourself, and always pushing it more. That doesn't mean you want to do it just because it is dangerous. It's a danger you are in control of and that's OK. You know you're doing something special and if you make a mistake you'll crash, but you've got it under control, that's the rush.

The words of Jacques Villeneuve, Mr Cool. His father made a mistake like that once, he had one of those crashes. It's true, but don't go thinking it's left too much of an impression on his son.

Villeneuve was heavily criticised for these statements. It really was time he grew up. Damon Hill even interpreted his words as a veiled death wish. Villeneuve retorted that too many drivers only thought about money instead of the sport. He also refused to join the GPDA because no one listened to drivers anyway.

The FIA called Villeneuve to account, but the result was a farce: of course, Villeneuve could say whatever he liked, he should just watch his language. It seemed a German magazine had quoted him expletives and all.

Meanwhile Imola was lost. As was Monaco. The high-tech Williams team forgot to look at the clouds before the race and sent their drivers out on the wrong tyres. Schumacher, with the right rubber, left both Williamses behind and was never seen again.

In Canada, in front of a home audience, the pressure was too much. At the end of the first lap, Villeneuve missed the chicane and rammed the wall. A beginner's mistake, he admitted that himself. Schumacher won again – after the race was halted following a severe crash by Olivier Panis. Panis was badly injured, both legs broken. A frustrated Villeneuve chided his colleagues for the subdued way they stood there on the podium: 'Two broken legs is nothing very bad. That happens to everybody in their lifetime. Just relax a bit.'

It didn't make him any more popular. To make matters worse, his sponsor was becoming annoyed by the eccentric, variable colour of his hair. And the FIA had begun lecturing Villeneuve for ignoring yellow flags. Yellow flags go out when dangerous situations have arisen on the track; after shunts, for instance. They're a warning for drivers to slow down. This is difficult to judge, but if nothing else, lap times must not be improved and overtaking is banned. Villeneuve had driven too fast a number of times and the FIA was threatening to suspend him. The pressure was mounting.

And Schumacher was getting into the swing of things: he won in France and Belgium and soared past Villeneuve in the world-championship tally. Villeneuve limited the damage with lucky victories in England and Hungary.

On the super-fast circuits of Hockenheim and Monza the championship contenders are nowhere to be seen. In 1997 Hockenheim belongs to Berger.

Berger's retirement has been in the air for some time. 1997 is a turning point in his life. After a trial that has dragged on for years, his father is sentenced to more than five years' imprisonment for embezzlement. Berger is constantly at odds with his team boss

Briatore. His third daughter is born, to his second wife. A sinus infection puts him out for three races, and in hospital Berger thinks for the first time about what would happen to his four girls if his number came up in the next race. Alexander Wurz shows himself an outstanding replacement: in England he even ascends the podium. Berger seems all washed up, especially after his father crashes his private aircraft while out on bail in July. Just a fortnight before the race at Hockenheim.

Berger is there, but Briatore openly questions whether he'll make anything of it after such a long break. During qualifying, Berger climbed into his car

> and drove a lap that was so smooth and forceful and perfect that it just had to be right. When I got the message 'pole position' during my slowing-down lap, tears came to my eyes for the first time in eighteen years of racing. I could only think of my father. All kinds of things ran through my mind: I saw the wrecked plane before me and thought about a few scraps from the priest's sermon at the funeral. It was, after all, the first time in my life that I had really listened to a priest. This pole position was actually more than enough for all the things I wanted to show and clarify, but before going to sleep, I thought that now I've come this far, I might as well go on and win the whole race.

And Berger won. Easily. In Austria he announced his retirement. According to many, Formula One lost its last human character with Berger's departure.

At Monza, Coulthard again showed that McLaren was on its way, beating Alesi and Frentzen in an unforgiving race. Villeneuve and Schumacher only came in fifth and sixth, respectively. Even worse for Villeneuve, he had raced past a yellow flag during the warm-up. He was given a suspended suspension.

With four races to go, Schumacher was ten points ahead in the championship: 67 to 57. Williams were worried, but Patrick Head insisted that nothing had been decided: 'All I can say is that Jacques has got to raise his game a bit – which he's capable of doing.'

In Austria, Villeneuve was handed another victory. Hakkinen, by far the quickest all weekend, dropped out in the first lap. And this time it was Schumacher who was involved in a yellow-flag incident. Schumacher overtook Frentzen while the yellow flags were out and was called in for a ten-second stop-go penalty. No arguing this time. Schumacher came in and fought back bravely in the final phases to finish sixth. Schumacher 68; Villeneuve 67.

On the Nürburgring, Villeneuve had even more luck. There was a chaotic shunt on the first corner, caused by Ralf Schumacher, yes, 'the brother of'. Ralf neglected to leave enough room for his team-mate Fisichella and the two Jordans collided. Ralf turned sideways, hit another car and took off, the rear of his Jordan skimming just over the head of brother Michael. Family drama. The Ferrari ploughed through the gravel, made it back on to the circuit, but turned out to be irreparably damaged.

Villeneuve settled in behind the superior McLarens of Hakkinen and Coulthard. Driving for the points – it wouldn't have occurred to Gilles. But towards the end of the race, both McLarens gave up the ghost: engine failure. Villeneuve benefited: Villeneuve 77; Schumacher 68. The world championship could be decided at Suzuka.

In Japan Villeneuve took pole. He was his old self again, keyed up, all the interviews and incidents seemed forgotten. But by Saturday evening, an ominous whisper was doing the rounds: Villeneuve had ignored yet another yellow flag. On Saturday morning Jos Verstappen had been stranded on the straight before the 130R. Yellow flags. But the situation seemed clear and safe and no less than six drivers in a row failed to lift off: Herbert, Barrichello, Frentzen, Katayama, Michael Schumacher and Villeneuve. All six were given a suspended suspension . . . until the stewards realised that Villeneuve already had one. Late that night, the decision came. Villeneuve was suspended for one race, tomorrow's. Williams appealed against the decision, and Villeneuve started the race under threat of disqualification.

The race became a tactical battle, with Ferrari coming out on top. A demotivated Villeneuve was really only driving to make things difficult for the Ferraris, but in the end it was Irvine who blocked Villeneuve and cleared the way for a Schumacher victory. Villeneuve ended fifth: Villeneuve 79; Schumacher 78. A week later Villeneuve was disqualified after all and the positions were reversed: Schumacher 78; Villeneuve 77.

A Clean and Fair Fight

The disqualification made a world of difference. Speculation was rife, Jerez was abuzz with Adelaide '94. There, with a one-point lead, Schumacher had rammed Damon Hill off the track – finally everyone dared to say it out loud. FIA boss Max Mosley warned: 'This time we want the fight to be clean and fair.' Villeneuve and Schumacher nodded politely, but Mosley insisted that he was also referring to team-mates, relatives, friends and enemies.

But the fun and games start first thing Saturday morning. More than once, Irvine cuts off Villeneuve. A furious Villeneuve marches up to the Ferrari pits, bends over Irvine and attributes him with a few undesirable qualities. One last hint of the ghost of '82?

On Saturday afternoon the knives are sharpened even more. After fourteen minutes, Villeneuve clocks up a fast lap: 1 minute 21.072 seconds. Fifteen minutes later, Schumacher is out on the track and squeezes his Ferrari dry. When he crosses the line, astonishment and disbelief is on everyone's face: 1 minute 21.072 seconds. Unprecedented! When Frentzen clocks up the same time just before the end of the session, everyone has to laugh – it's madness, frightening, and what do the rules say anyway, who has pole? Villeneuve. He clocked it up first. Beside him, Schumacher.

On Sunday the tension is almost unbearable. Not just in Jerez. In Italy the whole country is sending up prayers for those red cars. All over Germany, market squares are dotted with red caps, flags and stalls selling beer. Fans across the globe are on the edge of their seats. Experts tip Schumacher; experts tip Villeneuve; no one knows. Either way, this race is sure to be a thriller.

Schumacher. Schumacher has the best start. He's starting on brand-new tyres, after all. Villeneuve wasn't as cautious during practice and has to start the race on a used set. That's why he's careful now, so careful that even Frentzen slips past on the inside on the first corner. A few laps later, Frentzen lets his team-mate by again, but by then Schumacher is already more than five seconds in front. There doesn't seem to be much Villeneuve can do. 'It was a very tough race,' Villeneuve explains later, talking about the first phase, 'each lap was like a qualifying lap. Michael went flat out, all I could do was follow.'

The first pit stops. Schumacher first, on lap twenty-two. Villeneuve pitting one lap later. Frentzen takes over the lead, suddenly cutting two seconds off his lap times to slow things down and let Villeneuve get closer. When Frentzen stops for tyres and fuel, Schumacher retakes the lead, Villeneuve in his wake. Villeneuve is even considering an attack, then Fontana blocks him. Breathless, the world watches. Schumacher leads the dance, and yet the question is still there: will he make it? Jackie Stewart is willing to bet his house on it: Schumacher won't make it. Ralf . . . But Ralf is a good boy and lets the combatants past. The second series of pit stops approaches. Schumacher, first again, in the forty-second lap. Villeneuve two laps later. Perfect pit stops, all the Williams wheel nuts are on tight, Villeneuve is catching up. Villeneuve is hauling him in. In lap forty-six he's one and a half seconds faster, it's going to happen. A lap later and the difference is down to three-tenths of a second, the new tyres on the Williams are significantly better. One behind the other, the cars roar around the circuit. Curva Expo, Michelin, Sito Pons . . . Villeneuve is waiting his moment. 'I knew it was time to try, my tyres were still good. Of course, we could both go off, but hanging behind him was not an option. I never would have forgiven myself.'

Villeneuve creeps closer down the long straight. It's the forty-eighth lap; you can tell, it's now or never. In front of the Curva Dry Sack, a sharp right-hander, almost one-eighty degrees, Schumacher briefly leaves a gap on the inside and in a flash Villeneuve shoots alongside. 'Trying the move was a big risk. I knew Michael was capable of just deciding to take me off, but there was no point in just being second. I couldn't go more to the inside. I was actually on the grass.'

Schumacher is clearly surprised by Villeneuve's manoeuvre. When he goes to turn in, he realises that it's already too late. Villeneuve is next to him; you see Schumacher deciding to turn in hard, he rams the Williams. 'Either Michael had his eyes closed, or somehow his hands slipped on the wheel or something. I don't need to explain what happened, he turned in on me. But he didn't do it well enough because he went off and I didn't.'

'Adelaide revisited,' Frank Williams would say later, but in contrast to 1994, this time it was Schumacher who got the worst of it. The cars hit, the front right wheel of the Ferrari banging into the sidepod of the Williams. But Villeneuve held on to the corner and Schumacher slid out. The uncontrollable Ferrari plunged into the gravel trap, wheels spinning helplessly. Race over.

For a moment Schumacher stays sitting there. He gestures to the marshals that they should push him. That's forbidden and they know it. Schumacher is not being impressive. Then he gets out of the car, climbs on to a wall and stares down the long straight to see if Villeneuve is approaching. After about one and a half minutes Villeneuve comes past, something is hanging off the car, but he's still driving. In the lead. The championship has been decided.

Carefully Villeneuve drives out the last twenty-one laps. With the finish in sight, he even lets Hakkinen and Coulthard past; Hakkinen finally winning his first Grand Prix. 'Today the good guys are winning,' sniggers Ron Dennis. Villeneuve ends third and seizes the title in his second year of Formula One. Final scores: Villeneuve 83; Schumacher 78.

Three hours after the race Schumacher is finally available for comment. If his manoeuvre on the track was scandalous, his defence is truly grotesque: 'After my second pit stop I was a little slower than Jacques, but I felt that I could keep him behind me. His attack was rather optimistic. But fine, he had nothing to lose, in his place I would have done the same. I held off braking as long as possible, but he braked even later. I don't believe that I did anything wrong. If I hadn't been driving there, he never would have made that corner. I think he was counting on that and it turned out well for him. He is the champion. I have to live with that.'

Villeneuve, wearing a yellow wig and dancing in the pit lane, can only laugh scornfully: 'Who was talking about a clean, fair fight? The first chance he gets, he crashes into me. I would never have done that.'

The officials in Spain write it off as an incident, without consequences. But the international sporting press is in turmoil: journalists everywhere wipe the floor with Schumacher, even in Italy and Germany. In Maranello on the Tuesday after the race, Schumacher climbs down. The kid, always the kid, says he's sorry: 'I underestimated the situation. I didn't expect Jacques's attack. I wasn't trying to eliminate him, just instinctively defending my position. I didn't do it well, I admit it. I'm a man, not a machine. None the less, I consider the reactions I have heard rather exaggerated, worse things have happened.'

Finally the FIA gives Schumacher a dressing-down. Rumour has it that Schumacher will be suspended for all of 1998, but instead the FIA crosses him off the ratings list for the 1997 world championship, while still allowing him to keep his victories and points for the statistics. A mild punishment because 'all indications are that his action was instinctive and neither malicious nor premeditated'. Final score: Villeneuve 83.

'A hard break,' sighs Schumacher, 'that second place in the final ratings meant a lot to us.' The penalty is a joke, of course, but how else can you treat your main attraction?

Schumacher's reputation has been permanently damaged. Adelaide '94 was dubious enough; Jerez leaves no room for doubt, everyone saw Schumacher turn in. 'Schumacher shouldn't think he can keep on winning championships like that,' was Benetton team boss Briatore's snide but revealing comment. Damon Hill too seized the opportunity: 'Michael showed his true colours and got what he deserved. What he has done has underlined in people's minds just what his antics and tactics are. At least he is consistent.'

Hill. How were things with Hill in 1997? He did it again. The first half of the season was dramatically bad. At the opening race in Melbourne he only just managed to qualify and was out before the warm-up lap was even over. For a long time, he was looking like the worst ever defending champion in the history of Formula One. Even Pedro Diniz managed to occasionally qualify ahead of him. The first miserable point in England was celebrated as a victory. Two races later, on the Hungaroring, where the engine's lack of capacity counted less and the Bridgestone tyres were an advantage, Hill was suddenly there in third place on the grid. In the eleventh lap he passed Schumacher and took the lead. Hill dominated and left the others behind. The Arrows team's first victory was in the air, an outright sensation! But with just three laps to go, the hydraulics broke down. Accelerator and gearbox started to play up. Suddenly it was unclear whether Hill would even make the finish. His 33-second lead melted away and halfway through the last lap Villeneuve shot past. It was unbelievable, but not really: you'd actually been expecting it the whole race.

Intermezzo: The Point of Formula One

Nürburgring 1998. Turning into the Veedol S in the eleventh lap of the Luxembourg Grand Prix, Eddie Irvine slides straight ahead. Quick as a flash, Irvine corrects and jolts sideways left-right through the narrow chicane. 'Understeer,' Irvine complains later, 'murder on the tyres.'

Irvine is under pressure. Mika Hakkinen's menacing silver-and-black McLaren is behind him. Hakkinen is angry, desperate, inside the cockpit he shakes his fist. 'No, not at Irvine. I spotted some friends in the stand.'

Twelfth lap. In the Veedol chicane Irvine goes sideways again. Hakkinen searches – left, right – he's still too far away. Closing in is dangerous. Tucked in behind your adversary you lose a lot of downforce, the car becomes unsteerable and you glide straight ahead, through the corner. Modern Formula One's aerodynamic over-sensitivity makes overtaking especially problematic, risky, some say, impossible.

But Hakkinen has to get past Irvine. Because, in front of Irvine, Schumacher is getting further and further away, he already has a lead of six and a half seconds. Hakkinen and Schumacher are fighting for the world championship. That's why Hakkinen can't let him get away, but Irvine is Schumacher's team-mate . . .

Lap thirteen. Hakkinen watches and analyses. Irvine is having difficulties, especially in the chicane. Or is he playing a game, waiting for Hakkinen to attack so that he can punt him off the track, even if it means going off himself? Irvine is as hard as nails and with a carbon-fibre chassis, as Berger once claimed, a collision 'actually becomes an abstraction, a billiards situation'.

Through the Castrol S, the Dunlop hairpin, the RTL Kurve – this is the new Nürburgring, all the corners shamelessly bear the names of sponsors and TV stations – again the Veedol chicane. Irvine is more cautious this time, he takes it slower, now the Coca-Cola Kurve. Schumacher has got eight seconds already, Hakkinen needs to hurry.

Across the world, 350 million people spread over more than 200 countries are watching. And the insiders know: Hakkinen has to put up or shut up. No more whingeing. Overtaking might be problematic, risky, impossible even – a true champion still overtakes.

Fourteenth lap. In the ITT Bogen Irvine checks his mirrors again: Hakkinen is far behind. The Ferrari sails stylishly up to the Veedol chicane, brakes, and then suddenly Irvine sees the McLaren next to him. He's done it! Hakkinen is risking it! He's dived in on the left of the Ferrari and brakes centimetres later; with carbon-fibre brakes, that's light years. The McLaren slides into the bend, almost straight ahead, swaggers over the kerbs and is past. Leaving a baffled Irvine behind: 'I was driving on the ideal line and he still managed to wring his way through.'

Hakkinen takes off immediately. In search of Schumacher. He'll pass him too. But not on the track. Ultimately Hakkinen wins thanks to a better pit-stop strategy. Timekeeping mathematics, Formula One on a knife edge, but hard to take for outsiders.

That's why the director shows Hakkinen overtaking in the Veedol chicane over and over again. Super slo-mo. The cars gliding up to the chicane alongside each other, braking, turning in, the surroundings blurred. Irvine looks to the side, Hakkinen looks straight ahead, eyes wide open, grimly concentrated on the insanely twisting asphalt in front of his wheels. On the right he bangs over the kerbs, the whole car shudders, it's shaken up, the wings trill, flap, one by one the wheels lose contact with the ground, but the McLaren comes through it all and Hakkinen turns right in front of Irvine. Out of focus in the background, the Ferrari is lost. A ballet in silver and red.

The point of Formula One? Formula One is completely pointless, just like art. Formula One is art.

The Purpose

Nonetheless the first car races, famous epics traversing unsealed roads between major European cities, did serve a purpose: the propagation and perfection of a new invention – the automobile.

Initially it wasn't even about speed. Or rather, not about speed alone. In the first car race in history, Paris–Rouen 1894, the vehicle that covered the distance fastest was a De Dion steam car. It wasn't the winner. A jury declared steam power impracticable and divided the laurels between Peugeot and Panhard, both automobiles with internal combustion engines. They were much more practical and the future was theirs. Racing meant looking forward – the big manufacturers realised that – and creative interpretation of the rules was part of it from the very beginning.

Cars needed broad public acceptance. More than anything else, it was speed that appealed to people's imaginations, and that made speed the best publicity device. At the same time, testing and perfecting the cars remained important. Once racing had been banished to the motordromes because of the many accidents on public roads, cars began achieving tremendous speeds on the spectacular, banked tracks of Brooklands, Monza and Montlhéry, but the manufacturers soon stepped in. The high-speed tracks did not adequately simulate reality. For proper testing, more varied circuits were needed, and the variation would make racing more enjoyable for audiences as well. This led to the construction of circuits like Reims, Spa-Francorchamps and the old Nürburgring.

After World War II, with cars generally accepted and no longer needing promotion, racing developed into the highly specialised discipline it is today. In the 1950s and 1960s, Formula One was above all the domain of wealthy, single-minded amateur mechanics and racing teams with time-honoured traditions. But by the mid-sixties, the more experienced constructors began to realise that there were many more factors that could be exploited to get winning racing cars out on to the track. Colin Chapman made a deal with cigarette manufacturer Gold Leaf in 1968. In a sense, the tremendous boom in sponsoring that followed has brought motor racing back to where it all started: advertising.

Even if it's no longer advertising for cars as such. Today's hyper-specialised racing cars advertise cheese, lawnmowers, cigarettes of course, booze, computer systems, banks, condoms, energy drinks and various other daily needs.

The goal of perfecting the automobile fell by the wayside long ago. In fact, all kinds of driver aids that are increasingly common in ordinary cars are excluded from Formula One. Formula One mustn't get too comfortable; heroes should suffer. Inversely, important recent innovations in Formula One, such as the carbon-fibre chassis and carbon brakes, are unfeasible for mass production: too expensive.

Of course participating manufacturers occasionally learn something from Formula One, but generally slogans like 'we race, you win' are sheer nonsense: image making and pipe dreams.

Put simply, Formula One is an attractive, luxurious display case. Damn expensive but, considering the ratings, worthwhile.

But just when Ecclestone was planning to go public with his successful company, dark clouds blew over from Brussels. The European Union had decided to ban tobacco advertising. Large sporting events like Formula One are allowed to receive cigarette money until 2006, but by then they need to have made the change to alternative sources of finance. Or alternative continents, threatens Ecclestone.

Formula One defends itself like a major industrialist. In Britain

Ecclestone contributed a million pounds to Tony Blair's election fund. No strings attached and Ecclestone didn't need to spell it out. Blair knows very well that Formula One has become a vast amusement industry with thousands of employees in England alone.

Just as he might also realise that all those highly trained engineers, computer and media specialists could be doing much more significant work elsewhere. But what's significant?

Money, advertising, the car industry, employment, it's true, these are all significant aspects of Formula One. But the sport's true significance is much grander, much less tangible. Formula One is the embodiment of a dream, the dream of twentieth-century motorised man: speed, technology, control, new limits; vague romantic ideas and stories as by-products of an incorrigible belief in progress; but essential all the same. In Formula One, the West seems to cherish its own mirror image – hyper-capitalistic, rational and high-tech – but the underlying reasons for the embrace are a fiction, a dream.

Perhaps this dream is so important because it brings with it the absolute limit, the one thing that cannot be constrained by reason, finance or technology: death. Perhaps this is what Hemingway was getting at when he said: 'There are only three true sports. Mountain climbing, auto racing and bull fighting. All the rest are children's games played by adults.' Death is a draw.

Death

'The howl of the engines and the sponsors' glitter have won out over death. They have gagged humanity. Formula One has made a brutal spectacle of death' (*Osservatore Romano*, 3 May 1994).

The death of Ayrton Senna is a box-office success, it has brought a mythic aura back to Formula One.

Outsiders often claim that motor-racing fans all sit there waiting for a crash. This is complete nonsense. But it's not such a strange idea. The most-shown sporting moment of 1998 is undoubtedly the pile-up at Spa-Francorchamps. Thirteen cars written off right in front of the cameras.

Or take FOCA television itself: most of the replays during races are of crashes and shunts, all those comical scenes of Eddie Irvine and Jean Alesi bouncing over each other yet again. But I too disturb my family's well-earned peace on a Sunday afternoon most often when the debris is flying through the air.

And what about this book? Originally it was going to include a chapter entitled 'The Museum of Accidents', but gradually the book itself has developed into just such a museum. The reason is simple. Accidents are much more striking. More immediately than anything else, a crash shows what's at stake in Formula One, what's going on. A crash is also much easier to write about, it makes a better story than a magical qualifying lap or a stunning overtaking manoeuvre. Crashes are so much more provocative and disturbing, they have more repercussions.

But that doesn't mean that a true Formula One fanatic is just waiting for an accident to happen. When he stands there on some tree-and-shrub-covered hilltop, surrounded by thousands of other fans and watching the cars tear past on a narrow stretch of asphalt, awareness of the possibility of a crash is inherent, together with the fear that it might happen and a longing to avert it.

But when one of his heroes really does die, the Formula One fanatic is the first to turn away in tears, disgusted by the whole sport. Despondently, he'll admit that it's not a sport at all, it's a disease, an obsession . . . Sick at heart, millions of Formula One fans watched Ayrton Senna's funeral. But part of what's sickening them is their own character and the way they see the world.

And a fortnight later, most of them are simply back at their post. How could it be any other way? Formula One has become such an integral part of their lives, their nature, their sense of time, their biorhythm . . . What's more, the only solace available for this unrealistic grief for a lost hero is to climb back on to that same unrealistic merry-go-round, otherwise it would have all been in vain. In this sense, the madness of Formula One is exactly the same as the madness of life itself.

For motor-racing fans, death is simply beyond the limit. And yet it is at the heart of their fascination. Stirling Moss, a Formula One legend of the 1950s, once said: 'People come to see a man look death in the eye.'

Few contemporary drivers are willing to subscribe to this reality. They prefer not talking about the ultimate risk of their profession. When Jacques Villeneuve more or less repeated Stirling Moss's words by saying that it was the risk of a fatal crash that turned a limit into a real limit, he stood alone. Much to his displeasure because, in his vision, the imposition of drastic safety measures was taking away the magic of Formula One: 'What made Formula One so popular ten years ago was that the drivers were not normal human beings. Now we are presented as athletes but not anything special. You take more risks driving on the roads. Formula One has to be the ultimate or else why should it be called Formula One?'

Villeneuve has touched the essence here. Because it is the undeniable presence of death, in the past and in the future, which invests Formula One with a certain sacral character, distinguishing it from other sports and raising it above mere amusement.

This sacral character is present in all of the circus's fixed customs, its rituals. The set programme of a racing weekend: the arrival of the teams on Thursday, practice on Friday and Saturday, qualifying Saturday afternoon, the warm-up on Sunday morning, the briefing, the starting procedure, the race with all its rules and regulations, the slowing-down lap, the *parc fermé*, the ceremonies, the press conferences. But also the set features of the racing season: from the allocation of numbers through to the Grands Prix with their fixed place on the calendar. For Formula One fanatics the years pass through constantly recurring stations – Interlagos, Imola, Monaco and Monza – and after having paused at all these station, there is that comforting sense of a changing, yet always complete jigsaw puzzle of teams, drivers, constructors, engines, numbers, sponsors, circuits . . .

When Ecclestone began standardising more and more aspects of Formula One in the 1980s, he was probably hoping to make the sport more recognisable and accessible, but he also developed a sense of ritual, of continuity and certainty. This 'eternal return' is a perfectly fitting answer to the presence of death.

Hemingway has not been the only one to compare bullfighting and motor racing. Jackie Stewart also compared a lap around the old Nürburgring to a corrida.

But the comparison goes much further. Bullfighting too has its rituals and its recurring annual programme: drawing lots for the bulls, dressing the matador, the fixed stages of the fight. Bullfighting too is characterised by a confrontation between fervent opponents and a deeply enthusiastic following.

Like motor-racing fans, the fans of bullfighting, the aficionados, are not sitting there waiting for a bull to gore a torero. Above all else, they prize the courage of the matador, how closely he guides the bull past his body. They are especially grateful for style and beauty. Beautiful movements and shapes inspire them, they thrill to the sight of unified living sculptures composed of a steer, the red cloth and the matador's body. According to Hemingway, the true fans are there to see a highly stylised, artistic, emotional performance.

> The *faena* takes a man out of himself and makes him feel immortal while it is proceeding, that gives him an ecstasy that is, while momentary, as profound as any religious ecstasy; moving all the people in the ring together and increasing in emotional intensity as it proceeds, carrying the bullfighter with it. He playing on the crowd through the bull and being moved as it responds in a growing ecstasy of ordered, formal, passionate, increasing disregard for death that leaves you, when it is over, and the death administered to the animal that has made it possible, as empty, as changed, and as sad as any major emotion will leave you.

Bullfighting is art. Hemingway was convinced that only the unique and fleeting nature of the great matadors' performances prevented the corrida from being recognised as a leading contemporary art form.

And Formula One? In Formula One, style and beauty are no less fleeting and just as unrepeatable, what's more, they are taken for granted so often that they are hardly even noticed.

Beauty

Style in Formula One can best be applied to the driving style. An individual driver's driving style depends on the set-up of his car. Put very simply, the set-up swings between over- and understeer.

With oversteer, the front wheels have most of the car's traction. This makes it relatively simple for drivers who like to brake extremely late to turn in – the front wheels are always highly responsive. The problem is that the rear of the car is less stable and constantly threatening to overtake the front, to tail out. A halfway-decent driver has no problem at all with this kind of 'loose' rear. Oversteer looks spectacular. It's quick, but also dangerous.

Understeer is less spectacular, the car is less willing to turn in and tends to plough straight ahead because the rear wheels have most of the traction. Understeer is less risky: if a driver is in danger of missing a corner, he lifts off and turns the wheel again. Understeer generally means time loss; oversteer, the chance of spinning or worse. Despite this, most drivers prefer slight oversteer.

True champions, however, find a perfect balance between the two. That's why great drivers often have an unspectacular style. Purists value that: smooth generally means fast. Stewart, Lauda, Prost, Piquet and Senna were masters of accuracy. Listen to Jackie Stewart:

> A Formula One car is really an animal; a machine, yes, of course, but beyond that an animal because it responds to different kinds

> of treatment. A highly bred racehorse, a thoroughbred in its sensitivity and nervousness. To get the best out of it you must coax it, treat it gently and sympathetically. In a corner it's right on its tiptoes, finely balanced, on the very edge of adhesion, just fingertips on the road, and if you dominate it or try to push it around, it will go straight on or slide off or do any number of things that leave you without control. So you coax it – gently, very gently – to get it to do what you want. You point it and coax it into the apex, and even after you've pointed it and it's all set up, committed to the corner which might still be fifty or a hundred feet away, you must be tender with it, holding it in nicely, because it's got an angle on it, an angle of roll, and it's building to its climax of hitting that apex. You've set a rhythm and now you must keep it. And as it hits the apex, you take it out nicely; you don't say, 'You've got your apex, now I'll put my boot in it and drive however I want.' No, your exit speed is very important, so you've got to maintain that balance or rhythm which you've been building all along. You've got to follow through. Let the car fulfil itself.

Michael Schumacher can drive tidy laps too, but he still prefers a loose rear, a nervous, sliding car. As a result his fast laps often look very spectacular. That's won him a lot of fans, because when it comes to style, the majority of the race audience loves spectacle: sliding, drifting, going sideways, skidding, correcting, rough and tumble.

Staying quick despite all these 'inaccuracies' requires a special gift, something Gerhard Berger calls a 'dream-dancing instinct'. Drivers with this instinct are constantly going beyond the limit because they always manage to bring their car back. Drivers like Peterson, Gilles Villeneuve, Arnoux, Rosberg and Mansell wrestle with their cars, pushing them beyond their actual capabilities. Like true matadors they thrill audiences with their driving style, and in return their errors and blunders are more readily forgiven. Alesi was perhaps the last of the spectacular drivers.

Senna had this instinct as well, but only when he needed it. Schumacher is the same. Modern Formula One, with its extremely powerful brakes and insane downforce, leaves less and less room for this superior variety of slapstick. And computers only register speed, not style. You win races with speed, not with style.

Beauty doesn't win races either, but it does attract attention. Put a beautiful girl in a high-gloss racy catsuit on the nose of a Formula One racing car, and the photographers will swarm all over the pits. Photographers, they're as essential to Formula One as they are to haute couture or pornography.

In Formula One, beauty is generally instantly associated with women. More specifically: pit poodles. Although aesthetics are even more natural to Formula One than style, they are hard to pin down. Of course, the design and colours of the car are tremendously important for the advertising; even if it's not a winner, you'll still have a car to show off with. But how much easier it becomes when you put a seductive woman on or next to it. Never in it.

Only three women have driven in Formula One. The first female Formula One driver was Maria-Teresa De Filippis. Driving a rented Maserati, the *Pilotino* started in three Grands Prix in 1958. Full of regret, she explained later that the many fatal crashes around her robbed her of the desire to go on.

The only woman to score any success in Formula One was Lella Lombardi. The 'Turin Tigress' drove from 1974 to 1976, mostly at the rear of the field. But during the shunt operetta of Montjuich 1975, she steered her March safely through the debris. When the race was stopped early after Rolf Stammelen's crash, Lombardi was in sixth place. It scored her half a world championship point and is the first and only time a woman has scored in a Grand Prix to date. Because in 1992 Giovanna Amati drove, but failed to qualify three times.

In the world of the automobile, women are primarily there to drape over the bonnet, and Formula One does not seem to be an exception. Tall tales. Stirling Moss: 'There are always hordes of pretty girls hanging around the circuit. All women get tremendously excited by the impressions, the noise and the drama of the race. They're more willing than at other times . . .'

The cliché has it that racing cars are the apex of masculinity and that women on the circuits are dying to find out whether the drivers are as masculine as their machines. According to anonymous reports, the comparison can be quite disappointing: 'They go to bed with you to get rid of the stress from racing. They go to much less trouble than men who only have sex to score with. Well, maybe sex is just boring compared to a drive in a Formula One car . . .'

For a long time Formula One drivers automatically had a playboy image. Even today, the paragon playboy driver is still James Hunt, 1976 world champion. 'Sex,' declared one of the badges on his overalls, 'breakfast of champions.'

'Women,' according to Hunt, 'are attracted to racing drivers because they're nasty. You have to be nasty to be competitive and women always prefer nasty men.'

Hunt was just as clear about his own motives: 'Look, if I love something, I like to take it to bed: racing cars are too big, cups are too cold, what's that leave me?'

Niki Lauda, at the time Hunt's opposite in all things, thought that all that messing around on racing weekends was bad for your fitness. 'Worst of all is the hassle that comes with it. You meet someone, you go out to dinner, then to a bar, and you don't end up getting to bed until four in the morning. With your own wife or girlfriend you can have sex and still get twelve hours' sleep.'

In this regard too, Lauda was the herald of modern Formula One. Because Ecclestone's circus has now reined in women too. At least: for security reasons, access to the pits has been greatly restricted. A lot of pit poodles have had to pack their bags as a result.

Eddie Irvine, for many the last of the playboy drivers, laments: 'Senna ruled from 1985 to 1994, and Schumacher has ruled since, so there's been almost fifteen years of strait-laced boringness. Guys like them aren't interested in playing the field; it's seen as a sign of weakness or unprofessionalism. Now you've got to be boring to be perceived as able to win.'

Of course, they're still there, but often the ladies have only turned up for pre-arranged photo sessions with drivers or VIPs, or maybe just standard shots with the car body. In 1998 Eddie Jordan even had contracts with three models, who took turns to show up every now and then to straddle the nose of one of his cars. 'Jordan is a rock'n'roll team,' he explained, 'and you can't be a rock'n'roll team if you don't have nice girls. Some team owners would say Jordan is being distracted from core racing issues by using these girls. I'm saying quite the opposite – I'm attracting. There's been a yearning to look at shapely young girls since Adam and Eve. We have a very attractive car, so it's right that we should have the trimmings with it.'

The trimmings, the accessories, the eye-catchers. That's what it's all about. A woman in the immediate proximity of a Formula One car makes the true, mechanical beauty of the car visible, comprehensible. In their unzipped or low-cut suits, tops and skirts, preferably in the sponsor's colours, they are in a certain sense the redoubling, the human translation of the beauty of the Formula One racing cars.

In the popular imagination and for legions of psychologists, cars might still symbolise masculinity – Stirling Moss again: 'The car is the male organ, it can't be anything else. It is the dynamic element that attacks, conquering the corner . . .' – but in modern Formula One, this is no longer the whole story. Sticking to the classic distinctions, Formula One cars do possess a certain masculinity – in the engine, the noise, the capacity – but the design, the art of effectively placing all that horsepower on the track, is totally feminine.

To truly describe the aerodynamic elegance of a Formula One racing car almost calls for erotic poetry. Of course it does: what is aerodynamics if not the seduction of air?

Tastes differ, but one of the most beautiful cars in Formula One history was the 1973 Shadow DN1. Pitch-black, long and elegant, with a flamboyant, flowing shape, low broad flanks, a superb kink in the line of the cockpit and a magnificently pronounced airbox that firmly pressed the ethereal chariot down on to the ground, as did the generous rear wing.

The 1975 Shadow DN5 was possibly even more beautiful. Again pitch-black, wasp waist, wide chromed front suspension with a slight collarbone kink, the slim airbox floating high above the engine, and then, on the side, just in front of the radiators, the merging white-yellow-orange-and-red strip of colour that moved you to breathless enthusiasm as the car raced by. The DN7 even had a Matra twelve cylinder in the back, what a battery . . . Too bad it was a failure.

Another gorgeous car was the 1981 Ferrari 126 CK, with a broad front wing attached to a minimal nose that immediately gave way to the cockpit and the front suspension, behind it, bulging like a soft belly, the sidepods, and sticking up jauntily at the very rear, the cooling for the disc brakes. Or else the 1991 Jordan 191, in fabulous green and blue, streamlined panels all round, a pert upturned nose and a divine kink in the airbox . . .

Again the comparison with bullfighting. Don't matadors – courageous, desirable he-men each and all – don't they dress like graceful ladies with their gold-embroidered jackets, their lace and their frills, their ballet shoes and, as crowning glory, their pink tights? Formula One drivers also have a predilection for fine-looking overalls with elegant, brightly coloured shoes. More importantly, their bodies disappear into the car. Senna once said that he slipped into a car the same way he slipped into a coat, he wore his car.

What to make of all those euphoric moments when man and machine merge? Ever since the Dark Ages, it has been known that these mystical experiences are accompanied, or even driven by tremendous sexual energy. Arie Luyendijk, Holland's most successful car racer, just not in Formula One – Luyendijk won the Indianapolis 500 twice and in America he is *the* sex symbol for countless men and women – Luyendijk once admitted that every time he drove out of the pits he sighed, 'Oh God, racing gives me such a hard-on . . .'

Niki Lauda thinks it's all nonsense. 'I have every reason to be a car lover, but I feel absolutely no need to search for something profound behind it. There are some really amazing cars, but it has nothing to do with eroticism or something like an inflated ego. The stunning beauty of the back of a Ferrari Daytona, or the moment at which a Porsche 911 pulls up or a Ferrari 550 turns in, they're beautiful experiences with machines – nothing more, nothing less.'

The Show

Lauda's vision reflects modern Formula One: a level-headed, result-oriented business, in which values like sportsmanship, heroism and romanticism have essentially been reduced to the level of fossils.

But true heroes are still measured according to those values, and that probably explains why it is so difficult for today's Formula One to generate new heroes.

By late 1997 and early 1998, the Grand Prix victories were being all too obviously shared out between the chosen few, and the FIA immediately protested: the competition needed to stay hard and fair. But rather than a battleground for drivers, Formula One was increasingly becoming an arena for big investors who wanted their money's worth: a balanced, exciting well-directed show.

Back to bullfighting. Like the corrida, motor racing was almost the logical and inevitable product of cultural development – in this case the increasingly motorised culture of the twentieth century.

Now that the car has become commonplace and seems to be losing its primacy to electronic webs and nets, both function and content of racing are changing.

The French philosopher of speed Virilio expresses this quite radically. In his vision, the twentieth century has already overtaken its own symbol of speed, Formula One: ‘Formula One races are really only held now for the TV broadcasts, for a spectacle in which the race is reduced to a circuit of speed. The autodrome will finally become a manège with racing cars circling around like the circus ponies of yesteryear.’

The same arguments are invariably used by opponents of the corrida. According to them, bullfighting has degenerated into a soulless, meaningless show – cruel folklore – performed only for sensation-seeking tourists and a handful of mentally disturbed fanatics.

This cannot yet be said of Formula One. With its recent tradition, its links to motorised culture and its high-tech aura, the sport still commands respect. Yet it is not entirely implausible that in the coming centuries, when mobility has radically changed, Formula One might survive as a misunderstood and demonised folklore, just like today’s bullfighting.

Nürburgring 1975. Niki Lauda has just broken the record by going round the Ring in under seven minutes. This is the old Ring: 22.8 kilometres, 89 left-handers, 85 right-handers. Lauda took 6 minutes and 58.6 seconds; average speed 196.383 km/h.

When Lauda climbs out of his Ferrari, he is introduced to the writer Peter Handke.

‘Have you been to a race before?’ asks Lauda.

‘Not at all, I don’t even have my driver’s licence,’ answers Handke.

The driver shows the writer around the pits, explaining the special atmosphere of the circuit and telling him about his experiences and all the things that go with one of these races. Finally he asks: ‘And what, do you think, is the source of this tremendous fascination for car racing?’

The writer clicks his pen. ‘These people are all in search of a lost religion.’

PART 4: SUPERPOWERS

Ferrari versus McLaren: 1998–2000

It's come back at last. 6 August 2000. Zandvoort. A festive occasion. Flags flutter in the gentle sea breeze: Ferrari, Jos the Boss, West-Mercedes, Ferrari, Ferrari. A colourful procession shuffles towards the circuit in the dunes. And I'm no longer alone. For the first time, I have my son with me. Six years old. 'They're almost all boys!' he says with surprise, looking at the crowd of racing fans that have turned out for the tenth edition of the Marlboro Masters. Sixty thousand people. Of course, the Dutch Touring Car Championship, the Formula Ford 2000 and the Formula Three races are nice and entertaining in themselves, but ultimately all these people have come for the ten or eleven laps of Formula One. Last year there were already Ferraris to admire during the Masters, but this year, today, one of those racing cars from Maranello will be driven by the best driver of the current generation of Formula One stars: Michael Schumacher. That's not something you'd want to miss.

My son whirls ahead of me. We're getting close to the stalls of the Automobilia Market, he knows exactly what he wants: 'the V cap'. That's the cap Schumacher has worn for interviews and press conferences all season. The V stands for Deutsche Vermögensberatung, 'German Investment Advice', something Schumacher can no doubt use, because the German is costing Ferrari a fortune. When they signed him in 1996 he was already asking 25 million dollars a year, and in 1998 he extended his contract for an annual fee of no less than 30 million. Enzo Ferrari once claimed that 'victory is never too expensive', but whether the *Commendatore* meant such astronomical amounts is highly doubtful . . . And they've gone so long without success. Schumacher may have won twenty-one races for Ferrari, each more glorious than the one before, but the goal, the world title, has slipped through his fingers three times already, and this year too is threatening to become another disappointment. That's why my son wants a V cap – to turn the tide – and that's why I've decided that he's going to get one, even if it costs *me* a fortune.

The Myth versus the Company

After failing to defeat Williams in '96 and '97, Schumacher was confronted by competition from McLaren in the years that followed. For three seasons the struggle for the world championship developed into a blood-curdling duel between the two teams that represented Formula One at its most extreme. It was a duel between Mika Hakkinen and Michael Schumacher, Ferrari and McLaren.

By the end of the twentieth century, Ferrari and McLaren had emerged as the two superpowers of the grid. They were financially superior. In 1998 both teams had budgets of some 125 million dollars. Williams, number three in terms of money, spent 90 million. Minardi, at the bottom of the rankings, had to get by on 15 million. Their results were superior. In three seasons Ferrari and McLaren clocked up 45 of 49 possible victories, more than three-quarters of the podium places, and approximately 70 per cent of available points. And they were historically superior. On the circuit of Sepang, the last race of 2000, Ferrari started in its 636th Grand Prix. The *Scuderia* had won 135 of them. McLaren was up to its 509th Grand Prix and had won 130. In Malaysia, Williams was up to 428 and had won 103 times.

Ferrari and McLaren represented two extremes in Formula One history. Many people see Ferrari, with its time-honoured traditions, as the heart of Formula One. Ferrari is a myth. Even people who haven't got a clue about Formula One generally know what a Ferrari is.

The myth began with the *Commendatore* himself. Enzo Ferrari started out as an uneducated mechanic working for Alfa Romeo. In 1937 he set up his own racing section, and in 1946 he launched his own team, the *Scuderia* Ferrari. Ferrari's headquarters in Maranello developed into a typical Italian nest of intrigue, full of plotting, back scratching, patronage and behind-the-scenes politics. In his curtained room, a candle burning before a portrait of his prematurely deceased son Dino, an ageing Enzo Ferrari received the chosen few and then – after some twaddle about money, conditions and contracts – incorporated them into the myth. Often enough, years later, after the chosen one had been killed in one of his cars, he would carry his portrait into a side room. A gloomy mausoleum: Ascari, Carini, Castelotti, Musso, Collins, Von Trips, Bandini, Giunti, Villeneuve . . .

Every racer dreams of driving for Ferrari. 'In no other car is victory so sweet', according to Berger. In 1987 even Senna considered the journey to Maranello, but his price was too high. 'Senna and Ferrari is a forbidden love,' grumbled Enzo. Senna knew how much it would take to get the ramshackle *Scuderia* back on its feet, he preferred McLaren.

The myth was teetering. In 1979 Jody Scheckter had scored Ferrari's last world championship. Alboreto and Berger won races, but Ferrari was clearly falling behind the long-term factories McLaren and Williams. Mansell and Prost brought back some of the glory. In 1990 Prost even had a chance of claiming the championship, until Japan, where he was torpedoed by Senna in a McLaren.

After the *Commendatore*'s death, much of Ferrari was bought up by Fiat. There were several changes of direction, until finally Luca di Montezemolo was appointed president. Di Montezemolo had been team director in the glory days with Lauda. He brought Lauda back as consultant, made Jean Todt team director, and gradually

Ferrari began changing into a modern high-tech racing team. More business, less myth. Alesi was forced out to make room for Schumacher, at a salary many times the amount Senna had once asked. The *Commendatore* would never have tolerated it. In 1997 Marlboro dropped McLaren for Ferrari. A sponsor that had nothing to do with pure motor racing: Enzo turned in his grave yet again. At Schumacher's insistence, the money was deployed to recruit Ross Brawn and Rory Byrne from Benetton. With the technocratic troika Todt–Brawn–Schumacher, Ferrari's acceptance of the new businesslike mentality was complete.

In his memoirs Berger explains that for a long time Ferrari managed to keep a foot in both camps, combining 'the sweet madness that whipped us up' with 'level-headed use of state-of-the-art technology'. But the process of evolution proved irreversible, now they were just waiting for it to bear fruit. And a title was essential: without it the myth would not survive in its new form.

The history of McLaren is so different and yet so comparable. If Ferrari is the heart, McLaren is the brain, the grey matter of Formula One. Not a myth, but a company. McLaren never saw Nuvolari doing battle or Fangio driving in his polo shirt, they arose in the era of overalls and motor oil. In 1963 Bruce McLaren set up his own racing team. In 1966 he built his first Formula One car. Bruce himself was the first driver. Unfortunately he was also the first and as yet only driver to die in a McLaren. During private tests on the British Goodwood circuit, he slammed his powerful McLaren Can-Am car into a flag station, probably after part of the bodywork came loose. McLaren was alone on the circuit at the time of the crash. There were no witnesses.

The team was continued by McLaren's right-hand man, Teddy Mayer, who booked successes in the mid-seventies with Fittipaldi and Hunt. But with the emergence of wing cars and turbos, McLaren fell behind, until Ron Dennis arrived in 1980.

Like Enzo Ferrari, Dennis started out as a grease monkey – he'd been Jochen Rindt's mechanic at Brabham. But unlike Ferrari, who was proud of his nickname *Il Ingegnere*, Dennis doesn't want to hear a word about the old days. It's typical: for Dennis the only things that count are victory, prestige and status. The marble floor he had laid in the pits for some of the 1998 Grands Prix says enough.

Dennis wasted no time in taking things over – sidelining Mayer and dumping the likeable John Watson – then began an unprecedented series of successes. First with Lauda, Porsche and Prost. Most of the money came from Marlboro and TAG, the company of Mansour Ojjeh, the team's major shareholder. After the departure of Porsche and Lauda, Dennis pulled off his greatest coup, netting Honda and Ayrton Senna. McLaren was world champion four times in a row.

Perfectionist, successful, businesslike and clean, that is the image of McLaren. The team set a new standard in Formula One. Money was no problem. During their famous, ruthless negotiations, Dennis and Senna once tossed a coin to decide the last half million. Dennis: 'Our relationship is too valuable to allow it to be spoilt by side issues like money.'

But when Honda turned their back on Formula One, the lean years began. McLaren needed a new, reliable engine partner – since the turbo era, *the* essential prerequisite for Formula One success. Senna, spoilt and impatient, left for Williams; he wasn't interested in driving a car that couldn't deliver the world championship. It was a painful separation, but Ron Dennis was sympathetic: 'I understand Ayrton better than anyone. Of course, you can get all romantic and start talking about loyalty and the good old days, but this is business. This is about winning. And winning is everything to Ayrton.'

McLaren went through a very rough period with Ford and Peugeot. Things didn't click with a partner until 1995, with Mercedes. It didn't click with Mansell either. Literally: the perfectionists at McLaren built the cockpit too narrow for the stocky lion. Mansell and McLaren: just as much a forbidden love as Senna and Ferrari.

With Mercedes and a loyal Hakkinen, McLaren slowly fought

their way back to the top, even if Marlboro had had enough by late 1996; trading McLaren for Ferrari after an association of twenty-three years. A perfect opportunity to spray the cars silver, a reference to Mercedes' legendary Silver Arrows, invincible in the early fifties. 1997 saw the first victories, and the following year McLaren was once again a serious contender, with *two* potential champions, Hakkinen and Coulthard. By the first race of 1998, in Melbourne, the lead over their competitors was so compelling that the team pressured the drivers into making an agreement about who would win the race. The race was for the driver who led at the first corner. Dangerous games. But renowned as he was for his furious starts, Coulthard was willing to take the risk. It didn't pay off: 'We stood still too long, I got too hasty.' Hakkinen had the best start and beat him to the first corner. Halfway through the race, the team called Hakkinen into the pits by mistake and Coulthard built up a big lead until Ron Dennis called him on the radio to remind him of their deal. The loyal Scot let the Finn overtake. For the second race in a row, Coulthard followed Dennis's orders and gave the victory to Hakkinen.

Audience, media and organisers began to grumble: unfair! Shocked, the FIA even issued a decree banning team orders. Nonsense, of course. Team strategy and team orders were as old as racing itself. Highlight: at Monza in 1956 the young Ferrari driver Peter Collins, in the running for the title himself, gave up his car so that the old master Fangio could use it to win his fourth title. 'My time will come,' explained Collins. Two years later he died in a crash on the Nürburgring, without a title.

Noblesse does not pay in Formula One. Appropriately, these sporting gestures were the beginning of the end for Coulthard. Sure, he's one of the very quickest in Formula One, one of the smoothest drivers too, but he doesn't have the willpower. Coulthard doesn't have that killer instinct. That shows in his lack of consistency. One race there's no stopping him, two weeks later he's invisible. He doesn't have the temperament to always want to be number one. Coulthard is a fantastic racer, but Ron Dennis's orders in Jerez and Melbourne nipped the winner in the bud.

A Natural

'We don't issue team orders unless we need to,' insists Ron Dennis, but when pressed, the dispassionate manager admits he's closer to Hakkinen. Because of Mika's faithfulness, through the lean years as well, and especially after the almost fatal accident in Adelaide.

Hakkinen and McLaren became almost as synonymous as McLaren and Senna ten years earlier. But a closer analysis revealed nothing but differences. Senna pushed back the limits of Formula One, Hakkinen hasn't done that at all. But within those limits Hakkinen is the best when it comes to the essence of the sport: driving fast. Hakkinen epitomises unpolished natural talent. His life story confirms this image.

Mika was already into go-karts as a five-year-old. Even rolling on his very first lap couldn't dent his enthusiasm. His father had to moonlight as a taxi driver to pay for Mika's karting adventures, but rewards in the form of championships were not long in coming. And Hakkinen didn't stop there. In 1987, during a Marlboro talent quest at Donington, he put on an impressive show in front of an audience that included Ron Dennis. Other participants: Eddie Irvine, Mark Blundell, Jean Alesi, Gianni Morbidelli, Roland Ratzenberger and Martin Donnelly. Hakkinen's reward was a chance to drive in the 1988 Opel-Lotus series. He won the championship. The following year saw him in Formula Three, and for the first time Hakkinen failed to win the championship.

Yet there was no missing his natural speed. Hakkinen was compared to Ronnie Peterson, extremely quick, but without technical insight and incapable of analysis. The next year, with a better car, Hakkinen claimed the title after all. At Silverstone in 1990 he had his first drive in a Formula One car, a Benetton. 'Finally I was in the racing car that was ultimately quick,' Hakkinen told Christopher Hilton, 'the racing car that handled like a real fast car. You had to have fast reactions, you had to brake late, you had to turn into the corners late. All these elements were there and they were what I wanted, what I needed. It was absolutely something I had dreamed about for so long, and it just came true. I wanted to go flat out, I wanted to go so quick that nobody had ever gone quicker!'

After a two-year apprenticeship with Lotus, by now a dying swan, Hakkinen was keen to get ahead and took a risk: he became a McLaren test driver. Briefly his career seemed stalled, but when a disillusioned Michael Andretti flew back to the States in late '93, Hakkinen got his chance and was allowed to try his luck in the last three Grands Prix, promptly qualifying ahead of team-mate Ayrton Senna. 'He didn't like things like that,' recalls Hakkinen. 'He was studying the computer, he couldn't understand a couple of corners where this Hakkinen guy had been quicker.' The result was an immediate claim to fame, even if Hakkinen went off hard in the race itself.

Patient, loyal and trusting, Hakkinen slowly climbed to the top with McLaren and Mercedes. Until Adelaide 1995. During the Friday practice, Hakkinen loses control over his McLaren after a rear puncture in the bend before the Brabham Straight. Doing approximately 250 km/h, Hakkinen automatically tries to correct, but the McLaren shoots over the kerbs, takes off, bounces and slams into a tyre wall at around 200 km/h. Hakkinen's helmet hits the steering wheel so hard it breaks it. His head jolts back and forth, then falls gently to one side.

Rapid assistance saves Hakkinen's life. Specially trained doctors and marshals carefully lift him out of the wreck. Hakkinen's muscles are in complete spasm, his jaw is clamped shut, his airways are full of blood. An incision and the insertion of a tube into his trachea allow breathing to be re-established before brain damage can set in.

Hakkinen is lucky. He has a fractured skull, but no brain damage.

His recovery takes months, but on a cold February morning, Hakkinen climbs back into a Formula One car:

> I was pretty relaxed. Then I realised the mechanics standing around the car were pretty silent, which is unusual because all the time in Formula One something is usually happening. It was completely silent. I was putting my crash helmet and gloves on and I just started feeling a little bit nervous. As I got in the car and put on the belts I was looking at things, thinking of the past. Nervous is not quite the right word. I was not sure what I was feeling, but when they fired up the engine it sounded great. I selected first gear, went out of the pit lane and everything changed again. It was fantastic. The noise was really nice and the car felt good and I really knew what was going on. I thought, this is great, this is fun, I love it and I didn't feel scared any more.

In the next race, Melbourne 1996, Hakkinen is there in the third row of the grid as if nothing ever happened: 'The accident hasn't changed the way I think about Formula One.' 1996 is a year of recovery. In 1997 victory finally beckons. But when Coulthard scores McLaren's first win, Hakkinen seems almost happier than Coulthard himself: the Finn charges up to his team-mate, lifts him off the ground and dances around awkwardly. This kind of spontaneous behaviour, anything but orthodox in the world of Formula One, wins Hakkinen many fans. At last they can discern some human qualities in one of their idols.

Equally human and just as endearing is Hakkinen's abundance of bad luck in 1997. At Silverstone, on the A-1 Ring and on the Nürburgring, Hakkinen seems virtually assured of victory, but technology keeps on failing him. Gloomy racing fans compare him to the perennially unlucky Chris Amon, a driver of the sixties and seventies who led race after race but never won. But as Niki Lauda theorises, you can only have so much bad luck before it's no longer a question of luck: 'Good luck doesn't exist, neither does bad luck. You can be lucky twice or unlucky twice, but not three times. Then you're doing something wrong.'

This typical Lauda axiom exposes Hakkinen's weakness. In 1998 the Finn was unlucky twice: his gearbox seized up in San Marino and Canada. But the third time, it was no longer bad luck. While Schumacher confounded the McLarens in Hungary with a cunning pit-stop strategy, Hakkinen suddenly had problems steering. Later it turned out to be caused by a broken stabiliser. Bad luck? 'Senna,' relates Berger, 'would turn a stabiliser around ten times to look at it from every direction before he'd let them use it.' It wasn't bad luck.

The second half of 1998 made abundantly clear how much McLaren's golden years had owed to Senna's perfectionism. At Monza Hakkinen fell behind again with yet another obscure problem: incorrect pressure in his first set of tyres had taken too much out of his brakes. Hakkinen was forced to drive the last laps without any front-wheel braking power at all, and that at Monza with its chicanes and top speeds approaching 350 km/h. Although Hakkinen's natural talent still allowed him to come in fourth, Senna would never have let himself get into such a position in the first place. A gloomy Dennis worried that this lack of reliability might cost McLaren the title, but Hakkinen just took it in his stride: 'Reliability is one of the things you shouldn't brood over. If it goes wrong, it goes wrong. Leave that to others.'

This laconic approach, typical of those possessed of natural talent, guarantees that Hakkinen will never belong in the list: Lauda, Prost, Senna, Schumacher. It might make him a nice guy, but it will stop him from ever becoming a legendary champion.

Pressure

More than anything else, Hakkinen's success is the success of McLaren. With Schumacher and Ferrari, it's the other way round. Another one of those facts that Enzo could never have tolerated. But 'if Schumacher doesn't become world champion, it's our fault', declared Ross Brawn and Jean Todt. The pressure was on. After the 1998 Monaco Grand Prix, Hakkinen was already twenty-two points in front, and the McLaren was very clearly the faster car. But as Frank Williams knew from experience – 'Schumacher is always dangerous, even in a pram'. And Schumacher came back. With three consecutive victories, driving at the limit and beyond, with crashes and controversy.

In Argentina Schumacher punted Coulthard off the track with a dubious overtaking manoeuvre. Driving out of the pits in Canada, he ruthlessly pushed Frentzen's Williams off the track. Schumacher's comment: 'If I hindered him, I am genuinely sorry.' Understatement of the year. The press came up with a new title: 'The Red Baron'. In England Schumacher scored his next controversial victory by sitting out a stop-go penalty after the final lap. For the first time in history, a race was won in the pits! There were no rules against it and the title hung in the balance. Pressure was Schumacher's speciality, the insiders nodded. But was it? Or was Schumacher making mistakes that would keep the title out of his reach?

In Monaco Schumacher threw away six definite world-championship points by being impatient with Wurz. Although he knew that Wurz still had to go in for his pit stop, Schumacher squeezed his Ferrari alongside the Benetton in Loews. Side by side, the cars swung through the hairpin, Wurz not giving an inch. Wheel to wheel, they swooped down to Portiers, a right-hander, Wurz on the inside, hitting each other, another right-hander, Wurz too wide, Schumacher immediately taking the inside, hitting again, Schumacher in front. Brilliant but unnecessary. What's more, the Ferrari's rear suspension was damaged and Schumacher had to pit. 'A racing accident,' declared Schumacher, 'I'm not accusing Alexander of anything.'

But the accusations came thick and fast after a similar incident in the most spectacular race of the year, Spa-Francorchamps. It's pouring in the Ardennes, the track is awash, mist and spray. A year earlier under similar conditions, the race started behind the Safety Car and Schumacher, on intermediates – rain tyres with minimal tread – turned it to his benefit. Now almost everyone is on intermediates, but the stewards keep the Safety Car inside. One and a half laps later, everyone is sorry.

Hakkinen, Schumacher and Villeneuve get away well. They're the first to turn through La Source, a right-hand kink in the track before the descent to Eau Rouge. In the curtain of rain behind the leaders, the rest of the Grand Prix field become entangled in a massive pile-up. Only a handful of drivers manage to slip through unscathed.

Perhaps it began in La Source. Irvine and Coulthard touch each other, it seems innocent enough, Coulthard holds on to fifth place, but has to go wide, very wide and then, in the slight kink before the descent, he goes into a spin. Out of control, the McLaren flips diagonally across the track, hits the pit wall and bounces back. Immediately cars are hitting and hooking into each other everywhere.

On the right Barrichello, Diniz and Wurz form a rotating scrum. Trulli hooks into it. Herbert gets hit from behind and spins. On the left Coulthard bangs into the barrier. Behind him Salo rams Irvine, and together Salo and Irvine ram Coulthard. Panis and Takagi slide sideways into the enormous clump of cars. Takagi rams Wurz, Nakano rams Salo and lastly Rosset flies into Panis and Barrichello. Airborne debris everywhere – wheels, suspension, wings – miraculously no one gets hit. The fuel lines clamp shut the way they're supposed to, and the pile of wreckage slides helplessly downhill, on to the grass or against the barrier. Ten seconds, that's how long it's taken. Steaming wrecks, mist, in the middle the flashing lights of Prof. Sid Watkins's Mercedes. The red flag is already out.

Unharmed, the drivers climb out of their cockpits. Carbon-fibre chassis – billiards situation. Several drivers are already running back to claim the spare car. Barrichello has hurt his elbow. 'Twenty years ago,' points out Wurz, 'we would have needed eleven new drivers for the next start.'

With twelve damaged cars, Spa '98 went straight into the history books as Formula One's biggest pile-up. In Monza '78, Zeltweg '87 and Hockenheim '94 only ten cars had been written off. 'You all right?' Salo asked Coulthard. 'Fine, I'm perfectly OK,' answered the Scot. Only later did he reveal that it took him a few minutes to remember which circuit he was on.

During the restart Damon Hill's Jordan slips through between the two McLarens. Hill is the first to take La Source. Hakkinen and Schumacher are behind him, Coulthard falls back. And right away, it's on again. Hakkinen is on the inside, but he needs a lot of room. He forces Schumacher further and further to the outside. But Schumacher doesn't give way, their wheels hook into each other and, just at that moment, Schumacher puts his foot down. The Ferrari's right rear hits the McLaren's front left and Hakkinen does an immediate 180-degree spin. In the same instant the rest of the field comes storming through La Source. There's room on the right, but not for everyone. Herbert hits Hakkinen and knocks off his front left wheel. Race over. Safety Car. Clean up the mess.

In the pits Ron Dennis is furious. 'I'm not going to put fuel on the fire. The videos are clear.' Dennis suspects a deliberate move by Schumacher. Ross Brawn defends his driver: 'Hakkinen tried to put Michael off on the first corner. He makes no attempt to run tight at that corner, and he's tried to squeeze Michael against the wall. McLaren knew it was in a difficult position, that we were faster. The perpetrator failed and got his comeuppance.'

Hill in the lead! Eight laps. Then Schumacher's had enough. Visibly faster, he sails through Blanchimont, confidently puts his Ferrari alongside the Jordan, and brakes precisely enough to soar past and take the Busstop chicane perfectly. Schumacher in the lead. Meanwhile the rain is terrible. Irvine spins. Coulthard joined Wurz in an excursion over the grass and is now trailing along behind the others. One driver after the other goes in for full wet-weather tyres.

Schumacher has a comfortable lead. Rain, Spa, Hakkinen out,

Coulthard chanceless, everything is to the German's advantage. Ten points will give him the lead in the world championship . . .

Twenty-fifth lap. Schumacher is coming up to lap Coulthard, who has been taking it easy for a number of laps and radioing in to plead for the Safety Car – the conditions are too dangerous. Schumacher doesn't take it easy for a moment, that's his mistake. On the Kemmel he already has Coulthard in his sights, through Les Combes, Malmédy. The Ferrari gets closer. Schumacher shakes his fist and later declares: 'Coulthard suddenly started driving significantly slower. He was waiting for me.' Coulthard: 'The team had let me know that he was coming and that I should just let him overtake. I did not deviate my line or weave or brake. The stewards have access to our radio and telemetry. Ferrari can allege we did this, that and the next thing, but it's absolute bollocks.' After slinging through Rivage, Schumacher – now driving in Coulthard's wake – has minimal visibility, or rather, zero visibility. Like phantoms, the cars race down through the mist to Pouhon. Coulthard keeps to the far right: 'I accelerated out of the left-hander but not at full throttle. I expected him to overtake into Pouhon, not run into the back of me.'

The smash is enormous. Schumacher roars into the rear of Coulthard's McLaren. Fortunately he doesn't run over the rear wheel the way Pironi did when he hit Prost in the mists of Hockenheim in 1982, but Schumacher's car is still badly damaged. The right front wheel has disappeared, the suspension has been shredded. Race over. Isn't it? Schumacher races on *à la* Gilles Villeneuve on three wheels. Furious, he pounds the steering wheel.

There is tumult in the pits as the crippled Ferrari drives up, a dumbfounded Coulthard in its wake. Both cars immediately turn into their garages. Schumacher leaps out of his cockpit. You immediately sense what's going to happen. Boiling with rage, he strides, helmet in hand, to the McLaren pits. An alert member of the Ferrari crew tries to stop him, but Schumacher shoves him aside.

Coulthard is standing in the garage surrounded by McLaren

mechanics. In 1987 Mansell and Senna came to blows here at Spa, five years later Senna grabbed Schumacher by the collar, now Schumacher wants a piece of Coulthard. 'Are you trying to fucking kill me?' he screams at Coulthard before being dragged away by his crew. Flanked by the ever-respectable Jean Todt, he marches back to Ferrari. 'We were on the point of taking the lead in the world championship,' declares Schumacher later. 'We were the quickest today. I think it's suspect that a Formula One driver should lift off at 200 km/h. You don't do things like that. I had absolutely no intention of overtaking him there. I can only assume that he lifted off, and I think he did it deliberately.' Coulthard: 'Schumacher's behaviour is highly questionable. It isn't the first incident he's been involved in. I would never deliberately endanger a competitor, let alone try to kill him. His behaviour in coming into the garage is unacceptable and disgusting. To accuse me of doing it deliberately is paranoia in the extreme. He really needs to get some help for controlling his anger after such an event.' Outsiders backed Coulthard, the fair sportsman. Schumacher simply took too great a risk, especially considering his lead and the fact that Hakkinen was already out of the race. Ten sure points thrown away.

Only Eddie Irvine took Schumacher's side: 'If Michael had lifted off every time he couldn't see where he was going, he would have been last.' But not even Irvine believed that Coulthard had acted deliberately: 'He is not that kind of person. No driver would do that to a colleague.' No driver? Irvine has momentarily forgotten the past of his own team-mate. Damon Hill has a better memory: 'Blaming others is a tactic he often uses when he has made a mistake. He targets the innocent party to deflect from his own error.'

Hill! Suddenly Hill is back in the lead. And in the pits Eddie Jordan can't believe his eyes, because behind Hill is the second Jordan, Ralf Schumacher's! The last laps, with Hill in the lead, are nerve-wracking. Again you sense what's going to happen. Hill does, too. When Ralf starts to get threatening, Hill speaks to Jordan over the radio: 'Listen, Eddie, we can start fighting over it and both go off, or you can tell him to be a good boy and book a double victory. It's up to you.' Jordan orders Ralf not to attack Hill. But the pressure is still on because, behind Ralf, Alesi is pushing hard.

No one begrudges Eddie Jordan his moment. They've waited eight seasons for this, 126 Grands Prix. In late 1991 the team almost went bankrupt. Ecclestone lent a hand. Afterwards things improved. A major sponsor, good engines, and Jordan always had a nose for talent. He discovered Alesi and Frentzen, brought Irvine into Formula One, Barrichello, Zanardi, Michael Schumacher, he scored Fisichella, Ralf Schumacher, all talented drivers with beefed-up transfer clauses. And now Hill's experience is going to bring him his first victory.

The last lap. You still don't believe it, you still anticipate the Jordan skidding off everywhere – at Stavelot, going over Blanchimont, through the chicane, he almost missed it once already . . . But Hill wins, ahead of Ralf Schumacher. Jordan are clearly on their way to the top.

Finale

After a masterful Schumacher triumphed at Monza, and Hakkinen hit back just as masterfully on the Nürburgring, the margin going into the last race was just four points – Hakkinen's advantage.

Suzuka. Schumacher takes pole. Next to him, Hakkinen. Ferrari, McLaren. Eight years earlier Prost and Senna were next to each other here – Ferrari, McLaren – fifteen seconds later the struggle was decided. Warm-up lap. Heart pounding. Twenty-two cars roll out on to the grid and line up. Once they're all stationary, the red lights go on, one by one. But with all five on, Jarno Trulli in the Prost starts waving his arms – yellow flags, orange lights blinking above the reds: starting procedure interrupted. The rules are clear: Trulli, the cause of the delay, has to go to the back of the grid for the restart.

Second warm-up lap. Again, that tension. Schumacher leads the parade through the Esses, uphill to Dunlop Curve, through Degner Curve, under the overpass, then the hairpin and sweeping right on the way to the Spoon. Schumacher is driving in front, way out in front, unusually far ahead. All alone, he appears on the cross-over, reaching the 130R before Hakkinen is even in sight. Schumacher is much too far ahead, as a consequence he'll have to wait on the grid, the engine will heat up, it could boil, stall. But 'Mr Perfect' must know what he's doing. Schumacher slows down but still reaches the starting grid long before Hakkinen and the others. He takes up position and waits, waits and looks in his mirrors, hoping they won't waste any time. But just as the last driver, Trulli, pulls up, the Ferrari lurches forward and stalls. Yellow flags.

Schumacher holds up one hand. They haven't raced a single metre. The championship has been decided. Consternation. Again the mechanics run out on to the grid. Has Schumacher made a mistake? Did he drive too fast in the warm-up lap? Unbelievable. Ross Brawn explains that Schumacher deliberately drove that fast because the Ferrari's engine was overheating, the new control system for clutch and gearbox was malfunctioning; Schumacher was trying to suck in enough air to cool it down. Remarkable how far the Ferrari team will go to shield Schumacher. Just over twenty years earlier, Lauda's contract had stipulated that he never blame the car. Even after his crash on the Nürburgring, Lauda was obliged to hold his tongue.

But whatever the reason, Schumacher went too fast, needed to drop the revs to compensate, then stalled. Insiders recall something similar happening to Nigel Mansell, Canada 1991. On his way to victory in the last lap, he waved to his fans and stalled. Comparisons to Mansell? Had the superhuman, stress-resistant Michael Schumacher made yet another fatal mistake in a race that would decide the world championship?

But wait, the competition hasn't been decided yet. The Ferrari is still in the race. After the others have set off on a new warm-up lap, the Ferrari Number 3 tags along behind. Normally it would all be over bar the shouting, but this is Schumacher – as long as he's driving, he's still a contender.

The third start goes ahead without problems. Hakkinen takes the lead ahead of Irvine, Frentzen and Coulthard. At the back Schumacher overtakes five opponents before the first corner. After one lap he's already twelfth. In the next, he gets past Panis and Alesi. Of course, most drivers are looking in their mirrors more than at the track. No one wants to go down in history as the bozo who rubbed out Schumacher's championship aspirations. And yet . . . It's spectacular the way Schumacher worms his way past Fisichella in the hairpin. Next is Wurz. Schumacher and Wurz are old buddies from Monaco, but Schumacher has no time to stop and think, and overtakes Wurz on the outside climbing the hill after the Esses. A spot where it's not really possible to overtake, but this time Wurz leaves enough room.

Hakkinen has the lead and is extending it, but for now all eyes are on Schumacher. It's time for his little brother Ralf. In Austria the two Schumachers had a nice duel over a few laps, but now there's too much at stake: Ralf lets Michael overtake. He's seventh now, after just five laps, and in front of him is Damon Hill. Just as with Wurz, Schumacher tries it immediately after the Esses, but Hill doesn't give an inch. In the hairpin Schumacher tries the inside, but Hill keeps the door shut. The chicane then, but the Jordan has enough power, Schumacher can't get close enough. He can only threaten, showing that he's in a hurry. But Hill has no intention of letting Schumacher overtake just like that. In the hairpin Schumacher has to jump on his brakes to avoid a crash, Hill is unimpressed. But that's not all: in the next lap Hill even tries to overtake Villeneuve, in fifth place ahead of him. Schumacher can only watch, his advance stalled. The Red Baron concedes that 'Damon is a race driver and he has to do his job' but adds: 'Hill watched his mirrors more than the front of him, and it's not like this is the first time. His "Schumacher Complex" is becoming more and more evident over the years.' Ralf agrees with his brother: 'Hill was ordered three times to move over for Michael, but he didn't do it. That's a sign of poverty.' Hill: 'I'm not under any obligation.'

Of course Hill was paying Schumacher back. And even if he'd got past Hill, Villeneuve was waiting to settle up accounts for Jerez '97, and in front of him there was Coulthard with outstanding debts from Spa and Argentina '98, and in front of him, Frentzen with a bill from Canada . . .

But just when Hakkinen seems the furthest ahead, Schumacher pulls out his best card: the pit stops. Hill is the first to pit and seven laps later, when everyone has been in, Schumacher is in front of them all: Hill, Villeneuve, Frentzen and Coulthard. Incredible. Twenty-eight seconds behind Hakkinen. In between there is only Irvine. From the very back of the grid, Schumacher has fought his way to a highly favourable position. If Hakkinen is unlucky and breaks down, Schumacher will take the title. Unlucky. It never occurs to anyone that Schumacher can be unlucky as well.

But in the thirty-first lap Schumacher runs over debris from two crashed cars and punctures his right rear tyre. The German struggles to keep his car under control, then steers it through the next corner and on to the grass. Race over.

Head bowed, Schumacher sits down on a wall alongside the track. On the large screen behind him, the spectators watch Hakkinen coming in for his second pit stop. Singing into his radio, he drives back out on to the track. Ron Dennis warns him to take it easy.

The struggle has been decided. A disillusioned Jean Todt stares at his monitor on the pit wall. 'Statistically this was the best season in Ferrari's entire history,' mumbles Ross Brawn, but, in the garage, Ferrari boss Di Montezemolo is comforting weeping mechanics. Yet again tragedy has triumphed over technology. 'Next year,' declares a grim-faced Di Montezemolo, 'next year, we win!'

Zandvoort 2000. There is nothing the extended circuit would like more than to stage a Grand Prix. But there's still a lot to be done. A new grandstand, for instance. The old one has been demolished, spectators are obliged to find a spot on a constantly moving mountain of sand. My son, his V cap on his head, prefers the top of the dune on the far side of the circuit, near Gerlach Corner.

We watch the lacklustre Formula Three race. I point out a white car in sixth place, later in fifth: 'That's Tomas Scheckter, the son of Jody Scheckter, the last Ferrari world champion, but that's twenty-one years ago now.' After the Formula Three race, we stare up at the helicopters that come and go. Inside one of them is Schumacher. He's on a tight schedule and is being flown in direct from testing at Mugello. Tonight, still on that tight schedule, he'll fly home to his wife and children in Geneva. The helicopters recall that chopper at Silverstone '99, which in turn summons up memories of the drama of Imola '94 . . .

Crashes and Blunders

The 1999 season became another test of strength between Ferrari and McLaren. Both teams went to great lengths and great expense. The full intensity of the duel became apparent in Monaco.

Since it's virtually impossible to overtake in Monaco, the qualifying is at least as important as the race itself. Initially Ferrari seemed the strongest. During the free practice sessions, Schumacher and Irvine were a class apart and, during the qualifying session itself, the Ferraris seemed about to confirm their claim to the front row. Then, in the very last minute, Hakkinen produced a magnificent lap that Schumacher could not possibly better. It has become Hakkinen's speciality: when he has no choice, he comes up with a lap at the limit, or beyond. He himself is not that happy about it: 'In moments like those you drive like an idiot, beyond the limit. You try to keep the car under control, but it's not. Dangerous. I don't like racing like that at all.' According to rumours that circulated later, McLaren had reduced the tyre pressure below a critical level, increasing grip and speed but also the danger of a blowout –

Hakkinen on pole. But Schumacher had another ace up his sleeve. On the Friday off, Schumacher had jetted to Fiorano, Ferrari's test circuit, to practise his starts. In Monaco the start is even more important than the race and qualifying together, but test starts are banned in the principality itself. And it worked. When the lights went out, Schumacher showed Hakkinen the back of his car, dived through Ste Dévote ahead of the rest and wasn't seen again. Thanks to a brilliant tactical move, Irvine even managed to turn it into a double victory. Triumphantly, the two 'reds' drove side by side along the waterfront – 1999 finally seemed like it was going to be Ferrari's year.

Then came Silverstone. After a few lesser performances, Schumacher has ceded the lead in the championship to Hakkinen. The pressure is again building. They're next to each other in the front row. Schumacher messes up his start and has to let Hakkinen, Coulthard and even Irvine past. But somewhere in the middle of the grid, two cars haven't moved. Marshals run out on to the track to push them out of the way. The rest of the field races on through Copse and Becketts. The stewards see a potentially dangerous situation and decide to stop the race: red flag. The pack is already roaring down Hangar Straight at 250, 300 km/h. Most of the teams immediately relay the news that the race has been stopped, everyone flicks the switch to caution. Everyone, that is, except Schumacher. He alone has not received the news. Is super-strategist Ross Brawn relying on Schumacher's intuition and insight? Schumacher is going flat out. Into Stowe, he deploys a full-on outbraking manoeuvre. Irvine can hardly believe his eyes: 'Just when I touch the brakes Michael whizzes past like a lunatic with locked front wheels. He only just misses me and flies into the gravel . . .' Rear wheels spinning wildly, Schumacher shoots across the gravel trap and slams straight into a tyre wall in front of an embankment. The impact is tremendous. When the dust clears, the Ferrari has plunged cockpit-deep into the tyres. Schumacher moves. He throws out the steering wheel and goes to climb out of the car. No big deal, that's what it looks like. But then he gets stuck, he can't go any further. His body betrays pain. The marshals are already on the scene and helping him out of the car. Schumacher is laid down on the ground beside the Ferrari and immediately surrounded by doctors. The mood is suddenly sombre – memories of Imola 1994. No, it's abundantly clear that it's not that bad this time, but still: fate has once again laid its hand on the best of all and that's disturbing, frightening. Sid Watkins, one of the first on the scene, relates that Schumacher got straight to the point: 'It's my leg, Prof. And make sure Ferrari check the brakes on Irvine's car and give my wife a call to tell her I'm OK.'

The telemetry shows that Schumacher hit the brakes at 306 km/h, and that the brake fluid then escaped through an open nipple. The car hardly slowed down at all. The Ferrari knifed into the tyres, only meeting the first real resistance at the level of the suspension. The right front wheel, attached to the body with a kevlar tether (mandatory since 1999 in order to reduce the number of projectile car parts after crashes), smashed the chassis, presumably breaking Schumacher's leg in the process. The protective padding on the cockpit rim prevented serious head and neck injury. 'The best safety improvement in years', according to Watkins.

Of course afterwards, everyone is fixated on the bleed nipple that someone had neglected to tighten, but why wasn't Schumacher informed that the race had been stopped? And why such dramatic outbraking in the very first lap? Was Schumacher under pressure to keep up with the McLarens? Irvine's judgement was scathing: 'It was much too wild a move, even without the brake problem he would have gone off.'

While Schumacher is carted off by helicopter, the race, in fact the rest of the season, looks like it will be a walkover for Hakkinen. But with Schumacher out of the picture, 1999 now degenerates into one of the most farcical seasons in the history of Formula One. It starts right there in England, when the McLaren team mount Hakkinen's left rear wheel crooked during a pit stop. The McLaren goes out on to the track anyway, only to wobble back into the pits on three wheels a few laps later: race lost. McLaren and Hakkinen carry on like this and pile up mistake after mistake. What did Niki Lauda say about bad luck?

At Imola Hakkinen has a big lead when he cuts over the kerbs a little too deeply before start-finish. It happens to everyone sometimes, but it should never happen to a champion in the lead. The car flops uncorrectably left against the wall: race lost. After another amateurish pit stop in Germany, Hakkinen has a blowout at 300 km/h. He's lucky – nothing broken. Tyre manufacturer Bridgestone points the finger at McLaren, but McLaren denies fiddling the tyre pressure. In the next race, in Austria, Coulthard knocks his team-mate off the track on the second corner. Hakkinen is furious. He just avoids the gravel and mounts a phenomenal chase that is finally rewarded with third place. But the credit for the biggest blunder of all goes to Hakkinen alone. At Monza. By the thirtieth lap he's in the lead, eight seconds in front of Frentzen. For the thirtieth time, Hakkinen storms towards the Variante Goodyear, a double left-right-left-right chicane. Braking, 350 to 100 in just over four seconds, changing back from seventh to second. It's been years since drivers needed to wrestle with a gear lever, they now use comfy little all-electronic paddles on the steering wheel. Changing up takes fifteen milliseconds. Because of the automatic declutching, changing down takes a little longer: twenty to twenty-five milliseconds. You need a feel for it. If the driver presses a paddle too quickly, the software will interpret it as an error and won't change. Hakkinen takes his time changing down and gets it wrong. 'The whole weekend I've taken that corner in second and now I pull the paddle once too often.' A question of milliseconds. At 135 km/h in first gear the wheels lock: the McLaren spins inexorably to the left and slides sideways into the gravel. The engine stalls. Over and out. What did Niki Lauda say about bad luck?

Hakkinen hurls his steering wheel out of the cockpit, climbs out of the car, pushes the marshals aside, theatrically throws one of his gloves down on the grass and disappears behind some trees. There he sinks to his knees, puts his helmet down on the ground and bursts into tears. It's a performance worthy of Mansell. FOA Television – over 300 million viewers per Grand Prix and 'switched on' more than 75 billion times a year – seizes the opportunity and captures it all from a helicopter.

New Names

McLaren's bungling and the elimination of Schumacher allow new names to come to the fore in 1999. Names like Jordan and Frentzen, Irvine, Barrichello and, not really new, Stewart.

Jordan and Frentzen win twice and briefly look like real contenders. The victory in France is nothing short of brilliant. The circuit of Magny-Cours is harried by short but intense downpours. Eddie Jordan knows his classics: he quickly despatches one of the motorhome crew to the nearby airport with instructions to monitor the weather situation and report back on time . . .

The race starts on a dry track with lots of spectacular overtaking in the Adelaide hairpin. Hakkinen in particular puts on a wonderful show: brushing aside Schumacher, ruthlessly outbraking Frentzen and leaving Alesi behind as well. At that same moment the telephone rings in the Jordan pits. A few laps later all hell breaks loose. A cloudburst drenches Magny-Cours. Even wet-weather tyres can't stop the cars from sliding left and right off the track. Safety Car. This is just what Jordan has been banking on. Because midway through the race, fuel consumption becomes even more important than tyres. In the wet, consumption drops dramatically and, crawling along behind the Safety Car, it drops even more. In conditions like these it becomes possible to drive the whole race with just one pit stop – if your fuel tank is big enough. And Jordan has the biggest fuel tank in the paddock: 145 litres. The team has filled it to overflowing. 'The car felt very heavy,' relates Frentzen, 'I was wondering how I was going to be able to keep it on the road with all the aquaplaning.'

The Jordan engineers make furious calculations. Now and then there is contact with the driver. 'How much do I have on board now?' 'Enough. Another one or two laps and you'll make it.' Rain, mist, no overtaking. 'One more lap.' The lights on the Safety Car keep on flashing, the moment they go off the real race resumes. 'You'll make it.' 'OK.'

When the Safety Car leaves the track, Barrichello is leading, ahead of Hakkinen. Frentzen is third, but no one knows that he's still holding a big trump. Cleverly he remains aloof from the intense fighting on the track. After Hakkinen spins and falls back, a fantastic battle develops between Schumacher and Barrichello. Going into the Adelaide hairpin, Schumacher comes up from way back until he's alongside Barrichello, brakes, swings into the corner first, takes it on the inside so slowly he's hardly moving, then comes out of the corner slowly as well. Barrichello, on the outside, maintains just enough speed to re-pass Schumacher on the outside. Attack repulsed. Two laps later Schumacher tries it again, this time he does get past. 'Fantastic,' grins Barrichello afterwards, 'being able to take on Hakkinen and Schumacher in a competitive car . . .' All the same, the smile on his face is a little wry, because the tank of his Stewart only holds 118 litres . . . Schumacher has electrical problems and drops back, and seven laps before the end, Hakkinen and Barrichello have to pit for fuel. Frentzen stays out and wins.

Barrichello too is one of the revelations of the season. In Brazil he thrilled the whole nation by dominating the Grand Prix at Interlagos. Barrichello kept appearing at the front of the field, but all too often his Stewart broke down. Still, his remarkable achievements did not go unnoticed. At the end of the season, Barrichello received an invitation, or rather a summons, from Ferrari. And the Stewart team was bought up by Ford for no less than 70 million dollars. Ford had long been the driving force behind the team, and the automotive giant now thought that it could start racing under the name of its subsidiary Jaguar without losing face. A trend. Big car manufacturers see Formula One as a chance to raise their profile in the up-market sports section of the market. In well-considered steps, they have gradually increased their influence over the teams. BMW chased off Williams's sponsors so that they could have the car almost to themselves; Honda did a deal with BAR, and since then rumours of a complete takeover have been irrepressible; Toyota secured the last two open places on the grid by paying a deposit of some 50 million dollars; and even Renault reappeared in the back of the Benetton – if the team is successful they intend to take it over completely in a few years' time. Mercedes, to a degree the initiator of the whole trend, had already gone one step further, buying 40 per cent of the shares of the TAG-McLaren Group for over 300 million dollars, and announcing that the Mercedes 300 SLR would be built in a new McLaren factory. The old racing die-hards looked on sorrowfully. Eddie Jordan rejected a takeover bid from Honda: 'I want to keep on running my own team, because later when there's nothing left to win, they'll pull back and what will be left of the racing teams then?' After being taken over by Jaguar, Jackie Stewart had only one wish: 'I hope that the team wins a race under our name . . .'

But more than anything, 1999 is the season of Eddie Irvine. Irvine had already won the opening race after the withdrawal of the crown princes. No one in Formula One begrudged the Irishman his victory. For three whole seasons he had supported Schumacher as the ideal second driver. He was loud and romantic, but neither quick enough nor ambitious enough to rebel against the team's favoured scenario. Irvine's ego wasn't too big and it was solid enough to stand up to Schumacher's charisma. Irvine regularly praised Schumacher to high heaven, he stuck to the agreements, and uncomplainingly accepted the luxurious world of Ferrari. That's not to say that Irvine was unaware of the possibilities, the previous winter he had even whispered to journalists that Schumacher could always break a leg or something . . . You could expect quips like that from the laconic Ulsterman. Many saw Irvine as the last of the playboy drivers, a hedonist and a lady's man. 'If only he drove better,' sighed Niki Lauda, 'then he'd be the ideal racer.' But since Lauda's ascendancy, a wild life has been incompatible with the professional monomania of a Formula One driver.

But in 1999 things suddenly got serious. Thanks to Silverstone, McLaren's bungling and the fact that he scored regularly and even won, Irvine suddenly took the lead in the world championship! All over the world, people scratched their heads. Even in Germany newspaper headlines asked: '*Wieviel Schumi braucht Ferrari?*' Italians too began to question Schumacher's importance. Once it was clear that Schumacher would be out for a number of Grands Prix and no longer had any chance of claiming the title, the Italian press began singing Irvine's praises.

Fiat boss Agnelli set the tone: 'I love the way he's so thoroughly Irish, so romantic. He's like us Italians in that regard.' One newspaper wrote: 'We were like soldiers. We followed the logic of a factory instead of our own feelings. Irvine is real: when he wins, it's a victory for the people. When Schumacher comes back, will he find his car where he left it?' Irvine saw his chance: 'Listen, when Michael comes back, he'll have to drive in support of me, that goes without saying.'

But in Belgium and Hungary, circuits where Schumacher excelled with Ferrari, McLaren recovered and left Irvine out in the cold. It came as no surprise to Jean Todt, whose position in Italy also hung in the balance: 'Irvine needs Schumacher as a point of reference, he's better with Schumacher as a team-mate than he is without.'

Finally Ferrari too had a big share in the bungling of '99. When the rain came down in Magny-Cours, Irvine was one of the first to dive into the pits while the team was still getting ready for Schumacher. Irvine's wheels were whipped out of the pit box ready for mounting. But when the blankets were zipped open, they turned out to be dry-weather tyres. 'That won't happen to us again,' Ross Brawn insisted, 'in future we'll colour-code the blankets.' But on the Nürburgring the team stuffed up again. After some typically half-hearted Eifel rain, Irvine came into the pits but called out at the last moment that he wanted dry-weather tyres. No problem, the blankets are colour-coded. Irvine stops, wheels off, refuelling, everything goes fine, wheels on, hands go up . . . except at the right rear wheel. The right rear wheel is missing. Whoops! Three hundred million television viewers, a budget of over 100 million dollars, the status of a religion in Italy, and there you have it: a Ferrari on three wheels . . . Mechanics run into the garage. A wheel flies across the screen. It takes thirty seconds. Race lost.

The race on the Nürburgring is a caricature of the entire 1999 season anyway: comedy capers. First Pedro Diniz turns upside-down on the first corner. The rollbar breaks off and Diniz bounces along with his head in the gravel. Miraculously unharmed, the Brazilian gives the thumbs up as they slide him into the ambulance: Formula One 1999.

Then Hakkinen dives into the pits when it starts to spit. Frightened. Prematurely, because the track dries up again: race lost. Irvine misses a wheel. Frentzen has the lead – he can equal Hakkinen's score in the race for the title, until his clutch fails. Coulthard has the lead, he can come within two points of Hakkinen. But during the next squall Coulthard drives over a white line and slides off hopelessly. There goes his chance at the title; Coulthard will never be champion. Ralf Schumacher has the lead, his consistent performances in the substandard 1999 Williams have been very impressive. On dry-weather tyres he defies the rain. But during his last pit stop, Ralf runs over a screw and gets a flat. When it's dry again, Fisichella takes the lead – quick and talented. But 'Fisico' spins on a wet patch. Crying, he leans on the fence. Tears are all the rage, a little later Luca Badoer collapses weeping next to his Minardi, he'd suddenly found himself in fourth place . . .

Who does have the lead then? Herbert. Johnny Herbert books his third Grand Prix victory, the first and only win for Stewart. Herbert has kept an eye on the sky and pits at exactly the right moment. When a champagne-spattered Jackie Stewart raises the constructor's trophy on the podium, his son Paul wipes away a tear – and he's not the only one. This is not just any victory. This is a triumph for a whole life, an entire past set in the veiled continuity of motor racing.

1999 Finale

For the last two races of the season the Formula One circus sets off for the Far East. Hakkinen on 62 points, Irvine on 60. A week beforehand there was a press release from Schumacher: the German did not consider himself fit enough to drive the last two races. A few days later Schumacher was summoned to Maranello by Ferrari president Di Montezemolo. No one will ever know what they discussed, but that same day Ferrari announced that Schumacher had reconsidered and was fit enough to come out for Ferrari in the last two races after all. Of course Schumacher had no desire to help Irvine to the title. He was the one who had brought Ferrari this far and he wanted to reap the benefit himself. 'I will do my best to help Ferrari win the title,' declared Schumacher. Ferrari, not Irvine.

On the new Sepang circuit in Malaysia, Schumacher crushes all opposition, claiming pole with a lead of more than a second over Irvine. 'The car has been greatly improved,' explains Ross Brawn, 'new deflectors, a lighter engine, more capacity.' Is that possible, can a car suddenly be so much better? Just as in the Benetton years, rumours about outlawed traction control systems pop up. They don't find anything, but even FIA boss Max Mosley has to admit that 'the electronics have become so complex, a whole army of inspectors would not be enough'.

The race too is dictated by Ferrari. Schumacher lets Irvine overtake not once but twice, and manages to stay in front of Hakkinen. 'Ferrari did a brilliant job tactically, I have nothing to complain about,' Hakkinen admits after the race. Irvine is beaming, he's prepared his lines in advance: 'This was just a fantastic result for me and for Ferrari. What can you say about Michael? We knew he was the best number one and now he is also the best number two!' These words must make the German's blood boil, but the *tifosi* couldn't care less, in Maranello the bells are ringing. The resounding double victory has come in the nick of time.

Or hasn't, as it turns out two hours later. There's something wrong with the Ferraris. Jean Todt and Ross Brawn are called in by the stewards. According to the measurements, the new deflectors on the Ferraris are not consistent with regulations. Air deflectors, barge-boards: the terminology is as ugly and clumsy as the objects themselves. A lip on the barge-boards on the side of the Ferrari has turned out to be too small, ten millimetres too small to be precise. Todt and Brawn can't deny it. But it *is* minimal, they immediately add in their defence, a manufacturing error that provided no advantage at all. Disqualification follows. Hakkinen is the new world champion. In Italy all hell breaks loose. 'What kind of idiots can't even measure properly?' the newspapers scream. Calls go up for Jean Todt's head. 'I'll resign if you like,' answers Todt calmly. 'No way,' snaps Di Montezemolo, 'Todt stays.'

Ferrari appeal and the FIA promises to decide the issue in the coming week, before the Japanese Grand Prix. It's in the news all week, until finally the oracle speaks. Ecclestone: 'Perhaps we shouldn't make such an issue of these millimetre regulations.' Insiders know right away how the Ferrari appeal is going to turn out. McLaren and Stewart grumble that rules should always be enforced strictly, but television ratings will prevail over millimetres and thousandths of seconds.

A week later the FIA employs one technical and one legal ruse to reverse the disqualification. Viewed from another direction, the lip was only five millimetres too small. And well, five millimetres, that is just within the tolerance specified by the regulations . . . 'Difficult but fair', is Mosley's stoic reaction, but Niki Lauda calls it 'a catastrophic mistake. FIA regulations are obviously made of elastic. The Ferraris breached clearly defined regulations, Ferrari themselves admitted it! Deciding this world championship has become a farce. That's unacceptable. Formula One has suffered a heavy loss.'

But the tension was back. The show gained the desired denouement. Now it was all or nothing: Ferrari or Hakkinen.

Again Schumacher and Hakkinen are alongside each other in the front row at Suzuka. A crash now would be to the advantage of Ferrari, of Irvine. But those in the know don't believe that Schumacher will give his all for Irvine. He messes up his start and Hakkinen leads from start to finish. At the decisive moment, the Finn has what it takes – no problems, no bad luck. 'Why,' he sighs afterwards, 'wasn't it like this all year?' Maybe Hakkinen needs Schumacher as a point of reference as well, maybe he's better with Schumacher than without.

Ferrari takes the constructor's title, but that's cold comfort for the *tifosi* who have turned out in the early hours of the morning to watch the race on big TV screens all over Italy. For the third year running, they've seen their dream go up in smoke in the last race of the season.

Happiness. It goes right through my heart, my lungs and my intestines when a Ferrari V10 starts up in the distance, that first roar followed by quick impatient shrieks. Hooters go off *en masse* on the pile of sand opposite the pits. My son and I are on top of a dune next to Slotemaker Corner. 'Here he comes, now we'll get some real noise.'

The Ferrari storms out of the pits. We hear it taking the Tarzan, Gerlach Corner, Hugenholtz and then up Hunzerug, here he comes! We recognise the red-and-orange helmet: Michael Schumacher. The Ferrari curves past in front of us. The sound cuts through your body – pain, everywhere at once. Schumacher sweeps into Scheivlak and disappears.

Behind the dunes he races on. Through Marlboro Corner, heading away from the place where I once stood at the fence as an eleven-year-old boy, the place where Roger Williamson . . .

But here comes Schumacher again, that's what's so good about this spot, you can see the cars going past on the other side as well, on their way to Nissan Corner. From there Mitsubishi and Bos-uit take them to the straight. We hear the Ferrari racing past the pits at full speed. A few seconds later it reappears again at the top of the Hunzerug, an imposing sight.

My son cheers when the Ferrari passes by in front of us. He chose Ferrari three years ago – 'The red one! The red one's in it as well!' – later I told him that the driver's name was Schumacher. He cried when Schumacher went off the track at Jerez in '97, he could hardly believe it when Schumacher stalled his Ferrari at Suzuka in '98. 'He'll be back, won't he?' he asked in dismay after Silverstone last year. He knows I don't cheer with him, that I'm an inveterate Hill fan. But Suzuka '99 was Damon Hill's last race. He's given up. Fortunately, because the whole season was a fiasco. He simply couldn't win a thing, his motivation was gone. As far as Formula One was concerned, Hill's motto 'exhilaration through acceleration' was exhausted. 'Who are you for now?' my son asks occasionally. I don't know. Sometimes I pick a favourite for the day, Villeneuve, Trulli. For the time being, I have to get by without a hero.

The Ferrari approaches again. I notice my son slowly descending the hill, following a narrow path between the spectators, heading for the fence. I don't call him back. I know what he's doing. He wants to see the Ferrari from as close as possible, to feel it, almost touch it. Here it comes again, hurtling over the Hunzerug, you feel the suspension letting it go, then pulling it back, it's coming past nice and close to the fence and the barrier, curving beautifully into the uphill right-hander, the Scheivlak.

Towards the end of the demonstration I walk downhill, too. Schumacher passes for the last time, waving to his fans. Next to each other, we lean against the mesh fence.

'It was really him, wasn't it?'

'Yes.'

'And now the championship.'

A Flying Start

Hmmm, the championship . . . It all began so perfectly. For the first three races it looked like McLaren still had the quicker car at their disposal but, more than ever before, Ferrari were breathing down their neck and outdoing them in reliability and clever racing strategies. Schumacher won three out of three – Hakkinen dropped out twice with engine failure and was simply beaten in the other race: at Imola a cunning pit-stop strategy gave Schumacher the victory.

That was how to do it, Schumacher had always said. Get in there right from the start, put the pressure on McLaren and Hakkinen. And it was soon clear that the Finn didn't like this at all. 'The pressure to constantly win is hell,' he admitted. 'Hakkinen is getting bored', according to sniping journalists, 'he's lost his hunger.' Niki Lauda was convinced that a change of teams was desperately needed. Some journos even wrote that 'Mika should get his nose out of those brochures for nursery furniture'. It was true that Hakkinen had become a father, but that had nothing to do with his weak run. Still, things weren't coming together. It was up to Coulthard to resist Ferrari's dominance.

Coulthard smells his chance. He drives more forcefully and more consistently than in previous years and calls a halt to Ferrari's advance by winning in England. He triumphs again in Monte Carlo. Patiently Coulthard waits behind Trulli until he's forced to retire, and then, when Schumacher has to withdraw because of mechanical failures as well, victory falls into Coulthard's lap. 'I don't feel sorry for Michael at all,' declares the winner. 'I have had more than my fair share of reliability problems. I think it was time for him to have some problems, too . . .'

Amateur psychologists explain that the Scot has become stronger after narrowly surviving a plane crash in the spring. After Monaco Coulthard declares, 'This year I'm going for the title!' but Ron Dennis remains calm: 'Nothing's decided yet.' Schumacher knows the Scot's weak spot and shoots a poisoned barb at McLaren: 'Obviously I am disappointed but not too much. It's true I could have picked up ten points today, but the driver I consider my main rival could also have done so.' The hostility between Schumacher and Coulthard refuses to lie down. Undoubtedly this goes back to the 1998 crash at Spa-Francorchamps. Asked to comment on Schumacher's jibes, Coulthard answers, 'Unfortunately I'm not intelligent enough to understand it all.' Hakkinen remains aloof from the squabbling – 'a waste of energy'. With reactions like these the Finn cuts a somewhat bland figure, even Ron Dennis admits as much: 'Away from his car, Mika is not at his best. He's not a good communicator. But you win world championships on the track.'

Schumacher knows that, too. In Canada the McLaren mechanics don't get Coulthard's car ready in time for the warm-up lap: stop-go penalty, race lost. Hakkinen muddles along in the middle of the field, especially once it starts to rain. And Schumacher wins. Behind him Barrichello is faster, but Barrichello obeys team orders. Still, the hero of the race is Jos Verstappen. Jos is back in Formula One. After the disappointing years with Tyrrell, Jos's Grand Prix career seemed over. Until 1998, when he came out for Stewart for half a season. But Jackie Stewart's all too paternal concern didn't suit Jos, and once again Jos seemed condemned to the sidelines. But at the start of 2000 he suddenly reappeared, 'The Houdini of Formula One', according to Dutch headlines. Jos returned to Arrows and, in the wet at Montreal, he showed his stuff: quick and pugnacious. Wurz – no easy opponent – and Trulli – in a potentially faster car – were pushed aside mercilessly and, for the first time since Argentina '96, Jos scored world championship points.

The 2000 season is long and frenetic: from the start of March to the end of October a Grand Prix is held every two weeks. Halfway through, Schumacher – 22 points ahead of Coulthard and 24 ahead of Hakkinen – has a comfortable lead. But then – as if it could be any other way – the controversies and incidents begin.

In France Schumacher has another one of the poor starts that have dogged him this season, but immediately swerves across the track to cut off his opponents. Coulthard has to lift off to avoid hitting the Ferrari. Schumacher did the same thing at Imola, and at Magny-Cours he also hogs the track when Coulthard tries to overtake him. Coulthard is furious: 'I just don't think that Michael is sporting in the way he drives on the track. There are set rules governing the way you drive on the track, and to try to drive an opponent off the road is not within those rules. We all know very well whether something is acceptable or not. As drivers, we have to be able to trust each other. After all, we're risking our lives on the track.' It leaves Schumacher cold: 'I simply defend my line. Coulthard's whingeing, he's always trying to blacken my name.'

But Coulthard isn't the only driver who's noticed Schumacher's starting manoeuvres. Irvine in particular finds it hard to take: 'Schumacher is a bully! Someone should teach him a lesson. Next time, if I were Coulthard, I wouldn't lift off, instead I'd give him a taste of his own medicine.' Villeneuve gets involved as well: 'These things do bother me. There's not many people doing such things. It seems there's just one guy doing it and he always gets away with it, so why should he stop?' It all goes way back. Schumacher acts as if he doesn't understand what all the fuss is about: 'This is Formula One, isn't it? We get together to race each other, not for a tea party!'

But in Austria Schumacher is again the centre point of a controversial start. On the first corner he gets hit by Zonta, after which several cars collide. Schumacher tries to force a restart by letting his car roll back on to the track, but the marshals quickly push him out of harm's way. 'Zonta overestimated his speed and his ability, not deliberately, but I'm sure he will admit his error,' explains Schumacher in the pits, but Zonta and Trulli don't quite see it that way. According to them, the Ferraris made a mess of the corner because Barrichello was in such a hurry to make room for Schumacher. Coulthard's interpretation is crystal clear: 'I didn't see a thing, but I am certain that it was Schumacher's fault.'

In Germany the whole motordrome holds its breath as the red

lights go off. Coulthard and Schumacher are alongside each other in the front row. Schumacher has another bad start and Coulthard decides to give the German a taste of his own medicine. He shoots over to the left and Hakkinen, who has started brilliantly, races past on the right, boxing in Schumacher. Even worse: the German moves over so far that he doesn't leave room for Fisichella. The Ferrari and the Benetton hit and slide straight ahead into the gravel: race over. At the end of the pit lane, the two drivers have a long discussion about who was at fault. The stewards put it down as a 'racing accident', but Fisichella points out simply that he wasn't the one who deviated from his line.

McLaren is on course for their third consecutive double victory. In the rear of the field, Barrichello and Frentzen cause an uproar by coming from behind to overtake car after car on their way to fourth and sixth, but the front-runners have built up too much of a lead. Until suddenly, somewhere in the woods, a man in a plastic poncho pops out on to the track. A madman among racing cars doing over 300 km/h . . . The stewards call out the Safety Car and the lunatic is apprehended. It turns out he wanted to protest his dismissal by Mercedes! If nothing else, he has cost his former employer the victory, because now that the two McLarens have lost their comfortable lead, it starts to rain. With ten laps left to go, Hakkinen isn't taking any chances and goes in for rain tyres. Coulthard follows a few laps later. This gives the lead to Barrichello who, ignoring the advice of his team, decides to stay out.

Ten frightening laps. But the McLarens hardly draw closer at all. Barrichello defies the wet, like Senna at his best. Magic. In the style with which his friend and idol once won his most beautiful races, Barrichello is on his way to his first Grand Prix victory. No one begrudges the little Brazilian his moment. While the over-familiar melody of the Brazilian national anthem booms out over the podium, Barrichello jiggles the Brazilian flag and weeps openly. Every Formula One fan feels the proximity of Ayrton Senna. Senna, who once stood by Barrichello's hospital bed in tears, after he had crashed heavily as a harbinger of that dramatic weekend at Imola. 'He changed my life,' relates Barrichello afterwards. 'I think he definitely heard me today.' With a lump in my throat, I try to explain Senna to my son: the one with the yellow helmet, who was always very good, almost always the fastest at practice, he drove like that in the wet too, and shot off the track before you were even six months old . . . and I realise that Formula One is so much more than ruthless business and high-tech speed.

A week after Hockenheim, Schumacher is driving through the dunes at Zandvoort for an elated and grateful crowd. But a few jokers have hung up a banner at the top of the Tarzan: *Achtung Starkurve!* In the last two races he hasn't got further than the first corner. Schumacher seems to have lost his way and Hakkinen is drawing closer. Will the title slip through Schumacher's fingers for the fourth time in a row? When he comes down the Hunzerug on his way to Slotemaker Corner on a final lap of honour, flanked by a rally car and a motorbike, I want to call out to him: 'Hey, Schumi, just do it for my son, OK? Him here, with his V cap on and tired out from a long day's waiting, his face sticky from all those ice creams . . . For God's sake, do it for him . . .'

Tears at Monza

But things get even worse. In Hungary it's Hakkinen and Schumacher who charge into the first corner, wheel to wheel. Hakkinen a nose behind Schumacher, but on the inside. Schumacher forces Hakkinen right over to the side, but the Finn keeps pushing his McLaren, a crash is imminent. Until Schumacher very obviously makes room and Hakkinen slips through on the inside. This is a very different Schumacher, but for the first time in three races he's made it past the first corner and that's what counts. The only thing is, overtaking on the Hungaroring is even more difficult than it is in Monaco, so Hakkinen wins and takes the lead in the championship.

The next race is Spa-Francorchamps. Four-time winner Schumacher is one of the indisputable Kings of Spa, but in 2000 he's the one who has to bow. He has to bow to Hakkinen. And low. For a long time Hakkinen leads the race fairly comfortably. But in the twelfth lap he spins near Stavelot for no apparent reason. Bad luck. Schumacher shoots past. Now he's the one who leads the dance, but eventually, after the second pit stop, Hakkinen starts to haul him in. Lap after lap Schumacher's lead diminishes. The McLaren is quicker, but in Formula One catching an opponent and overtaking him are two very different things. With just six laps to go, Hakkinen is up under the rear wing of the Ferrari. Through La Source, downhill, almost full speed through Eau Rouge, uphill, over the Kemmel, 280, 330. Suddenly Hakkinen darts out from behind the Ferrari, but Schumacher reacts instantly, slamming the door and turning into Les Combes ahead of Hakkinen. The whole Formula One world holds its breath, everyone knows what's at stake, everyone knows about Schumacher's ruthless racing tactics. Once he managed to keep Damon Hill behind him lap after lap, weaving over the Kemmel. Hakkinen approaches again. With four laps to go, the two cars roar up Eau Rouge once again. Again Hakkinen has slipped in under Schumacher's wing. In front of them, Ricardo Zonta. Zonta looks in his mirrors, later he admits that he had no idea that Hakkinen was anywhere in the vicinity. Les Combes ahead, Zonta driving in the middle of the track. There's more room on the left, Schumacher chooses left and in the same instant, Hakkinen dives out from behind him and takes right. A question of millimetres. Hakkinen goes over the grass with two wheels, but manages to turn his McLaren into Les Combes just in front of Schumacher and Zonta. Brilliant. Risky. If Zonta had moved just a centimetre over to the right . . .

Schumacher was beaten. Hakkinen's hat trick almost seemed a foregone conclusion and the press couldn't stop talking about Spa. The best overtaking manoeuvre of the year, of the decade, in Formula One's entire history. The superlatives gushed. And all over the world, the same question was posed: who was actually the best, Hakkinen or Schumacher? Just a few races earlier it would have been inconceivable, but three titles in a row, that was something that only Fangio had ever managed – even if he immediately went on to his fourth.

Three consecutive races without scoring, then defeated twice in one-on-one duels by their greatest rival. The pressure was back on Ferrari. And on Schumacher, and the next race was in Italy, at Monza. But Ferrari comes back. Schumacher and Barrichello take the front row of the grid. This will be the race of truth, it's in the air.

They negotiate the start and the feared first chicane flawlessly. Only a handful of cars are forced on to the grass. Salo and Irvine collide, sending Irvine on a spectacular detour through a polystyrene roadblock. At that same moment Schumacher is already taking the Curva Grande in front of the two McLarens, with Barrichello between the two Jordans. Ten seconds later it is complete havoc. Approaching the Roggia chicane, speed approximately 330 km/h, Barrichello moves left in an attempt to outbrake Trulli. Frentzen immediately takes Barrichello's line. Later Barrichello blames Frentzen: he braked much too late. Frentzen blames Barrichello: he braked too soon. The stewards just put it down as a racing accident. And what an accident! Frentzen hits the back of team-mate Trulli. Both Jordans turn sideways, Frentzen hits Barrichello, Trulli takes out Coulthard. And behind them the entire field storms closer. In the mêlée of braking and dodging cars, dust and components, Pedro de la Rosa runs into the back of Johnny Herbert's Jaguar. The Arrows takes off, cartwheels four times through the gravel and slams down next to Barrichello's Ferrari. Everyone seems to have come through unscathed yet again, but then it turns out that a marshal on the left of the track has been hit by a wheel launched from Frentzen's Jordan. Thirty-year-old Paolo Ghislimberti dies in hospital soon after the race. A terrible drama. The drivers express their sympathy and pass the hat around. Calls go up for better protection for marshals. Nothing changes.

The Safety Car is out on the track for eleven laps. Afterwards Schumacher dictates the race. Hakkinen chases him for forty-one laps but is unable to mount a real challenge.

Immense euphoria erupts as a victorious Schumacher tears across the finishing line. Tens of thousands of *tifosi* storm the track. In the *parc fermé*, Schumacher looks happier than ever as he embraces his mechanics. On the podium too he seems beside himself, eye to eye with jubilant masses, flags and banners, bonfires. Monza, Ferrari. The myth. There's nothing like it. It's not just the dead that elevate Formula One above sport and business, here it is almost a religion . . .

The tide has turned and Schumacher knows it. He stays up on the podium even longer than usual, sprays some more champagne over his crew and the fans crowding up behind them, then heads off to the press conference.

Most after-race press conferences are obligatory affairs full of banal, standard phrases. But when the questioner follows his congratulations by asking Schumacher how he feels now that his forty-one Grand Prix victories have brought him up to the same tally as Ayrton Senna, the ever-cheerful, unflappable German suddenly caves in and weeps uncontrollably. All over the world, dumbfounded Formula One fans stare at their TV screens: there's that fifteen-year-old kid again, everyone had forgotten all about him.

'It was too much for me,' explained Schumacher afterwards, 'the euphoria mixed with my own memories of the death of Senna. I'm only human.' Hakkinen and Schumacher's brother Ralf lay their hands on his shoulders. Hakkinen doesn't want to speak either, and like a robot – 'this is live television' – the interviewer turns to Ralf, who delivers a standard spiel alongside his still-sobbing brother.

It was the pressure. The pressure of five years of work, of four years of fighting for the championship, of five lost races in a row. Schumacher knew he had stopped McLaren's roll, he knew that the title was within reach again, and all that on the hallowed ground of

Monza. Stopping to think for a moment after all the adrenalin and euphoria, he realised that he was on the verge of becoming an absolute legend, comparable only to greats like Fangio, Senna and Prost.

2000 Finale

The last three races of 2000 were held outside Europe: Indianapolis, Suzuka, Kuala Lumpur. For the first time since 1991, the Formula One circus visited the United States of America. And straight to the heart: the Indianapolis Motor Speedway. In the 1950s, the Indy 500 still counted towards the Formula One world championship – explaining the presence of all kinds of highly obscure Americans in the most comprehensive Formula One statistics – but the race was always the odd man out. The parting of the ways came in 1960, and since then CART (Championship Auto Racing Teams) and Formula One have been separate worlds. Ignoring the disapproval of CART traditionalists, circuit director Tony George opened the Motor Speedway to other classes of racing in the 1990s, paving the way for Formula One as well. A new circuit was built, leading partly over the oval and partly through the infield. The infield section is winding and slow, the oval section is fast: a wide slightly banked bend and a long straight, together some 1.8 kilometres, in other words twenty-one seconds, flat out. That sloping bend in particular inspired dread: would the tyres stand up to it, and what about the suspension? 320 km/h was terrifyingly fast to be skimming past a concrete wall. 'Fast,' sneered Villeneuve, 'what's fast? During the Indy 500 you take it at 380 km/h. That's fast.' But after the first practice sessions, most drivers were disappointed in Turn 13. Schumacher: 'It's more exciting from the outside than it is from in the cockpit. It's too slow.' And Frentzen: 'You could do it with one hand on the wheel . . .'

In an unrivalled setting and with 250,000 people on packed stands in the oval section, the race begins with Coulthard jumping the start. Instead of watching the lights, the Scot counts down to himself and shoots off too early. By doing so he does succeed in taking the lead from Schumacher. With a stop-go penalty coming, Coulthard starts blocking Schumacher to allow Hakkinen to get closer. Impatiently Schumacher opts for a daring overtaking manoeuvre. At the end of the flat-out section, Schumacher comes up on the outside next to the McLaren. Both drivers brake late for the right-left combination that follows. Coulthard forces the Ferrari to the outside, the cars touch, but Schumacher maintains enough speed for the left-hander and takes the lead. 'Coulthard knew he would get a penalty, everything he did was on the limit again. He wasn't driving, let me put it this way, a particularly tight line. A crash was in the air', according to Schumacher. Coulthard disagreed. 'Nonsense, I could have pushed him off like that if I'd wanted to.'

After Coulthard has sat out his penalty, Schumacher seems set to dominate the whole race until Hakkinen suddenly gets closer. Hakkinen is quicker, each lap shaves a few tenths of a second off Schumacher's lead. The fans are already getting nervous, everyone's thinking of the duel at Spa-Francorchamps. But suddenly it's over. With smoke, and even flames, coming out of his engine, Hakkinen rolls down the pit lane. It's been a long time since the Mercedes broke down, but this is a crucial moment. With relative ease Schumacher and Barrichello drive out the race to score a double victory. Even if everyone's heart misses a beat along the way when Schumacher goes on to the grass of the infield with his right front wheel and spins. A lapse of concentration. But Schumacher is lucky: he is able to keep going and is rewarded with an eight-point lead in the world championship.

Even if Hakkinen wins the following two races, two second places will still secure the title for Schumacher. But before the Japanese Grand Prix, Schumacher, grown wise through too many disappointments, states that he would prefer not to let it come down to the last race. Hakkinen is determined to go all out. Asked about his battle plan, the Finn answers: 'Brake three metres later for each corner.' Schumacher's response is immediate: 'Then I'll brake five metres later.' Hakkinen: 'See you in the gravel.' No trace of a dirty war, and as the rivals take up position next to each other in the front row in Japan for the third year running, no one is thinking of Suzuka 1990. Again Schumacher has a mediocre start. And again he veers over to the right, forcing Hakkinen to the side of the track, but the Finn knows he has more speed, doesn't give in and takes the lead. A furious race begins. They make it look easy, but Schumacher and Hakkinen are harrying each other into producing razor-sharp lap times. It's a matter of tenths of seconds – clever, faultless pit stops and quickly passing the back markers. Both Schumacher and Hakkinen have opted for two stops. After the first series, Hakkinen holds on to the lead by 2.4 seconds. But then he has problems with some back markers and it starts to drizzle as well. Ideal conditions for Schumacher. In the thirty-seventh lap Hakkinen stops for the second time and Schumacher knows that he can stay out for another three laps: it's now or never. And while Hakkinen struggles on the wet track with a heavy fuel tank and new tyres, Schumacher clocks up a few super-fast laps before pitting. Eighteen men around the car. Tyres off, on. Refuelling. Meanwhile Hakkinen sails through the 130R on his way to the chicane. Schumacher is stationary for six seconds. Driving off, he shouts into the radio, 'Tell me where Mika is!' And crawling through the pit lane with the revs limiter on, he hears Ross Brawn's voice inside his helmet, 'It's looking good . . . it's looking good . . .' Schumacher still doesn't trust it. But as he drives out of the pit lane, Brawn shouts: 'It's looking damn good!' Then Schumacher sees Hakkinen in his mirrors on the straight and he knows he has the title. 'Also,' explains Schumacher later, 'because Ross let me go on used tyres, I immediately had more grip, Mika couldn't do a thing.' Thirteen more laps. But the Ferrari F1-2000 can't break down now. Ferrari can't lose it now. 'Reliability has been the key this season,' admit Mercedes. 'Mika's engine failure at the start of the season and in

Indianapolis cost him the title. But it's still 2:1 our way and we'll be back next year.'

It's a glorious moment when Schumacher thunders across the line to claim the title. The mechanics are in tears, Jean Todt is in tears and, inside his car, Schumacher is in tears. World champion. After five years. Losing twice on the brink and almost killed once. Now the championship is his.

Ferrari has had to wait twenty-one years for this moment. Jody Scheckter can laugh about it: 'Of course all those times Michael blew the championship, I celebrated with a glass of champagne. Being the last Ferrari champion has given me a lot of success with the girls. Now I have to come up with a new intro.' Alain Prost doesn't take it quite so lightly: 'With the same management and the same organisation they have today, I would have won this title in 1990,' he asserts. 'I lost it only because of political comments, strange decisions, political reasons.' Poor Alain, always the bad loser. And he knows that Schumacher is on the verge of leaving him behind in other areas as well. If Schumacher wins in Malaysia (and he does), he will be just eight Grand Prix victories away from Prost's record of fifty-one. And that fourth title will come as well.

Hakkinen shows himself a much better loser. 'Michael deserves this title. Moaning about tactics, start manoeuvres and mechanical failures would only detract from his success. I don't begrudge him his happiness, that's the way it should be with top sportsmen.' 'Mika is the fairest and most likeable adversary I have encountered,' responds Schumacher, 'and the strongest.'

'I feel just like I did at Monza,' Schumacher explains when asked about his emotions, 'but this time I won't burst into tears. This championship can't be compared to 1994 and 1995. I've worked five years for this. And with all due respect, Benetton is not Ferrari. Ferrari has a much more impressive history than Benetton. This title means much more to me. It is an indescribable feeling. Especially when I think about everything that's happening in Italy right now.'

Schumacher has heard about the reaction in Maranello over the phone. Ferrari chairman Luca di Montezemolo has not travelled to Japan 'to avoid bringing bad luck'. Now he's shouting into the telephone. 'I'm calling right away,' Di Montezemolo yells, 'because in half an hour I'll be too drunk!' Fifteen thousand *Ferraristi* have watched the race on an enormous TV screen in Maranello's Piazza Liberta, some of them employees appointed by Enzo Ferrari himself. The euphoria is overwhelming. The bells ring, the local cellars hand out Rosso di Maranello.

At last Ferrari has triumphed in the digital techno and business era. The myth lives on, but in a new form. 'Is this the most beautiful moment of your life?' someone asks Di Montezemolo. 'Come on now, I'm a father too, you know . . .'

In the kitchen my son is eating a late breakfast. His V cap next to his bowl. He never expected anything less.

Supremacy: 2001

With the title won at last and the enormous pressure off, there was really only one question left in 2001: who would be capable of beating Schumacher in the seasons to come? 'I haven't had enough for the time being,' declared the German. 'I want to continue to dominate.' And dominate he did. In 2001 Schumacher was in his element. He underlined his rule by claiming a fourth world championship; scoring a record number of points in one season – 123; finishing with the biggest lead ever over the number two; equalling the record for victories in a season – nine; and, much more importantly, at Spa, exactly ten years after his Formula One debut, winning his fifty-second Grand Prix, passing Alain Prost in both all-time ratings *and* total world-championship points: Schumacher 801, Prost 798. Only two records were left unconquered: the number of pole positions: Senna has sixty-five compared to Schumacher's forty-three by the end of 2001 – that seems safe – and the number of world championships: Fangio scored five, but Schumacher will definitely come up alongside and probably leave him behind as well. Who's going to stop him?

Even before the summer of 2001, Schumacher had drawn the thickest line of all under his sovereignty: for an annual salary of some 30 million dollars, he extended his contract with Ferrari until the end of 2004. Until then at least, everyone else in Formula One will have to deal with Michael Schumacher.

His secret? Seemingly elusive. Prost was calculating and smarter than the rest, Senna had his mystical obsession and was quicker than the rest, but Schumacher? Schumacher has it all. Driven by tremendous willpower, he has an enormous talent for organisation. Schumacher is anything but a pampered prima donna. His attention to detail seldom lapses, he inspires the whole team but demands the right people in the right place. Add to that his tactical acumen. He knows exactly when he needs to go fast and then he goes all the way to the limit. And yes, there's his incomparable control. You can't miss it: when Schumacher puts his foot down, he drags his car around the circuit, the Ferrari swings tightly through the big sweepers and on the other corners it's just that little bit more aggressive, throwing up an extra tuft of grass or a bigger cloud of sand . . . Schumacher is simply the best.

In 2001 his dominance was so great that even the scandals and controversies were kept to a minimum. It won't stay that way. A new confrontation is in the air, the fans have already caught wind of it.

On the way to his fourth title, no one was really able to defeat Schumacher. McLaren, the company with the advantage of Hakkinen's raw speed, lost the campaign right at the start of the season. In Australia and Malaysia, McLaren were clearly too slow. In Brazil Hakkinen came to a standstill right after the start. In Spain it was even worse: after leading for almost the entire race, Hakkinen broke down in the final lap. When he got no further than the grid in Austria as well, the Finn had had enough. Hakkinen decided that he wanted time to enjoy fatherhood and began secretly negotiating a year's sabbatical with Ron Dennis.

It's an opportunity for Coulthard, who begins by scoring points and even wins in Brazil, but in Spain it's his turn to stall. McLaren just can't get going in 2001.

From the Spanish Grand Prix on, electronic aids are again allowed in Formula One. After years of being helpless in the face of electronic skulduggery, the FIA has decided to scrap all restrictions. Traction control, which maximises engine output without allowing the wheels to slip, is loathed by almost all drivers and fans. Niki Lauda boldly asserts that with traction control even a monkey could drive a Formula One car. Schumacher's assessment is milder; in fact, he's happy about the changes: 'Traction control makes it possible to drive more precisely, I like that.'

More problematic is the launch control, the electronic system regulating the start. Many drivers are left stranded on the grid. Among them, David Coulthard. Team boss Dennis is quick to judge: 'I am afraid to say that David had a bit of a brain fade on his part.' Coulthard's angry response: 'I think Ron has suffered a brain fade. He has not spoken to me or to my engineers yet.'

Relationships within McLaren are immediately strained. Coulthard manages to hit back with a victory in Austria, but in Monaco he wastes his crucial pole position by again failing to get the McLaren started in time. A reckless chase is finally thwarted by the Arrows of newcomer Enrique Bernoldi. For thirty-five laps, Coulthard is unable to get past the Brazilian. Of course, overtaking is impossible in Monte Carlo, but if you want the championship, you have to do it. Coulthard is no killer, and after Monaco things go completely downhill. In the next six races he scores just eleven points. In the end Coulthard finishes the season second with 68 points, a little over half of Schumacher's 123 . . .

Williams puts up more of a fight. But Williams still haven't solved their reliability problems, and in their first year with Michelin tyres, performance is not yet optimal. What's more, the rest of the field still has to get used to the power of their BMW engines. It seems as though the enormous straight-line speed requires an unusually long braking distance. In Australia Ralf Schumacher is hit from behind by Jacques Villeneuve in one of the season's most hair-raising crashes. Using the Williams's left rear wheel as a launching pad, the BAR takes off, spins high in the air, scrapes along the wire fence – sending debris hurtling into the crowd – flips over, and lands in a gravel trap. Villeneuve climbs out unharmed, but a wheel has flown through a hole in the fence and hit a marshal in the chest. He dies on the way to the hospital. The second dead marshal in five races. Safety must be improved, everyone agrees, but a much worse crash will need to happen before something is finally done about it.

In the next race, Ralf is rammed again, this time by Barrichello, and in Brazil it happens again. In that same race his team-mate, Montoya, falls victim as well. Just when he, in his third Grand Prix, has been dictating the race, lap after lap.

Montoya – insiders know him from Indycars, but in Brazil he gives the Formula One fans something to think about as well. In the third lap, after a short Safety Car period, Montoya uses the BMW power to his advantage. On the straight he tucks in behind the leader, Michael Schumacher, then cold-bloodedly puts his car alongside the Ferrari in the Curva del Sol, forcing Schumacher all the way to the outside of the track – not off it – and slipping through on the inside himself. Everyone is enthusiastic: at last, a driver who dares to use his elbows on Schumacher. Unfortunately Montoya is unlucky. Halfway through the race, he laps Jos Verstappen. A simple procedure: Jos moves over going into a left-hander, Montoya goes past and Jos can come up behind him again as they brake for the corner. But then it goes wrong. Suddenly Jos slams into Montoya's rear wing, briefly mounting the back of the Williams before both cars spin helplessly off the track. Race over. Montoya is disappointed, but doesn't blame Jos: racing accident. The FIA penalises Jos with a hefty fine anyway. Jos is furious, but Arrows let it slide. For the next race, Williams places a warning on the rear wing: 'Keep your distance!'

And it works. Ralf scores his first Grand Prix victory. The first for Williams in three years. At Imola, Ralf is in a class of his own and leads from start to finish, proving that for now he is more experienced and a more complete Formula One driver than Montoya. In Canada too Ralf demonstrates how much the erstwhile tearaway has changed: for half the race he seems stuck behind his big brother, but a delayed pit stop allows him to come back out in front of the Ferrari. 'I knew I was on more fuel and therefore quicker, I just needed to be patient.' At Williams Ralf has matured into a winner: hard, quick and clever. In 2001 he also demands his own chief engineer, someone he can work perfectly with – organisational talent runs in the family. Williams immediately extends Ralf's contract until 2004 for 14 million dollars a year, more than his brother Michael was earning at the same age! 'Ralf is a champion,' observes his big brother, 'if I ever decide to retire, he can take over.'

Big brother. His place in the family is Ralf's only handicap. But what a handicap: no matter what he does, he'll always be '*der Kleine*', six years younger than the brilliant older brother who paves the way in everything he does. That goes deep. When Ralf wins, Michael is the first to congratulate him. Patting him on the helmet, on the shoulder, compliments – well done, kid, big brother is proud of you. It's not like that the other way round. And in Michael's reflections about his succession, it's clear that Ralf inherits the crown when he retires, not before.

Even worse for Ralf, their relationship is like that on the track too. At the start of the European Grand Prix, in Germany, the Schumis share front row. Michael on pole. But Ralf has the better start. Immediately, however, Michael slants across the grid in one of his controversial diagonal manoeuvres, pushing his brother towards the pit wall. Ralf lifts off to avoid a crash, and Michael takes the lead. Again, later in the race, when Michael goes too wide in the Dunlop hairpin, Ralf has a chance to get past on the inside, but Michael blocks him ruthlessly, forcing Ralf on to the grass with two wheels. Afterwards Ralf is angry and refuses to congratulate Michael. When he has calmed down, he explains away the incident at the start: 'Can't be helped, in Michael's position I would have done the same.' Probably not. With any other driver he would have done the same, but not with his big brother. Big brother, the only person he can't compete with. That was decided long ago. That's why

Montoya, quite possibly a lesser driver than Ralf, is still the only one who can take on Michael Schumacher.

Montoya would not have lifted off. In Austria he shows that he has no intention of allowing Schumacher to intimidate him. It's the sixteenth lap, Montoya is leading, but Schumacher is faster this time and wants to get past. Well ahead of the second corner, Schumacher comes alongside on the left; wheel to wheel, they race into the sharp right-hander. Braking late, Montoya *too* late. The Williams keeps going straight ahead, sliding, but the Ferrari has no choice and has to go with it on the outside. Schumacher brakes and goes over the grass while Montoya jolts through the gravel. By the time they make it back on to the track they've fallen back to sixth and seventh. Schumacher is furious: 'There was no way he could make that corner and all he was trying to do was take me with him.' Montoya is unimpressed: 'I just defended myself, we both missed the corner. Surely it can't be that he just needs to say, "Hey, I'm Michael, so let me go by."'

Montoya manages to anger other drivers as well. Irvine accuses him of dangerous driving during practice, and Villeneuve criticises him as well. The envy of speed demons on the wane. When Montoya taunts Villeneuve with the shunt in Australia during an altercation, they even come to blows. Montoya obviously has what it takes. In Monza he grabs his first victory, and in Indianapolis he comes up with an unexpected overtaking manoeuvre to demonstrate yet again that Schumacher is not invincible.

Formula One needs fresh blood – Eddie Jordan is convinced of that – young drivers who can beat Schumacher. Jordan obviously suspects talented drivers like Trulli, Frentzen, Fisichella, Barrichello and even Coulthard of having resigned themselves, albeit subconsciously, to the German's supremacy. Perhaps that's why Formula One is being flooded with youngsters. Since Jenson Button's dream debut in 2000 – before the season Button's eligibility for a super licence was doubtful and the FIA forced him to take a driving test, but by Spa people at Williams were already comparing him to Alain

Prost – cradle snatching has been all the rage. Sauber came up with Kimi Raikkonen, Benetton scored Alonso and immediately lent him out to Minardi, and Arrows have Bernoldi.

The arrival of Bernoldi demonstrated that talent and experience have become side issues in Formula One and that contracts are virtually meaningless: you only sign them with a view to the buy-out fees. Arrows were so keen to acquire Bernoldi's financial backing that they immediately dumped De la Rosa – after months of faithful service. Prost knew that a driver like De la Rosa was too good to leave out in the cold, but Niki Lauda, the new helmsman at Jaguar, snapped him up first, callously dumping Luciano Burti to make room. Burti was able to start right away with Prost, because now that Mazzacane had delivered *his* sponsor, he could make himself scarce. Things are no more genteel further up the grid. After the British Grand Prix, Frentzen received a short, sharp fax stating that Jordan no longer required his services. Frentzen switched to Prost, whose 'great friend' Alesi could suddenly relocate to his 'great friend' Jordan. These were Alesi's last five Grands Prix. In Indianapolis he drove his 200th, but then had to cede his place to the talented Japanese Sato. His friend Jordan needed to think of his future with Honda.

With Prost, Frentzen immediately shows that he is still quick. At Spa he puts the substandard car in fourth place on the grid. But at the start, he stalls and has to move to the back for the restart. Belgium is not going Prost's way at all because, just a few laps later, people are fearing for Burti's life.

In Germany Burti had already had one of the season's most spectacular shunts. At the start at Hockenheim, Schumacher's Ferrari stops after just a few metres. Cars shoot by left and right, only Burti fails to avoid the Ferrari and rams it at some 200 km/h. Catapulted up into the air, his Prost cartwheels and lands on its rear on the asphalt just between the two Arrows. A wheel slams down on to Bernoldi's car, and Burti slides off the track into the tyre barrier. The Brazilian is unharmed, to the point of even managing a restart, but ends up in the same tyres twenty-four laps later after losing control because of the pain. At Spa things look much worse. Coming out of Stavelot, Burti starts an overtaking manoeuvre on Irvine. Overtaking on Blanchimont, at around 300 km/h – impossible and highly dangerous. Undeterred, Burti pushes his Prost up alongside the Jaguar. Irvine doesn't flinch and when the gentle left-hander comes, there's no room left for Burti. He's forced on to the grass, the cars touch and slide hopelessly into the gravel. Irvine spins and stops with a bang, but Burti loses his front wing and jolts straight ahead over the stones before slamming into a four-deep tyre wall. The impact is enormous. A wave of tyres rises metres in the air. When the dust clears, the car is embedded past the cockpit. Everyone watches the images with dismay: the replay, the impact. The red flag is already out. When the tyres are lifted, they reveal a glimpse of the driver, slumped forward in the cockpit . . . Everyone fears the worst. Spa and its merciless speed and surroundings, but maybe things have turned out well after all . . . News dribbles in: Irvine has told Lauda over the radio that Burti is conscious and can move everything. And in the end, it does turn out well. Badly bruised and slightly concussed, Burti is admitted to hospital for observation. The race is resumed.

Briefly it was back again, the absolute danger of motor racing, but the fear that cut to the bone soon made way for paeans to the safety of modern Formula One. Not untrue, but one smash could end it all. In 2001 that was shown outside of Formula One. In America the NASCAR (National Association of Stock Car Auto Racing) legend Dale Earnhardt died after a hard but relatively innocent collision. On the Lausitzring Michele Alboreto died when his Audi got a blowout, took off and landed on top of the barrier. Formula One too mourned the loss of the gentleman racer. Months later, on that same Lausitzring, during Europe's first Indycar race, Alex Zanardi's car was sliced clean in two when he went into a spin coming out of the pit lane. Zanardi survived – just – but has to go through life as a double amputee.

Off the tracks, more legends died. The 'Monza gorilla', Vittorio Brambilla, died of a heart attack while gardening. The fans will never forget his lap of honour in his badly dented March in the 1975 Austrian Grand Prix, the only race he ever won. Sports-car hero Bob Wollek (fifty-seven years old and thirty starts at Le Mans) died after qualifying for the twelve-hour race on the Sebring – he was hit by a truck while out cycling. Ken Tyrrell, 'Uncle Ken', the very British war-horse from the motor-oil era, with whom Jackie Stewart won all of his world championships, died of cancer.

'I'll be back,' states a resolute Hakkinen, when announcing his one-year sabbatical. Not everyone is convinced. Life outside of the frantic world of Formula One will be too enjoyable. What's more, there's no guarantee that McLaren will be able to maintain its position at the absolute top. Either way, the team secures the services of the promising young Finn Kimi Raikkonen for the next six years.

It seems that Ecclestone's circus will survive the loss of tobacco sponsoring: the 1970s image of adventure and freedom has given way to state-of-the-art technology and reliability – banks, telecommunications and computer giants are more appropriate sponsors than cigarette manufacturers. The differences of opinion with the European Commission about Ecclestone's supposed monopoly have also been laid to rest. But the sale of a large package of shares has set big money in motion and the car manufacturers are determined to increase their influence over how Formula One is run. Their main interest, freely accessible world-wide advertising, is at odds with the goal of maximising profits by selling the TV rights to the highest bidder. A schism that could overshadow the 1980s' FISA-FOCA crisis threatens. The manufacturers seem increasingly serious about setting up their own Formula One series, something that would obviously mean the deathblow for Formula One in its present form.

All this high-level financial wrangling has not improved the position of the smaller teams. Alain Prost's team goes bankrupt even before the first race of 2002. A disillusioned Prost turns his back on Formula One.

With Frentzen suddenly available, Arrows promptly shows Jos Verstappen the door. In 2002 Jos had demonstrated one lightning start after the other, he'd fought hard, even taking on Hakkinen and Schumacher in the wet in Malaysia. 'Jos was flying,' the German explained afterwards. 'On rain tyres he was the fastest car out there. He was going very well and made it very difficult for me. Just like it should be.' But in 2002 it's still a case of no money, no car.

But Arrows really do need to scrape all their pennies together, and according to rumour, Jordan and Minardi are also having great difficulties balancing their budgets.

Despite the difficulties, Formula One continues to beckon. After a year of testing, Toyota joins the grid in 2002 with a clear programme: participate in the first year; win in the third; in the fifth, go for the title. Because in five years' time, yes, by then, Schumacher's reign *should* finally be over.

Too Much: 2002

'I've had it!' I yell from the kitchen, 'I'll never watch it again!'

'Yes, you will!' my children reply in chorus. For them a Schumacher victory is the most natural thing in the world, and they know that I too will resign mysel to it eventually. Just like everyone else. But this. This really is too much. The Austrian Grand Prix. All weekend Barrichello has been faster than his team-mate. He takes pole and leads the race, Schumacher leaves him to it, and then, one hundred metres before the line, the Brazilian lifts off and Schumacher roars past. Enraged, I run out of the room – this is too disgusting for words.

Of course, Ferrari are thinking of the title. But Schumacher is already 21 points ahead after just five races. This will take him to 54 from six, double the score of his closest 'rival', Montoya. Of course, the season can flip at any time: an accident like 1999's, a miraculous Michelin tyre, a run of obscure bad luck. Imagine ending four points short at the end of the season . . . Ferrari are right.

But still. The Austrian audience is booing and whistling. On the podium Schumacher realises that he has overplayed his hand and pushes Barrichello up on to the highest step. The Brazilian accepts it as his due. A distasteful performance. The FIA takes the affair seriously and promises an investigation. Months later the verdict will be handed down: a hefty fine for Ferrari. No, not for the team orders, you can't ban them, but for disrupting the protocol of the official ceremony.

At the press conference after the race, Schumacher tries to save face: 'It wasn't my decision.' I don't believe a word of it. Everything at Ferrari revolves around Schumacher. The team, the management and Schumacher himself are so intertwined that a decision like this could not possibly be made without his involvement, let alone against his wishes. 'At least we still let our drivers compete against each other,' Ron Dennis grumbles, harking back to the battles between Senna and Prost. His string-pulling with Hakkinen and Coulthard has momentarily slipped his mind.

And the season doesn't flip. Schumacher wins and keeps winning, shredding record after record: the most points, the most victories in a season, the fastest title. No, that wasn't actually the intention, he'd planned on seizing the title in front of a home crowd at Hockenheim, but after Raikkonen slips on oil dropped from McNish's Toyota with five laps to go, Schumacher wins the French Grand Prix as well. Never before has the championship been decided so early in the season.

His competitors have no reply. Ralf wins in Malaysia, but after that he's invisible. Montoya shows his speed with five pole positions in a row, but in the actual races the Ferraris prove faster. Coulthard wins Monaco because no one can get past him, but in the course of the season, his team-mate Raikkonen turns out to be quicker. But how quick is quick? At Hockenheim McLaren simply get lapped. Mika Hakkinen announces from his backyard that he will definitely not be returning to Formula One.

Behind the top three, the middle of the field stagnates: Renault, Jaguar, Jordan, BAR. How long will the big manufacturers bear the sight of their cars hopelessly limping along behind? And what will happen then? 'Next year we want to be the best of the rest,' announces Toyota's Ove Andersson. They put up a good debut performance and have little to lose. But in the rear of the field the problems are mounting. Arrows tumble into an abyss of debt. By mid-season each race could be the last and in France Frentzen and Bernoldi deliberately fail to qualify – the financial and legal soap of Formula One. Later in the year, Minardi's Paul Stoddart is threatening to quit as well, the field is thinning out . . .

But Ferrari drive on. At the end of the season Schumacher and Barrichello clock up double victory after double victory, sharing out the spoils between them. In Indianapolis Schumacher goes so far that he 'accidentally' gives away the victory while attempting to finish equal first with Barrichello. Anger on the stands. Incomprehension in the racing mags, even in Germany: '*Soll dass Motorsport sein*?' But Ferrari go on. The Scuderia scores the constructor's title for the fifth year running. A record. And not once, not once are they forced to withdraw. Another one of those records: in Japan Schumacher completes his twenty-second consecutive race, one more than the legendary Fangio. And that other record? His fifth championship brings Schumacher level with Fangio and – considering Ferrari's supremacy at the end of 2002 – he will go on to win his sixth title as well. Then he really will have ascended to lonely heights. Schumacher himself claims that records and statistics don't interest him, he'll keep driving as long as he enjoys it. As terrible as it sounds, all we can do now is wait for him to get bored. Then the importance of the Schumacher factor in Ferrari's series of victories will finally be revealed. Until then, every second week sees me sitting among the surging Ferrari T-shirts and caps, listening to 'Schumacher songs'. I resign myself to it and think of the wise words of Jody Scheckter (once the 'last Ferrari world champion'): 'Winning never gets boring. Losing does.'

Virtual Reality

The moment I'm back in the pits, I get new tyres fitted and adjust the wing angle, one per cent more, front and rear. I make fifth and sixth a bit tighter and then I'm all set. At least half a second and maybe more is there for the taking. As long as I make it through the chicanes in one piece . . .

Simulation. I've got it at home now as well. At the insistence of all the friends and family I've terrorised long enough with my obsession. 'Just try it,' they said, 'virtual reality, it's made for you.'

They were right. And I can't bear it. I, who always looked upon computers and 'their infinite possibilities' with the greatest contempt – the emperor's new clothes – I too have finally succumbed. No matter how much I insist that it's a simple con, the digital puppet show really does give you a sensation, an experience that at least corresponds to reality. But it only works if you already feel some kind of passion, if you have some degree of fanaticism before you even start. That's scary if you consider how many people get into 'games' like Doom, Carmageddon or Holocaust.

It happened on an ordinary Tuesday afternoon during practice at Monza. I'd only just started and couldn't get the thing – I'd chosen a Ferrari – to corner decently anywhere. I just kept on skidding, jolting, spinning and detouring over the grass or, even worse, into the gravel. After a few cautious laps without crashing, I drove back to the pits in desperation, selected the set-up menu and slightly increased the wing angle. Without too much hope, I drove out of the pit lane, carefully negotiated the chicanes and put my foot down.

Curva Grande, 280, 290, a right-hander, fifth, sixth gear, barriers and trees on my right; on my left, the depth of an enormous gravel trap. Like always, the speed pushes the car to the outside. But then suddenly I feel it – grip. I feel the car sticking to the track. It's no fantasy, it's not just in my head, it's in my shoulders too, in my backside, in my whole body, I fly over the asphalt like a magnet . . .

Astonished, I realise that the Ferrari is taking the double Lesmo smoothly as well, as if it's on rails. I do the second corner without even braking, it feels just like the way drivers describe a 'flying lap' – as if you're floating, tickling the kerbs with a rear wheel, a slight shock passes through the car, just enough to make you realise that you're still of this world.

The car is perfect. Totally confident that it won't fly off, I note the way it races beyond the limit, and I'm inside it. Monza has become a feeling. Smoothly taking the Ascari, slightly losing the rear of the car, turning the wheel to correct that terrifying, blissful slip, then exiting perfectly into the straight that follows.

It's only in the gravel alongside the Parabolica that I come to my senses. Obviously this corner doesn't allow itself to be taken at, or more correctly, just over the limit . . . Fortunately I've set the program to 'invulnerable', otherwise I'd be like Jochen Rindt now and bleeding to death in a wreck. The computer automatically turns my Ferrari around to face the right direction.

Stunned, I hobble back to the pits. Did I really surge around Monza at 320 km/h with perfect grip and 700 horsepower? Or was it just a fantasy?

Since then I have combed all the circuits for another glimpse of that weightlessness, but even at Monza I rarely recapture it. Perhaps it has already become routine, because by now all the circuits have been entered into my muscles, nerves and blood: every movement, every braking point, every millimetre of kerb.

And then Monaco. The ride through the labyrinth really is astonishing. The terrifying chase through the trench around the swimming pool, brushing the barriers, the treacherous zebra crossing before Rascasse. A chance to catch my breath – the trees above start-finish – then immediately back through the eye of the needle: Ste Dévote. Avoid the white lines, I think, quickly climbing to Beau Rivage. I'm surrounded by voices, the words of drivers, colleagues – somehow the accumulated madness is pre-programmed. It's inside you. Faster, Daddy! Sometimes I saw two or three McLarens in front of me. Almost hyperventilating, I begin the classic outbraking manoeuvre at Mirabeau. Perverse, you have to skim the barriers at a couple of points. Well beyond my conscious understanding. I could see a lot more than I think she intended me to. I'm not accusing Alexander of anything.

Coming out of Portiers I always think of Senna, the way his car sat there against the barrier in 1988. Tunnel. Twilight, and every time I hope I'll see them, I hope I'll have caught them up as I appear out of the tunnel: Stewart and Peterson, the Tyrrell and the Lotus racing along the waterfront towards the Virage du Tabac . . .

In the not-too-distant future it will be possible to race against the heroes of yesteryear. The Valhalla of Formula One (system requirements: 8 Mb ram, VGA, double speed CD-ROM; price $ 19.99) offers the true fan the chance to form his own grid: see how Clark does against Senna, Peterson against Hakkinen, Lauda–Schumacher, Gilles versus Jacques, and of course, you can climb in behind the wheel yourself to take on Stewart, Prost or Rindt.

But even before then, the Multi-Death Vision series will appear with highly detailed renditions of Lauda's inferno, the fraction of a second in which Gilles Villeneuve made his decision at Zolder, and the horror of the Tamburello, ending with the suspension component darkening the screen . . . The blurb on my CD case already says 'create beautiful crashes', and no doubt somewhere a group of digital obsessives are already hard at work on the pile-up of Spa 1998, so that soon we will be able to experience the accident from the perspective of all twelve drivers. The possibilities are infinite.

But for now I'll stick to my simple, straightforward game. Tweaking the wing angle, a few laps to test it out, putting on new tyres, sometimes adjusting the brake balance: getting down to the nitty-gritty. Even if I don't dare fiddle with the sorcery of the spring adjust or the bump and rebound. It's enough as it is, I'm part of it all.

Monza, line-up. Slowly, exasperatingly slowly, I roll out of the Parabolica. Oh God, the gigantic square in September's dusty golden glow, the heat of the cars. The champions are in position, already pulling down their visors. Hundreds of thousands of fans are up on their feet in the stands, craning their necks so as not to miss a thing. At home the viewers are almost crawling into their TV screens. None of that's visible on my monitor, but I know it's all there. Just like I know about the filtered light and the scattering leaves soon, when we come storming over the Serraglio. I take up position, the sign with my number on it disappears off screen. I'm in the third row behind Coulthard and Irvine, Hill is next to me and in my mirrors I can see Villeneuve and Fisichella – not bad for someone who doesn't even have his driver's licence.

Concise Glossary

Aerodynamics: 'The golden key to today's Formula One', according to Niki Lauda. Designers use various means (wings, flaps, panels and clever curves and kinks in the bodywork) to affect airflow over and under the car so that it is pressed firmly down on to the surface of the track.

According to technicians, modern Formula One cars can be pressed down on to the track with a force double their own weight.

Back markers: Drivers at the back of the field who are lapped by the lead cars.

Brakes: In 1958 the disc brake was introduced. Steel discs were long used, but in 1978 Brabham introduced carbon-fibre brakes, now universal. Braking power has increased tremendously and decelerations of 4.5 Gs are not uncommon.

Carbon fibre: Until the early 1980s, Formula One cars were made of aluminium. Carbon fibre, originally developed for spacecraft, is a third as heavy and four times as strong. Brabham were the first to experiment with carbon-fibre components. In 1981 McLaren's John Barnard designed the first full-carbon-fibre chassis. Carbon fibre soon became standard in Formula One. Many drivers owe their lives to their carbon-fibre chassis. The highly expensive material is moulded, then baked in special furnaces. The larger teams work shifts around the clock producing parts.

Chicane: A slow corner shaped like a narrow Z, generally placed just before a high-speed corner to prevent drivers from taking it at excessively high speed.

Circuits: Most countries have a designated Grand Prix circuit; some countries have more than one. In the following list, the circuits currently being used are named first. In the past some countries, such as Spain and Britain, alternated their Grands Prix between two circuits.

Australia:	Albert Park – Melbourne
	Adelaide (until 1995)
Austria:	Zeltweg/A-1 Ring (until 1987, since 1997)
Belgium:	Spa-Francorchamps (until 1970, since 1983)
	Zolder (until 1984)
	Nivelles (1972, 1974)
Brazil:	Interlagos – São Paulo
	Jacarepagua – Rio de Janeiro (until 1989)
Canada:	Circuit Gilles Villeneuve – Montreal
	Mosport (until 1977)
France:	Magny-Cours
	Paul Ricard (until 1990)
	Dijon-Prenois (until 1984)
	Reims (until 1966)
	Rouen-Les Essarts (until 1968)
Germany:	Hockenheim
	Nürburgring (until 1976)
Great Britain:	Silverstone
	Brands Hatch (until 1986)
	Donington (1993 only)
Hungary:	Hungaroring – Budapest
Italy:	Monza

Japan:	Suzuka
	Fuji International Speedway (1976, 1977)
Luxembourg:	Nürburgring (Südschleife)
Malaysia:	Kuala Lumpur
Monaco:	Monaco
San Marino:	Imola
Spain:	Circuito de Catalunya – Barcelona
	Jerez de la Frontera
	Jarama – Madrid (until 1981)
	Montjuich (until 1975)
USA:	Indianapolis (since 2000)
	Watkins Glen (until 1980)
	Long Beach (until 1983)
	Dallas (1984)
	Detroit (until 1988)
	Phoenix (until 1991)

No longer included on the Grand Prix calendar are:

Argentina:	Buenos Aires (until 1998)
Holland:	Zandvoort (until 1985)
Mexico:	Mexico City (until 1992)
Pacific:	Aida (Japan, 1994, 1995)
Portugal:	Estoril (until 1996)
South Africa:	Kyalami (until 1985, and 1992, 1993)

Electronics: In the late 1980s electronic driver-aid systems were increasingly incorporated into Formula One cars. These systems included active suspension, in which the computer anticipates the track surface to increase grip and speed; traction control to prevent wheel spin; electronic accelerator and ABS (anti-lock braking system). Driving became more comfortable, faster and, above all, constantly subject to computer adjustment. More dangerous and less human in the judgement of the FIA, and in the early nineties all of the above-mentioned aids were banned.

Later, in 2001, the FIA allowed the reintroduction of launch and traction control systems because of the impossibility of policing a total ban.

FIA: Fédération International d'Automobile, the leading organisation in the automotive world.

FISA: Former sporting arm of the FIA.

Flags: Track marshals posted around the circuit use flags to signal the drivers. The meanings are:

yellow flag (stationary): danger, reduce speed.
yellow flag (waved): danger, reduce speed, do not overtake.
yellow-and-red striped flag: slippery track.
green flag: all clear from this point.
blue flag (stationary): a faster car is following.
blue flag (waved): a faster car wants to overtake, give way.
white flag: slow vehicle (ambulance) on the circuit.
red flag: race must be stopped.
black flag (with white number): the driver is disqualified and must stop in the pits.
chequered flag (only at the finish): the race is over.

The first flags (red and yellow) were used in 1899.

Since 1998 flags have been supplemented by warning lights on the dashboards of the cars.

FOCA: Formula One Constructors' Association, the voice of the teams and since the 1980s the most powerful organisation in Formula One. FOCA gave birth to the FOA, the Formula One Association. The FOA, led by commercial mastermind Bernie Ecclestone, controls the overall organisation of Formula One and arranges transport, the media and, above all, finance.

Formula Three and *Formula 3000*: the most important lower classes of motor racing. This is where talent develops: in cars that are lighter, less powerful and less technologically advanced. All drivers want to graduate to Formula One; the competition is killing.

G-forces: In Formula One the forces produced by braking or in crashes are expressed as G-forces. If a driver is subjected to a force of three Gs, it is equivalent to his momentarily carrying three times his body weight. G-forces can work in any direction – neck muscles in particular are exposed to great strain.

GPDA: Grand Prix Drivers' Association, the Formula One drivers' 'union'.

Grand Prix: The first Grand Prix was held in France in 1906. Winner on the circuit near Le Mans was the Hungarian Ference Szisz in a Renault.

Gravel trap: Fine or coarse gravel, sand and other materials alongside the track are used to slow down cars before they hit guard-rail, wall or tyre barrier.

Indycars: A distinct racing series in the United States. Nothing to do with Formula One. Indycars are heavier, sturdier and at their best on purpose-built Indycar circuits or 'ovals'. Washed-up Formula One drivers sometimes make the transition to Indycars, moves in the other direction are rare and usually fail. Exception: Jacques Villeneuve.

Inspections: During practice sessions, cars are selected at random for official inspections. All dimensions and weights are checked. After the race, cars are subjected to another thorough inspection. Fuel samples are taken regularly.

Kerbstones: Red and white paving stones on the edge of the track, especially on corners. The kerbs are designed to jolt and slow the cars in order to convince drivers that they really have reached the outermost edge.

Overalls: All drivers wear 'fire retardant' overalls. Special sandwich-weave nomex fabrics guarantee twelve seconds before drivers suffer serious burns. The mechanics in the pits also wear fire-retardant overalls, especially since Jos Verstappen's pit fire at Hockenheim 1994.

Overtaking: A problem in modern Formula One. The enormous downforce and powerful brakes greatly reduce the scope for overtaking adversaries.

Drivers are not meant to block each other and are not allowed to deviate from their line without reason. In corners, however, there are several lines and it is possible to 'slam the door', in other words, to cut off an opponent mounting an attack. The basic principle is that the driver who reaches the corner first can choose which line to take.

Back markers generally wave to signal their intention to make way for a faster competitor.

Paddock: Place behind the pits that is open only to teams, organisers and guests.

Parc fermé: Place where cars are parked ready for inspection after the race.

Pits: The garages in which the teams work. The name dates from the French Grand Prix of 1908, when the mechanics really did work from 'pits' dug alongside the track.

Pit stops: Pit stops to change tyres have been usual since 1983. Refuelling has been allowed since 1994 and has become more or less essential because of the smaller fuel tanks.

Drivers are informed to come in for the pit stop by radio and through pit signs.

The speed limit in the pit lane is set at 80 km/h (cars are fitted with a speed limiter). Approximately twenty men work on the car at once. Cars remain stationary for between seven and twelve seconds (depending on how much fuel is pumped). The total pit stop generally costs between twenty and thirty seconds (depending on the length and difficulty of the road to the pits).

Pit-stop strategy: In modern Formula One, pit stops are a weapon for overtaking opponents. Using a computer and their own insight, teams decide the number of pit stops in advance. Having less fuel on board means they can go faster, but it also obliges them to pit more often. What's more, it is also advantageous for drivers to pit before they get caught up among the back markers, this gives a relatively open track for the last and fastest laps.

Points: The first six cars to finish a Grand Prix score world-championship points. The winner scores ten points; second scores six; third is worth four; fourth place, three; fifth place, two; and sixth place, one point. Until 1990 the winner scored nine points, and only the best eleven results from the sixteen races counted.

Pole position: The driver who achieves the fastest lap time on Saturday afternoon starts from the front in the race on Sunday.

Practice: A Grand Prix weekend is made up as follows: on Friday there are two free practice sessions; another free practice is held on Saturday morning, after which the teams choose which tyres they will use for the rest of the weekend. The qualifying session follows on Saturday afternoon. Qualifying lasts one hour and the drivers are allowed to drive a maximum of twelve laps. The qualifying times determine the starting order. On Sunday morning, there is another thirty-minute warm-up.

Race: During the season the race starts on every second Sunday afternoon, generally at one p.m. GMT. A Grand Prix lasts a maximum of two hours, or 300 kilometres.

Safety Car: In extremely dangerous conditions, the stewards can decide to bring the Safety Car out on to the track. Participants must drive behind the Safety Car and overtaking is not allowed. After the Safety Car returns to the pits, the race resumes from the start line. Any time differences from before the Safety Car period are no longer relevant.

Shunt: An accident.

Stop-go penalty: Drivers who drive irresponsibly or in breach of regulations can be penalised by having to drive into the pits and stop, usually for ten seconds, without any work being done on the car.

Teams: The following is a list of current Formula One teams. Hyphenated names give the engine partner. The team director, manager or owner is given in brackets:

Ferrari (Jean Todt)
McLaren-Mercedes (Ron Dennis)
Williams-BMW (Frank Williams, Patrick Head)
Renault (Flavio Briatore)
Jordan-Ford (Eddie Jordan)
BAR-Honda (Dave Richards)
Sauber-Petronas (Peter Sauber)
Jaguar (Niki Lauda)
Minardi (Paul Stoddart)
Toyota (Ove Andersson)

Illustrious teams that have disappeared from Formula One include Lotus, Tyrrell, Brabham, BRM, Alfa Romeo, Ligier, March, Shadow, Wolf, Hesketh and Penske.

Telemetry: Countless aspects of a Formula One car are continuously monitored by sensors that instantaneously transmit data back to the pits. The handling and condition of the vehicle can be studied at any time, even during the race. Problems that might arise can be detected in an early phase. The telemetric data is also used to analyse the performance of the drivers. Since 2002 the use of telemetry to change the settings of the car has also been allowed.

Tests: Formula One teams test constantly throughout the year, but especially in the winter. Tests are held on circuits designated for this purpose by the FIA. Generally a number of teams test simultaneously because of the cost of renting a circuit: security in particular needs to be optimal. Most teams employ a special test driver.

Timing: The days of stopwatches are long gone. Times are now logged through transponders inside the cars. When a Formula One car races over an antenna embedded in the asphalt, the antenna picks up the signal of the transponder and relays the time to the main timing centre.

Turbo: Turbo engines were introduced to Formula One by Renault in 1977. A turbine driven by the exhaust gases forces air into the engine. Increasing the air supply to the engine improves combustion, thus increasing output or capacity. From 1983 turbo engines were essential. Engine capacity kept increasing until 1987, when the FIA decided to limit boost pressure by introducing pop-off valves. In 1989 turbos were banned.

Tyres: Tyres differ in tread and in the composition of the rubber. There are hard, soft and very soft rubbers; the softer the rubber, the more grip and the faster the wear. The tread depends on the weather conditions: lots of rain requires 'full wet-weather tyres' with deep tread that is capable of displacing large volumes of water; semi-wet conditions require 'intermediates', tyres with less tread; in dry conditions, tyres with minimal tread are used.

Between 1971 and 1997 drivers generally used treadless tyres, 'slicks'. Since 1998 grooves in the tyres have been mandatory.

Formula One tyres have a high operating temperature. Before use, they are warmed up with electric tyre blankets.

World championship: The first world championship for car marques was held in 1925. Winner: Alfa Romeo. The first world championship for drivers was in 1950. A separate title for constructors was introduced in 1958.

World champions:
1950 Guiseppe Farina, Alfa Romeo
1951 Juan Manuel Fangio, Alfa Romeo
1952 Alberto Ascari, Ferrari
1953 Ascari, Ferrari
1954 Fangio, Maserati and Mercedes
1955 Fangio, Mercedes
1956 Fangio, Ferrari
1957 Fangio, Maserati
1958 Mike Hawthorn, Ferrari
1959 Jack Brabham, Cooper
1960 Brabham, Cooper
1961 Phil Hill, Ferrari
1962 Graham Hill, BRM
1963 Jim Clark, Lotus

1964 John Surtees, Ferrari
1965 Jim Clark, Lotus
1966 Brabham, Brabham
1967 Dennis Hulme, Brabham
1968 Hill, Lotus
1969 Jackie Stewart, Matra
1970 Jochen Rindt, Lotus
1971 Stewart, Tyrrell
1972 Emerson Fittipaldi, Lotus
1973 Stewart, Tyrrell
1974 Fittipaldi, McLaren
1975 Niki Lauda, Ferrari
1976 James Hunt, McLaren
1977 Lauda, Ferrari
1978 Mario Andretti, Lotus
1979 Jody Scheckter, Ferrari
1980 Alan Jones, Williams
1981 Nelson Piquet, Brabham
1982 Keke Rosberg, Williams
1983 Piquet, Brabham
1984 Lauda, McLaren
1985 Alain Prost, McLaren
1986 Prost, McLaren
1987 Piquet, Williams
1988 Ayrton Senna, McLaren
1989 Prost, McLaren
1990 Senna, McLaren
1991 Senna, McLaren
1992 Nigel Mansell, Williams
1993 Prost, Williams
1994 Michael Schumacher, Benetton
1995 Schumacher, Benetton
1996 Damon Hill, Williams
1997 Jacques Villeneuve, Williams

1998 Mika Hakkinen, McLaren
1999 Hakkinen, McLaren
2000 Schumacher, Ferrari
2001 Schumacher, Ferrari
2002 Schumacher, Ferrari

Bibliography

No images without the images of others. From a vast sea of information, I would like to gratefully acknowledge a particular debt for the guidance and inspiration I found in the following books:

Gerhard Berger, *Zielgerade*, Edition Autorevue, 1997
Adriano Cimarosti, *The Complete History of Grand Prix Motor Racing*, Aurum Press, 1997
Timothy Collings, *The New Villeneuve*, Bloomsbury, 1997
Gerald Donaldson, *Gilles Villeneuve*, Motor Racing Publications, 1996
Maurice Hamilton, *Frank Williams*, Macmillan, 1998
Alan Henry, *Damon Hill. On Top of the World*, Patrick Stephens, 1996
Alan Henry, *Formula 1. Creating the Spectacle*, Hazleton, 1998
Alan Henry, *McLaren. The Epic Years*, Haynes, 1998
Damon Hill, *My Championship Year*, Warner Books, 1996
Christopher Hilton, *Alain Prost*, Partridge Press, 1992
Christopher Hilton, *Ayrton Senna. The Legend Grows*, Patrick Stephens, 1995
Christopher Hilton, *Ayrton Senna. The Hard Edge of Genius*, Corgi Books, 1997
Christopher Hilton, *Michael Schumacher. Controversial Genius*, Haynes, 1997
Christopher Hilton, *Mika Hakkinen*, Haynes, 1997
Peter Lanz, *Niki Lauda, Der Weg zum Triumph*, Ullstein, 1984
Niki Lauda, *Mijn derde leven*, Elmar BV, 1997
Nigel Mansell, *My Autobiography*, Collins Willow, 1995
Jan Segers, *Senna. De rechtervoet van God*, Roularta/Fontein, 1994
Sid Watkins, *Life at the Limit*, Macmillan, 1996

Lastly, I also derived a great deal of information from Heinz Prüller's *Grand Prix Story* series and Ulrich Schwab's *Grand Prix* series.

A Note on the Author

Koen Vergeer is the author of two novels and is a reporter for the Belgian daily *De Morgen* where he regularly covers Formula 1 and other motor-racing events. He lives in Utrecht.

A Note on the Translator

David Colmer is the translator of 'An Autumn Day in Bohemia' by Benno Barnard for *Leopard, The House of the Seven Sisters* by Elle Eggels and of two children's books by Bart Moeyaert, *Bare Hands* and *Hornet's Nest.*

A Note on the Type

The text of this book is set in Bembo, the original types for which were cut by Francesco Griffo for the Venetian printer Aldus Manutius, and were first used in 1495 for Cardinal Bembo's *De Aetna*. Claude Garamond (1480–1561) used Bembo as a model, so it became the forerunner of standard European type for the following two centuries. Its modern form was designed, following the original, for Monotype in 1929 and is widely in use today.